BULLS

BEARS

AND THE

BALLOT BOX

BULLS
BEARS

AND THE
BALLOT BOX

*How the Performance of Our Presidents
Has Impacted Your Wallet*

BOB DEITRICK & LEW GOLDFARB

Published by Advantage, Charleston, South Carolina.
Member of Advantage Media Group.

ADVANTAGE is a registered trademark and the Advantage colophon is a trademark of Advantage Media Group, Inc.

Printed in the United States of America.

ISBN: 978-1-59932-288-9
LCCN: 2012932176

This publication is designed to provide accurate and authoritative information in regard to the subject matter covered. It is sold with the understanding that the publisher is not engaged in rendering legal, accounting, or other professional services. If legal advice or other expert assistance is required, the services of a competent professional person should be sought.

Advantage Media Group is proud to be a part of the Tree Neutral® program. Tree Neutral offsets the number of trees consumed in the production and printing of this book by taking proactive steps such as planting trees in direct proportion to the number of trees used to print books. To learn more about Tree Neutral, please visit www.treeneutral.com. To learn more about Advantage's commitment to being a responsible steward of the environment, please visit www.advantagefamily.com/green

Advantage Media Group is a leading publisher of business, motivation, and self-help authors. Do you have a manuscript or book idea that you would like to have considered for publication? Please visit www.amgbook.com or call 1.866.775.1696

"Don't just buy a single copy of this book. Buy dozens, send them to everyone you know, and do it now! In a clear, concise, and accessible style, Bob Deitrick and Lew Goldfarb have written a book that, finally, lets the facts speak for themselves. In doing so, they have turned a whole lot of what stands for conventional wisdom on its head. Necessary reading before family gatherings, high school reunions, elections, or turning on Fox News or MSNBC...wherever and whenever the discussion is likely to turn to politics. Deitrick and Goldfarb are not politicians and they are not from the Beltway, and perhaps that's why this book contains more common sense per page than just about any other book of this sort I know of".

– David Wilhelm is the past Chairman of the Democratic National Committee, Senior Political Adviser to Bill Clinton in 1992, and Owner of Woodland Venture Management and New Harvest Ventures, LLC; Education: Harvard University Kennedy School of Government and B.A. from The Ohio University.

DEDICATION

This book is dedicated to my father,
Thomas Carter Deitrick,
who died during the research of this book.
He was the smartest and the most well read man I ever knew.
I would rarely see him watching television,
but I often did catch my father reading at 3 a.m.
when he could not sleep.
He was the inspiration for the writing of this book.
This book is for you, Dad. I love you.

– Bob Deitrick

To the memory of my mother,
Jean Goldfarb,
who died during the writing of our book.
She was a special person, mother and friend, and a crusader
for the rights of those who did not have the resources
or voices to be heard.
Consider yourself hugged, Mom.

– Lew Goldfarb

ACKNOWLEDGMENTS

This book could not have been completed without the assistance and dedication of a small army of people who contributed in various ways to turning our dream into reality. We'd like to thank our entire team who spent many hours researching information about our U.S. presidents and their parties, including Justin Buntain, Ben Goldfarb, Josh Goldfarb, Colin Ketterer, Christian Conner and Nick Snow. We were helped by many undergraduate students at the University of Cincinnati who gave up part of their winter break to do fact checking and footnote drafting, including Kiley Brodeur, Garrett Cummins, Samantha Miller, Scott Schrider, Lauren Stanfield, Erin Shayne Williams, and Holly Yurchison. Many thanks also to Shannon Kemen for helping us with fact checking and to Aaron and Eli Fellows for their insights regarding the data collection and compilation.

We owe special thanks to several people who went above and beyond the call of duty and exceeded our expectations to make this project a great success. We are deeply indebted and thankful to each of them. Sean Graves was instrumental in researching and compiling data for our PRES Rankings, assisted in writing chapter drafts, and developed visually appealing depictions of the data collected. Cynthia Hilliard, our lead editor, used her "magic pen" to polish our drafts and make our words, sentences and paragraphs flow. Steve Morgan helped provide critical input, helped us synthesize our data, and he did yeoman's work handling the day-to-day responsibilities of Bob and Steven's wealth management practice, Polaris Financial Partners, LLC while Bob was writing in St. Croix for three months. Pink Johnson, a client of Bob and Steven's and Steve's uncle as well, was instrumental in assisting us in the marketing of this book. Jeff Nein did a terrific job in helping us anticipate criticisms of our book and providing insights as to potential responses. Dr. Ben Passty and Paul Reuther of the University of Cincinnati's Applied Economics Research Institute performed the important task of verifying the accuracy of our data. Dr. Jonathan Fox of The Ohio State University provided expertise and consultation regarding the statistical analysis used in our book. Sharon Goldfarb, Lew's beautiful wife, helped with the fact checking and footnoting and showed extraordinary patience during the writing of the book.

We extend our gratitude to the University of Cincinnati College of Law and the Harold C. Schott Foundation for the grant Lew received in the summer of 2011 to help fund the research and writing of this book. Additional thanks are due to the University of Cincinnati College of Law for funding the work of student research assistants and supporting Lew throughout this project. We also want to thank Bob and Steven's broker/dealer, Cadaret, Grant & Co., Inc. and B.J. Johnson and Art Grant specifically, who were very supportive of our endeavor from day one.

We could not have achieved our goals for this book without the expertise of our publisher, Advantage Media Group, and its professional staff, and the talents of our publicist, KBC Media, led by its charismatic founder, Karen Ammond. They guided us every step of the way. Finally, we thank Chad Frye and Kory Crabtree as well as Tim Sullivan who were of tremendous assistance with respect to developing marketing strategies for this endeavor.

Also, we would be remiss without acknowledging all of our friends, clients, students, fellow faculty and family members for their patience and perseverance during the writing of this book. Specifically, thanks to our children, Mallory, Mitchell and Meredith Deitrick and Ben and Josh Goldfarb for being so terrific and patient with us.

To everyone involved in this four-year mission, your time and effort have been genuinely appreciated – more than you will ever know. Thank you to all.

PREFACE

As the owners of Polaris Financial Partners LLC, a financial and wealth management practice in Columbus, Ohio, Steven Morgan and I develop strategies for the nearly $50 million invested by our company's clients. In February 2008, my colleague, Nick Snow and I were studying historical stock market trends to prepare for an upcoming presentation to my clients when I discovered some intriguing facts that piqued my interest. There seemed to be a correlation between the political party of the president and the strength of the stock market, and I wondered whether that same relationship would hold true for other indicators of a strong economy, for example: GDP growth, unemployment rate, personal income growth, corporate profits, fairness of income distribution across the socioeconomic classes, low inflation, etc. Moreover, I realized that during the 80-year time period we were examining (1929-2008), the Democratic Party and Republican Party had occupied the Oval Office for precisely 40 years each.[i] We realized this was a unique and historic opportunity for an in-depth comparative analysis.

I approached Lew Goldfarb, a client and friend, who attended my presentation that cold winter day shortly after Bear Stearns had collapsed, about doing an in-depth analysis of the subject and coauthoring a book about it. Lew, a CPA and law professor, was excited about the notion and agreed. Thus began our journey to answer the many questions regarding the economic stewardship of our nation's chief executive officers, which we have described in *Bulls, Bears, and the Ballot Box*. We believe you will find those answers interesting and enlightening, or at the very least, surprising.

Every president plays a vital and unique role in the performance of our nation's economy. In fact, each president in our view since Herbert Hoover has been the de-facto chief executive officer (CEO) of the country. As our commander-in-chief, the president decides whether we go to war. As CEO, he decides whether to be proactive or reactive in issues of fiscal and monetary policy. He has a major influence on how money is appropriated in the federal budget and presents his own budget to Congress for approval. It is his role to ensure that our laws are enforced at the federal level, and he wields veto power when bills or budget appropriations from Congress are not to his liking. The president has tremendous influence on tax and investment policy and suggests whether we should increase taxes to balance the budget or to deficit-spend to resuscitate a depressed economy. Our president recommends how capital should be deployed in order to move the country forward.[ii] He owns the bully pulpit and can use it to champion or attack policies and programs. We assert that the president of the United States is the single most important leader in our three branches of government as it relates to the stewardship of the nation's economy.

Yet curiously, there has not been, up to now, a comprehensive historical analysis of the past 80 years that illustrates how each president has performed during his tenure in office as it impacts the American consumer, shareholder, investor and business owner in his or her wallet or purse. There has never been such a thorough review that compares and contrasts how each of our presidents has performed from the vantage point of real economic results for the

American people. That is up until now. This book will fill that gap with a thoughtful, objective review of the past 80 years concerning lower and middle- to upper-middle class consumers in America – the taxpayer, the shareholder, the 401(k) and 403(b) holder, and the IRA owner. We believe wholeheartedly that the middle class is the backbone of this great country. Our book is written for all of them: the hard-working Americans who go to work each day striving to build the American Dream for themselves and their families.

Our journey will end in 2009 as it begins in 1929, with a depressed economy and a high rate of unemployment. Sadly, over those intervening years we did not learn from our mistakes, which is why we nearly experienced a second Great Depression in 2009.[iii] We will first discuss the events of the 1920s that led us into the Great Depression, and we will conclude with what almost led us to the identical result just three short years ago.[iv] The foundation for this book rests on our study of a private citizen who became our first Federal Reserve Chairman – Marriner Stoddard Eccles.[v] We will discuss and venerate this unsung American hero who was a banker, entrepreneur and a Republican.[vi] Marriner Eccles defined the word *statesmanship*. His wisdom and economic prowess were crucial in moving the country from calamity to recovery in the 1930s.[vii] Eccles believed one of the primary reasons for the Great Depression was rampant leverage and over-speculation that created a casino on Wall Street, one that siphoned an increasing portion of the then-currently produced wealth into the hands of the few. According to Eccles, it was this inequitable distribution of wealth that was a primary reason that led us to the Great Depression – taking money out of circulation and putting it into the hands of those who would hoard it instead of putting it into the hands of those who would spend it.[viii] Eccles was the first Federal Reserve chairman under Franklin Delano Roosevelt in the early 1930s, and we have studied his life from the 1920s, when he created the first and oldest multi-bank holding company in the U.S., First Security Corporation, through his tenure at the Federal Reserve that ended in 1952.[ix]

Our study of the life of Marriner Eccles and his significant role in rescuing the U.S. economy during the Great Depression inspired the development of *our Presidential Rules for Economic Success (PRES Rules)*, which we utilize throughout the book to explain each president's economic successes and failures. These five powerful and simple rules are as follows:

1. **ADVANCE THE COMMON GOOD AND NOT SOLELY THE INTERESTS OF THE ADVANTAGED FEW.**

   Questions explored: Did the president promote policies that spread the wealth among all economic classes or was he beholden to special interests? Did he advocate policies that advanced the interests of the bottom 99% and not solely the top 1%?

2. **THE MIDDLE CLASS IS THE ENGINE THAT DRIVES THE ECONOMY.**

   Questions explored: Did the president promote monetary, fiscal, tax, trade and other policies that recognized the importance of the middle class to the strength of the nation's economy?

3. **THE FEDERAL GOVERNMENT PLAYS A VITAL ROLE IN CREATING AND MAINTAINING A HEALTHY ECONOMY.**

Questions explored: Did the president follow Eccles' basic economic philosophies: Deficit-spend during recessionary times; balance the budget during times of business prosperity; avoid excessive inflation at all costs; leverage government spending; implement reasonable (not excessive) regulation of the economy and business; and provide basic necessities for the least fortunate?

---

4. **TAKE BOLD ACTION AFTER CAREFUL AND INNOVATIVE THOUGHT.**

Questions explored: Did the president appoint and consult with experts? Did he adjust his approach/decisions based on changing circumstances? Was he a student of history? Did his decisions have factual support? Did he study and evaluate all available options and relevant data? Did he make mid-course corrections as they were needed?

---

5. **LEAD AS A STATESMAN, NOT AS A PARTISAN.**

Questions explored: Were the president's actions consistent with what he said? Did he demonstrate leadership in critical times? Did he lead or did he follow? Was he a conciliator (look for win-win solutions) or adversarial in his approach to getting the task done (win at all costs)? Did he show respect for all, even those who disagreed with him? Did he set the agenda, lead, and was he able to work with Congress? Did he do the right thing on behalf of the American people, not the popular or partisan thing? Did he demonstrate honesty and integrity?

It is our belief, based upon our study of this 80-year period of presidential history that those presidents who governed consistently with the PRES Rules presided over the strongest economies and provided the best results for all Americans, consumers and business owners alike. In Chapters 3 through 13, we more fully explain the PRES Rules and specifically examine the actions and policies of each of the nation's chief executive officers from 1929 through 2008, and whether those actions and policies followed or deviated from the Rules.

In Bulls, Bears, and the Ballot Box, we review how the income disparity between the bottom 99% and top 1% of income earners has grown dramatically, especially over the last 30 years. In the middle of the Reagan years, there were a paltry 13 billionaires in the United States.[x, xi] Today, there are more than 1,000. According to the Federal Reserve, the wealthiest 200,000 households in the United States each have a net worth exceeding $20 million.[xii] Of those households, 49,000 have a net worth between $50 million and $500 million and 125,000 have a net worth between $25 million and $50 million.[xiii] To those who have made it or inherited their way to this rung on the ladder, we say congratulations! This group is very fortunate in that there are few places on earth where one can accumulate this much wealth. This group defines the term "super rich": They represent less than 1% of our population, yet they possess more than 32% of our nation's net worth.[xiv] To put things in perspective, a small city the size of Akron, Ohio (excluding its suburbs) controls one third of the wealth in the nation. By contrast, the bottom 99% of our population comprises households having an annual income of less than $360,000 per year, with most well below that; in fact approximately 66% of those households make less than $65,000 per year.[xv] Our focus in *Bulls, Bears, and the Ballot Box* is to enlighten those in this substantial group.

There is tremendous misinformation in the public domain about the role each United States president has played as it relates to actual economic results. There is too much mantra, hyperbole and incantation for most people to discern the wheat from the chaff; therefore, most walk away confused, bewildered or even disgusted with our political process. Voters often make their decisions at the ballot box on social and cultural issues such as same-sex marriage, illegal immigration, or whether the president is wearing a flag pin on his lapel. They also vote based on who has the best sales pitch and the best campaign slogan instead of voting on the facts that affect their own economic interest. While both parties do their best to cherry-pick the statistics and facts that best support their cause and omit those which contradict it, the Republican Party has been much more effective at conveying and communicating its message than the Democratic Party.[xvi] Many of us intuitively believe that Republican presidents bring shrewdness and a sense of business acumen to the White House; that when a Republican resides at 1600 Pennsylvania Avenue the equity markets perform better, the economy overall works better, we have fewer recessions and so on.[xvii] Surprisingly, the facts do not support this hyperbole. In fact, Republican economic dominance is a myth, yet it is one that is widely believed.

Our primary motivation is to educate the American voter. Most people are poorly informed about personal finance and consumer economics, which is why we believe that financial literacy is critically important. Again, most individuals make voting choices based on sound bites, which divert attention from the real problems we face as a country.

Bulls, Bears, and the Ballot Box is a pilgrimage on behalf of all Americans who work hard and play by the rules each day to provide for their families. It evaluates how each of the past 13 presidents has performed as a steward for the U.S. economy and your wallet. It assigns each president a rank using our system, *The Presidential Rankings of Economic Stewardship (PRES Rankings)*. The final ranks were based on scores from 12 consumer-based economic indicators compiled for the time period that each president held office. We assign an overall ranking to each president, in addition to assigning a rank for each of *three economic pillars: (1) the U.S. Financial Health Pillar, (2) the Personal Wealth Pillar, and (3) the Business Prosperity Pillar*. This system allows each president to be evaluated from the perspective of various constituents of the American electorate. The PRES Rankings, including a detailed explanation of the three economic pillars and 12 economic indicators, are described in more detail in Chapter 2.

Most Americans get excited and enjoy the banter of presidential politics every four years. This book will provide our readers with a newfound understanding of the president's unique impact on our nation's economic results, and it will become a road map to select the best candidate for the White House to achieve your economic goals. We urge Americans to cut through the campaign rhetoric and thwart those who strive, often with malice, to divert our attention from the real issues just to keep their party in power. Having been in the professions of law and wealth management for a combined 52 years, we have witnessed first-hand how little attention the average American pays to his or her financial well-being. Our primary objective is to inform our readers that the choice they make at the ballot box can have a significant impact on their personal bottom line. We hope the readers of *Bulls, Bears, and the Ballot Box*, when casting their ballots for president, will place their own family, their financial security, and children's education on the front burner – perhaps for some – for the first time. The secondary and tertiary cultural issues, which take center stage, are important but be advised they are often disguised as red herrings and are distractions. We hope that our book serves as a wake-up call to Democrats, Republicans and Independents alike to STAND UP and *vote your economic pocketbook.*

Bob Deitrick
Polaris Financial Partners LLC

Lew Goldfarb
University of Cincinnati College of Law

December 2011

PREFACE ENDNOTES

[i] Miller Center of Public Affairs, "American Presidents: A Reference Resource." Accessed December 12, 2011. http://millercenter.org/president.

[ii] The White House, "The Executive Branch–The President." Accessed December 12, 2011. http://www.whitehouse.gov/our-government/executive-branch

[iii] Economist's View, "A Second Great Depression Is Still Possible." Accessed December 12, 2011. http://economistsview.typepad.com/economistsview/2009/10/a-second-great-depression-is-still-possible.html

[iv] The Economist, "A refresher on the 1930s." Accessed December 12, 2011. http://www.economist.com/node/165701?story_id=E1_TGVSDT

[v] The Federal Reserve Bank of Minneapolis, "The Tale of Another Chairman." Accessed December 12, 2011. http://www.minneapolisfed.org/publications_papers/pub_display.cfm?id=3562

[vi] Sidney Hyman, *Marriner S. Eccles: Private Entrepreneur and Public Servant* (California: Stanford. 1976), 3-8

[vii] Utah History, "Marriner Stoddard Eccles." Accessed December 13, 2011. http://www.media.utah.edu/UHE/e/ECCLES%2CMARINER.html

[viii] Utah State History, "People Who Made a Difference: Marriner Eccles." Accessed December 12, 2011. http://history.utah.gov/learning_and_research/make_a_difference/eccles.html

[ix] Salt Lake City Tribune, "How Marriner Eccles Saved America." Accessed December 13, 2011. http://www.sltrib.com/sltrib/opinion/51046418-82/eccles-economy-president-federal.html.csp

[x] Number of Billionaires, "Number of Billionaires." Accessed December 13, 2011. http://hypertextbook.com/facts/2005/MichelleLee.shtml

[xi] Miller Center, "American President: Ronald Wilson Reagan." Accessed December 13, 2011. http://millercenter.org/president/reagan

[xii] Library of Economics and Liberty, "Distribution of Income." Accessed December 13, 2011. http://www.econlib.org/library/Enc/DistributionofIncome.html

[xiii] MSNBC, "CNBC Special Report: Who Are the Super Rich?" Accessed December 13, 2011. http://www.msnbc.msn.com/id/25244140/ns/business-cnbc_tv/t/cnbc-special-report-who-are-super-rich/#.Tud-j5h6421

[xiv] United Nations University, "The World Distribution of Household Wealth." Accessed December 13, 2011. http://www.wider.unu.edu/publications/working-papers/discussion-papers/2008/en_GB/dp2008-03/_files/78918010772127840/default/dp2008-03.pdf

[xv] My Budget 360, "How much do average Americans make after the Great Recession?" Accessed December 13, 2011. http://www.mybudget360.com/how-much-average-household-income-us-recession-income-distribution/

[xvi] The New Republic, "Left Behind: How Democrats are Losing the Political Center." Accessed December 13, 2011. http://www.tnr.com/article/the-vital-center/95296/democrats-ideology-republicans-independents

[xvii] The White House, "Corresponding with the White House." Accessed December 13, 2011. http://www.whitehouse.gov/contact/write-or-call#write

TABLE OF CONTENTS

CHAPTER 1

MARRINER ECCLES

AN ECONOMIC STATESMAN
AND UNSUNG AMERICAN HERO

"As in a poker game where the chips were concentrated in fewer and fewer hands, the other fellows could only stay in the game by borrowing. When their credit ran out, the game stopped." [xviii]

– Marriner Eccles on what led to The Great Depression –
Autobiography, *Beckoning Frontiers*

Born in Utah in 1890, Marriner Stoddard Eccles served as the first Federal Reserve Board chairman of the United States under Franklin Delano Roosevelt.[xix] Few Americans know his name or his many accomplishments despite the fact that Eccles is arguably one of the most important and influential men of the 20th century. Marriner Eccles was a successful businessman, an entrepreneur, a Republican, a Mormon, and a millionaire by the age of 22.[xx] As a young man, he believed that any individual could succeed through thrift, hard work and perseverance. Though his name is rarely mentioned in the history books, Eccles' prophetic and visionary views on fiscal and monetary policy rescued the United States from the depths of the Great Depression.[xxi] Furthermore, this gentleman defines the quality that has made our nation great over time and which it desperately needs more than ever today: *statesmanship.*

Mr. Eccles' life, his dedication to public service, his leadership and pragmatism in time of crisis, and his thoughtful and humanitarian economic philosophies were a great inspiration to the co-authors in the writing of this book, leading us to create a customized system to evaluate presidential economic performance. This system has two components. The first is a quantitative analysis, which we call the Presidential Rankings of Economic Stewardship (PRES Rankings), that grades and ranks each U.S. president in terms of his specific economic performance while in office and how he performed as a steward on behalf of the consumer, the business owner, and the general health of the economy. The other component is a qualitative analysis, known as the Presidential Rules for Economic Success (PRES Rules), which we apply to each occupant of the Oval Office. We believe each president's economic successes or failures can be explained by whether he adhered to, or deviated from, the PRES Rules. Our book is designed to evaluate how these men performed as individuals and how their political parties performed in aggregate over the past 80 years so that you, the voter, can cast a vote that makes the most sense relative to your economic interest.

When we started this analysis and selected our data points almost four years ago, we did not know what we would find. While we conducted our research, we watched the economy slide downhill. Now, we have some startling conclusions to share with our readers, and our readers have an important vote coming up: the 2012 presidential election. Politically speaking, the past two decades have been an atrocity perpetrated on the American people. Politics has become tainted with partisanship, heckling, cynicism, and red herrings, all of which are exacerbated by the 24/7 news cycle.[xxii] It is difficult, if not impossible, for most Americans to see the forest through the trees in order to make an intelligent and informed decision. Our goal is to have our readers digest the results of our PRES Rankings, understand the importance of our PRES Rules, and take into account lessons learned from past presidential successes and failures in order to become more enlightened voters.

Getting back to our story, Marriner Eccles was the 14th of his father David's 22 children, and when his father died in 1912, Marriner picked up the pieces of the family business and turned it into an empire.[xxiii] Continuing to build on his father's success, Eccles went on to establish the first multi-bank holding company in the nation, First Security Corporation, which owned 28 banks at its height and still exists to this day. Besides banking, Marriner Eccles was extensively involved in the lumber, sugar and construction industries.[xxiv]

Eccles' business and political philosophies were unique, and he proved to be decades ahead of his time. When the Great Depression hit during the autumn of 1929, Marriner volunteered for the Utah Committee for Relief.[xxv] It was there that his belief in the relationship between hard work and the fruits of that labor were challenged for the first time. The Depression opened his eyes to the fact that hundreds of thousands of good, hard-working people were unable to make ends meet regardless of how desperately they tried. Hunger, homelessness, and an overall sense of helplessness ran rampant across the country. This period in Eccles's life prompted an epiphany that changed his life mission. Before, he had devoted his time and energy toward the pursuit of profit, but now he adopted a new purpose – the creation of a stable national economy for all Americans.[xxvi]

Eccles believed the economy had faltered in 1929 for a variety of reasons but primarily because of over-leverage, rampant speculation, and no regulation on Wall Street. In addition, he felt too much wealth had become concentrated in the hands of the top 1% of the economic ladder; he realized that the affluent did not have to spend their wealth during bad times; instead they could hoard it or delay spending. Consequently, the affluent unintentionally had become a huge drain to the free-market system.[xxvii] Eccles believed that the only way to get the slumping economy primed and running in 1932 was to get money back into the hands of those who would spend it instead of in the wallets of those who would hoard it. [xxviii] Eccles also believed that the gross production by business needed to be matched by mass consumption, and that mass consumption required an equitable distribution of wealth.[xxix] Moreover, he believed that the nation needed to provide its citizens with an amount of buying power equal to the amount of goods and services offered by the nation's economic machine. Over the course of the 1920s, culminating in 1929, rampant leveraging and speculation created a giant suction pump, which siphoned an increasing portion of the currently produced wealth away from the middle class and into the hands of the wealthiest Americans. Eccles observed about the Great Depression, after his tenure at the Fed, that, "as in a poker game where the chips were concentrated in fewer and fewer hands, the other fellows could only stay in the game by borrowing. When their credit ran out, the game stopped."[xxx] By taking purchasing power out of the hands of consumers and putting it in the hands of the most affluent, business owners ironically denied themselves the very demand for their products they needed to justify reinvestment of their own capital accumulation.[xxxi] A vicious downward spiral resulted, and by 1929, 42% of the nation's wealth was accumulated in the top 1% of society.

In February of 1933, Marriner Eccles was invited to Washington D.C. to testify before the Senate Finance Committee.[xxxii] Addressing a predominantly Republican lame duck Senate, Eccles was the last of approximately 50 people to testify on various proposals to save the faltering economy. Repeatedly, the committee listened to men testify with two basic themes:

- *I don't know the solution.*
- *Reduce spending and balance the budget.*

The senators had heard it all, or so they thought until Marriner Eccles stepped up to the plate and spoke. Eccles became the sole voice of dissent and he woke up the committee members by saying, "The government should put idle men, money and material to work. If the government spent enough money, it would put more money in the hands of consumers, stimulate business, and begin a cycle of recovery".[xxxiii] In essence, he suggested that the only viable pathway out of the mega-recession was through a government policy of deficit spending.

When Franklin Roosevelt was elected, his views were firmly in the mainstream conservative camp of creating a balanced budget. Marriner Eccles impressed the Senate committee so much that he was then invited to meet the president, where he conveyed the same message to FDR as he had to the Senate.[xxxiv] He stressed that using government leverage and deficit spending was the only means to spur growth in a depressed economic environment and that the government needed to be the spender and investor of last resort. Eccles was able to convince Roosevelt to alter his strategy and he changed the course of American history in one single meeting. In addition, Eccles argued that spending on public works projects, such as the Hoover Dam, would be a key facet to ending the Great Depression. In fact, unknown to most, Eccles, a Republican, went on to become the architect of many New Deal programs, such as the Works Progress Administration, the Federal Housing Authority, the Federal Deposit Insurance Corporation, a centralized Federal Reserve Board, and the Banking Act of 1935, among others.[xxxv] He firmly believed that in a depression the federal government's role should be to implement an expansionary fiscal policy, but in a boom economy the opposite should be the case.[xxxvi] This savvy Utahan persuaded the United States Senate and FDR to take profoundly bold steps that had never been discussed, let alone attempted, steps that had the net effect of borrowing money from those who had it in order to get it into the hands of those who would spend it, to keep the momentum of the economy going in order to get us back on stable ground.

Eccles originally agreed to stay in Washington D.C. at the Treasury Department for 18 months. He was asked to form a committee to come up with a new housing program, and because nearly a third of the nation's unemployed had been in the building industry, the committee sought to stimulate housing construction. Eccles sat through a few meetings and listened to vague ideas circle around the room. Later, he would comment that the committee members sounded, "like a bunch of social workers who could only think in terms of public housing."[xxxvii] Eccles envisioned a private/public investment project on a much grander scale – one that would not only help the disadvantaged but would also stimulate the nation's economy, and thus the Federal Housing Authority (FHA) was born. Eccles believed that a maximum amount of private spending could be and should be stimulated by a minimum amount of public investment.[xxxviii]

Eccles was also the first person to introduce the concept of the subcommittee to Congress, and the suggestion worked so well that Eccles was named subcommittee chair of the FHA. The plan he and his group hammered out would alter conventional mortgage design forever. In essence, Eccles realized that to make loans more affordable so millions of Americans might have the opportunity to own a home, the government should insure home mortgages, thus allowing the banks to lend for a much longer term. Prior to 1933, banks would lend only up to 50% of a home's value, and the loan had to be totally repaid in a *five-year term*, making homes beyond reach for most Americans. Building and loan associations would lend up to 80% of a home's value, but only at sub-prime rates, forcing homeowners to take out second and third mortgages.[xxxix] During the Depression, if a homeowner defaulted on one loan, he defaulted on all, and faced foreclosure.

Eccles proposed three new concepts in tandem with the FHA:
- A single mortgage loan given on a much higher percentage of the property value – up to 80%.
- Lower interest rates.
- A much longer maturity of up to 30 years on all mortgage loans.

These three changes made homes much more affordable for Americans. In order to induce banks to make these loans, the federal government promised to insure the loans by adding 1% to the interest fee, creating an insurance fund with the proceeds. The government would then make up the difference in the case of a default, using the insurance fund. Eccles' theory was shrewd. He was using a small government investment that would stimulate a great deal of private spending. This was Eccles' concept of government leverage.[xl]   The FHA bill met with some serious opposition in Congress, but ultimately it did pass and became a law from which millions of Americans benefited and continue to benefit today.[xli] Eccles had done what he had promised. His vision changed the economic landscape of our country, making homes affordable for tens of millions of Americans who otherwise would have spent their lives renting, and by doing so, the nation's recovery from the Great Depression was accelerated. This idea of Eccles' was one of the cornerstones that built the middle class in America over the next 60 years.

After Marriner Eccles spent 16 months in the Treasury Department creating the template for the FHA, he had established himself as one of the president's most astute advisors. In August of 1934, Marriner was stunned to learn that FDR had nominated him to become the first chairman of the Federal Reserve Board.[xlii] Eccles' 18 months at Treasury would evolve into a 17-year sojourn in Washington. FDR stressed to Eccles that there would be considerable opposition to his appointment as the new Fed chairman. But when FDR pounded his desk emphatically saying, "I don't give a damn." Marriner replied, "Well, Mr. President, if you don't give a damn, I don't see why I should either." [xliii] However, Eccles proposed a number of conditions before he would ultimately agree to this new role as Fed chairman, and he asked for a month to prepare his proposal for the president. His conditions to FDR were substantial and compelling:

1. He wanted the role of the Federal Reserve to be altered to become a wholly autonomous arm of the Treasury Department.

2. He wanted all Fed powers centralized in Washington D.C. – far away from the politics and bankers of New York City.

3. He insisted that the Fed's role be subordinated to the

executive branch so that the Fed and Treasury would
become two separate and distinct entities, granting
the Federal Reserve full authority over monetary policy
and the Treasury complete control over fiscal policy.

Roosevelt listened intently to Eccles' presentation for almost two hours. Although he knew this would be another battle with the bankers and the "good ol' boy network" in New York City and Congress who were intent on the status quo, FDR said with indignation, "It will be a knock-down, drag-out fight to get it through, but we might as well undertake it now as at any other time." FDR granted all of Eccles' requests and nominated him to become the first Federal Reserve Board chairman in 1934.[xliv] Both FDR and Eccles were unprepared for just how strong the opposition would be. Powerful interests in Congress, lobbied heavily by New York bankers, were determined to defeat both Eccles and the Banking Act he proposed. Despite the rancor, the Senate finally confirmed Marriner Eccles in February of 1935.[xlv]

As Fed chairman, Eccles began to examine the commingling of commercial and investment banking activities on Wall Street, a practice that began in the early '20s. He discovered that there were innate conflicts of interest and fraud in some banking institutions' securities activities, and he realized the need for powerful new legislation. Eccles' ideas led to the Banking Act being passed in 1935 and the Glass-Steagall Act, sponsored by Carter Glass and Henry Steagall, being passed as well.[xlvi] This was the country's first genuine effort to curtail excess speculation and excessive leverage on Wall Street. The Glass-Steagall Act created a giant firewall separating commercial banking firms (checking, savings, loans) from investment banking firms (stocks, bonds and other securities). The law was designed to protect investors from the integration of these two facets of the banking industry and the fraud that frequented such commingling. Eccles' goal was to promote sound business practices resulting in greater consistency, predictability and stability (CPS) for the average Main Street investor as well as fewer pitfalls for those on Wall Street.

Marriner Eccles' career embodied the spirit of the word statesmanship, making him one of the most compelling economists and leaders in America's 20th century. His vision was to create a stable national economy, and that is what he accomplished during his tenure in Washington. He did not parse words when he believed he was correct. A radical among his peers, Eccles detested politics; albeit in many respects, he turned out to be a savvy politician. He once said: "I believe that inefficiency and waste should be eliminated. I abhor politics and favoritism in any phase of government expenditures. I am as anxious as anyone to see the federal budget balanced."[xlvii] But he believed that the federal government was the lender of last resort and that if the government were proactive it could end the Great Depression. At the end of the day, Eccles was right. Eccles did not believe in partisanship. He believed in putting his country first, and it was this Republican and colleague of a Democrat – Franklin Delano Roosevelt – who brought the country back from the ashes to the economic juggernaut it is today. It was Eccles who persuaded Roosevelt to move forward with a radical set of untested policies. This progressive, sagacious Republican persuaded a Democrat, Franklin Delano Roosevelt, that draconian government involvement and deficit spending could lead the country out of the Great Depression.[xlviii] As history will testify, Eccles was correct.

CHAPTER 1 ENDNOTES

[xviii] Sidney Hyman, *Marriner S. Eccles: Private Entrepreneur and Public Servant* (California: Stanford. 1976), 95.

[xix] Marriner Eccles, *Beckoning Frontiers: Public and Personal Recollections* (New York: Alfred A. Knopf Inc., 1951) 26.

[xx] The Federal Reserve Bank of Minneapolis, "The Tale of Another Chairman." Accessed December 13, 2011. http://www.minneapolisfed.org/publications_papers/pub_display. cfm?id=3562.

[xxi] Utah State History, "People Who Made a Difference: Marriner Eccles." Accessed December 13, 2011. http://history.utah.gov/learning_and_research/make_a_difference/eccles.html.

[xxii] Brookings Institute, "The CNN Effect: How 24-Hour News Coverage Affects Governments Decisions and Public Opinion." http://www.brookings.edu/events/2002/0123media_journalism.aspx.

[xxiii] Marriner Eccles, *Beckoning Frontiers: Public and Personal Recollections* (New York: Alfred A. Knopf Inc.., 1951) 39-47.

[xxiv] The Federal Reserve Bank of Minneapolis, "The Tale of Another Chairman." Accessed December 13, 2011. http://www.minneapolisfed.org/publications_papers/pub_display.cfm?id=3562.

[xxv] Utah State History, "Marriner Eccles." Accessed December 14, 2011. http://history.utah.gov/ learning_and_research/make_a_difference/eccles.html.

[xxvi] Utah State History, "Marriner Eccles." Accessed December 14, 2011. http://history.utah.gov/ learning_and_research/make_a_difference/eccles.html.

[xxvii] Marriner Eccles, *Beckoning Frontiers: Public and Personal Recollections* (New York: Alfred A. Knopf Inc.., 1951) 71-80.

[xxviii] Marriner Eccles, *Beckoning Frontiers: Public and Personal Recollections* (New York: Alfred A. Knopf Inc.., 1951) 81.

[xxix] Sidney Hyman, *Marriner S. Eccles: Private Entrepreneur and Public Servant* (California: Stanford. 1976), 94.

[xxx] Sidney Hyman, *Marriner S. Eccles: Private Entrepreneur and Public Servant* (California: Stanford. 1976), 95.

[xxxi] Sidney Hyman, *Marriner S. Eccles: Private Entrepreneur and Public Servant* (California: Stanford. 1976), 94.

[xxxii] Marriner Eccles, *Beckoning Frontiers: Public and Personal Recollections* (New York: Alfred A. Knopf Inc.., 1951) 91.

[xxxiii] Utah State History, "Marriner Eccles." Accessed December 14, 2011. http://history.utah.gov/ learning_and_research/make_a_difference/eccles.html.

[xxxiv] Sidney Hyman, *Marriner S. Eccles: Private Entrepreneur and Public Servant* (California: Stanford. 1976), 110.

[xxxv] Sidney Hyman, *Marriner S. Eccles: Private Entrepreneur and Public Servant* (California: Stanford. 1976), 190-197.

CHAPTER 1 ENDNOTES

[xxvi] The Federal Reserve Bank of Minneapolis, "The Tale of Another Chairman." Accessed December 14, 2011. http://www.minneapolisfed.org/publications_papers/pub_display.cfm?id=3562.

[xxvii] Sidney Hyman, *Marriner S. Eccles: Private Entrepreneur and Public Servant* (California: Stanford. 1976), 143.

[xxviii] Sidney Hyman, *Marriner S. Eccles: Private Entrepreneur and Public Servant* (California: Stanford. 1976), 143.

[xxvix] Sidney Hyman, *Marriner S. Eccles: Private Entrepreneur and Public Servant* (California: Stanford. 1976), 145.

[xl] Utah State History, "Marriner Eccles." Accessed December 14, 2011. http://history.utah.gov/learning_and_research/make_a_difference/eccles.html.

[xli] Sidney Hyman, *Marriner S. Eccles: Private Entrepreneur and Public Servant* (California: Stanford. 1976), 150.

[xlii] Utah State History, "Marriner Eccles." Accessed December 14, 2011. http://history.utah.gov/learning_and_research/make_a_difference/eccles.html.

[xliii] Marriner Eccles, *Beckoning Frontiers: Public and Personal Recollections* (New York: Alfred A. Knopf Inc.., 1951) 175.

[xliv] Marriner Eccles, *Beckoning Frontiers: Public and Personal Recollections* (New York: Alfred A. Knopf Inc.., 1951) 175.

[xlv] The Federal Reserve Bank of Minneapolis, "The Tale of Another Chairman." Accessed December 15, 2011. http://www.minneapolisfed.org/publications_papers/pub_display.cfm?id=3562.

[xlvi] Marriner Eccles, *Beckoning Frontiers: Public and Personal Recollections* (New York: Alfred A. Knopf Inc.., 1951) 232.

[xlvii] Utah State History, "Marriner Eccles." Accessed December 15, 2011. http://history.utah.gov/learning_and_research/make_a_difference/eccles.html.

[xlviii] Utah State History, "Marriner Eccles." Accessed December 15, 2011. http://history.utah.gov/learning_and_research/make_a_difference/eccles.html.

CHAPTER 2

RANKING THE PRESIDENTS

★ ★ ★ ★ ★ ★ ★ ★ ★ ★ ★ ★

Americans have a voracious appetite for rankings, reviewing and relying on rankings of the best and worst new cars, athletes in a particular sport, restaurants, colleges, or places to live – to name a few. In this chapter, we will satisfy that appetite by ranking the U.S. presidents on their stewardship of the U.S. economy, a topic of the utmost importance to each and every one of us. We evaluate the performance of the U.S. presidents for the past 80 years, from Herbert Hoover and the Great Depression (1929) through George W. Bush and the Great Recession (2008). During this 80-year period, Democrats and Republicans shared the Oval Office for precisely 40 years each, creating a unique opportunity to compare and contrast the performance of each of the political parties. We do that in Chapter 14. Our rankings of the presidents (Chapter 2) and their political parties (Chapter 14) will be based upon our Presidential Rankings of Economic Stewardship, which will be referred to throughout this book as the PRES Rankings.

The PRES Ranking System is a customized system for ranking and evaluating economic performance and was developed by the authors specifically for use in this book.

For now, let's look at how all the presidents over the past 80 years have fared as CEOs and chief stewards of the economy. Two of them, John F. Kennedy and Gerald Ford, did not serve full terms. Since neither served long enough to fairly evaluate their performance in office, for purposes of our rankings we have combined JFK with his successor, fellow Democrat Lyndon Baines Johnson, and Ford with his predecessor, fellow Republican Richard Nixon. At the time of the writing of this book, approximately three years of data (2009-2011) were available for President Barack Obama, insufficient to include him in the rankings. However, we will provide some information and analysis regarding his economic stewardship in this and later chapters. Figure 2-1 depicts how the presidents are sorted.

★ ★ ★ ★ ★ ★ ★ ★ ★ ★ ★ ★

DATES IN OFFICE	U.S. PRESIDENT (CEO & CHIEF ECONOMIC STEWARD)
March 1929 - March 1933	Herbert C. Hoover
March 1933 - April 1945	Franklin Delano Roosevelt
April 1945 - January 1953	Harry S. Truman
January 1953 - January 1961	Dwight D. Eisenhower
January 1961 - January 1969	John F. Kennedy and Lyndon B. Johnson
January 1969 - January 1977	Richard M. Nixon and Gerald R. Ford
January 1977 - January 1981	Jimmy Carter
January 1981 - January 1989	Ronald Reagan
January 1989 - January 1993	George H.W. Bush
January 1993 - January 2001	Bill Clinton
January 2001 - January 2009	George W. Bush

FIGURE 2-1 [xlix]

As asserted in the preface to this book, we believe the president of the United States is the chief executive officer (CEO) of this country and the chief steward of its economic fortunes. Some may argue that Congress determines this country's economic plight. We disagree. Consider that the president sets the tone for the country, he appoints people to influential positions within his Cabinet and various government agencies (including the Federal Reserve Chair and U.S. Treasury Secretary), possesses broad power to enact executive orders, has access to the "bully pulpit" at any time, can significantly influence the confidence and attitudes of the American public through his leadership, and holds the ultimate legislative weapon – the presidential veto.[1] In other words, we assign credit or blame to a president for what happens on his watch. Whether you are the CEO of a company (or the country), or work in the mailroom, whether a teacher, or a plumber, or a nurse, everyone expects to be measured on the results under their tenure. Even if you inherit a lousy set of circumstances (or a lousy economy) from your predecessor, your boss will still evaluate you on what you did. And American voters evaluate the president in like manner. We have followed this familiar and fair system in ranking the presidents for the past 80 years.

The PRES Ranking System rests upon three separate but distinct economic pillars: (1) the U.S. Financial Health Pillar, (2) the Personal Wealth Pillar, and (3) the Business Prosperity Pillar. Each pillar is in turn made up of four to six economic indicators pertinent to the health of that sector. Each of the 11 presidential administrations is assigned a PRES Indicator Score based upon how it ranks under each economic indicator, with a score of 1 (worst) through 11 (best). The PRES Indicator Scores are added together under each pillar to obtain the PRES Pillar Scores, which are then added together to obtain the PRES Economic Stewardship Score. The PRES Rankings (1st through 11th) are based upon the PRES Economic Stewardship Scores of the respective presidential administrations – the highest score wins. This PRES Ranking System is depicted on the spreadsheet contained in Appendix A.

Our goal in developing this system was to inform our readers which presidents and political party were the best and worst economic stewards during this 80-year period, based on their across-the board performance for the nation, the average worker, and the business owner. In selecting which economic indicators to use, the goal was to present quantifiable facts from reliable and reputable sources, not innuendo, hyperbole, or subjective opinion coming from political candidates and their advisers or political pundits on various talk shows. In searching through the voluminous data available, we sought to level the playing field by using only statistics calculated and maintained as far back as 1929 – when Herbert Hoover took office. Using only such long term and time-tested statistics did limit us to some extent; however, we believe the economic indicators chosen provide a sound and fair measurement of a president's economic performance.

We calculated many of the indicators on a per capita basis to eliminate the impact of a growing population, a factor outside the president's control. We also converted dollar amounts into 2010 dollars to eliminate the impact of inflation. Of course, we did include inflation as a stand-alone economic indicator under the Personal Wealth Pillar, using a statistic that measured "% of Years of Acceptable Inflation." Many of our indicators reflect the average annualized change in a given economic indicator to reflect how a president handled the situation he inherited from his predecessor – did he make it better or worse? Moreover, calculating an average annualized change eliminates the impact of the length of the president's term in office, allowing for a fairer comparison. In short, we have done our best to optimize the fairness and objectivity of the PRES Ranking System. We had no predetermined outcome in mind when compiling the statistics and rankings and let the data lead us to our (surprising) conclusions.

Ronald Reagan suggested that the American voter, when casting his/her vote for a presidential candidate, must answer the question: "Are you better off now than you were four years ago?"[li] When developing our rankings, we recognized that the answer to that question may vary depending upon your relationship to the U.S. economy. The country's gross domestic product (i.e., the value of goods and services produced) and national debt may be meaningless to you if you are someone without a job or a business owner struggling to make a profit or to raise capital. It is extremely frustrating to hear on the nightly news that our country's economy is doing well because GDP is up or national debt is down, neither of which measures the plight of the American worker or business owner in any real or significant way. Those statistics are "bigger picture" statistics applicable at a national level, which form our U.S. Financial Health Pillar. Economic indicators that may directly impact or measure the thickness of the average American worker's wallet are compiled in our Personal Wealth Pillar. Lastly, economic indicators that may directly impact or measure business performance are compiled in our Business Prosperity Pillar. Taken together, these three pillars allow for a fair, complete, and thorough look at our economic health.

We did repeat one economic indicator for two of the pillars and one for all three pillars. Our economic indicator that measures income inequality, Average Annual Change in the Top 1%'s Share of Income, was used for the U.S Financial Health Pillar and the Personal Wealth Pillar, as we believe that statistical measure has a significant impact on both the financial health of the country as a whole and the personal wealth of individuals in the bottom 99% of income earners.

Consistent with the name of our book, the economic indicator Average Annual Stock Market Return was used for all three pillars. We believe the average annual compound return of the stock market is a good indicator of: (1) the country's financial health, acting as a catalyst for the entire economy; (2) personal wealth, indicating whether the average American's retirement plan or personal investments are generating good returns; and (3) business prosperity, indicating whether publicly owned companies are profitable and growing and whether the climate is good for businesses to raise capital. The title of this book is meant to convey that there is a startling and important link between the political party affiliation of who is elected president and the performance of the stock market.

Economists and statisticians who have studied this link agree the party affiliation of the president is correlated to performance of the stock market. Pedro Santa-Clara and Rossen Valkanov studied and analyzed this phenomenon and published their findings in the Journal of Finance, Vol. LVIII, October 2003, hypothesizing as to why the stock market has performed so much better under Democratic presidents.[lii] We will take a further look at this study and phenomenon in Chapter 14, when we look at how the political parties fared under our PRES Rankings.

The economic indicators and the three economic pillars that make up the PRES Ranking System are described in more detail in Figure 2-2 below and in Appendix A.

ECONOMIC PILLAR	ECONOMIC INDICATOR
U.S. Financial Health	Average Annual Stock Return
	Average Annualized Change in GDP Per Capita
	Average Annualized Change in National Debt Per Capita as Percent of GDP
	Percentage of Months in Recession
	Average Annual Change in Top 1% Share of Income
Personal Wealth	Average Annual Stock Return
	Average Annualized Change in Average Personal Disposable Income Per Capita
	Average Unemployment Rate
	Average Annual Change in Unemployment Rate
	Percentage of Years of Acceptable Inflation
	Average Annual Change in Top 1% Share of Income

FIGURE 2-2

EXPLANATION

Used a blend of the Dow Jones Industrial Average, S&P 500, and NASDAQ as those indices became available.

Measured rate at which gross domestic product per capita increased or decreased; GDP=total value of goods and services produced.

Good indicator of country's ability to pay debt; measures whether national debt is excessive.

National Bureau of Economic Research (NBER) defines recession as "a significant decline in economic activity . . . lasting more than a few months, normally visible in real GDP, real income, employment, industrial production and wholesale-retail sales."[liii] NBER determines when it begins and ends.

Measured income inequality – whether the income gap widened between the bottom 99% and top 1% - calculating the average annual percentage change in that gap during the president's term.

Used a blend of the Dow Jones Industrial Average, S&P 500, and NASDAQ as those indices became available.

Disposable Income is gross income less tax paid.

Sum of unemployment rates each year divided by number of years in office.

Measured average by which unemployment rate increased or decreased on annual basis during presidential term (i.e. unemployment rate in last year of term minus unemployment rate in year prior to beginning of term divided by number of years of term).

Inflation reflects the price of goods and services; i.e., the average American's purchasing power. Acceptable inflation range of .95%-3.05% is a reasonable range based upon our readings of the opinions of well-respected U.S. economists, as confirmed by economists at the University of Cincinnati.

Measured income inequality – whether the income gap widened between the bottom 99% and top 1% - calculating the average annual percentage change in that gap during the president's term.

ECONOMIC PILLAR	ECONOMIC INDICATOR
Business Prosperity	Average Annual Stock Return
	Average Annualized Change in Index of Industrial Production
	Average Annual Trade Balance/Deficit
	Average Annualized Change in Corporate After-Tax Profits

Graphical illustrations of the rankings of the presidents under each economic indicator, economic pillar, and their overall PRES Economic Stewardship Score are presented over the next eight pages. You will be surprised!

U.S. FINANCIAL HEALTH PILLAR

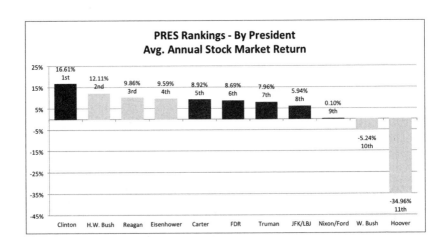

EXPLANATION
Used a blend of the Dow Jones Industrial Average, S&P 500, and NASDAQ as those indices became available.
Index of Industrial Production measures industrial output.
Positive balance if exports exceed imports; i.e., more money coming into U.S. than going out. Otherwise, there is a trade deficit.
Measured whether corporate (business) profits are increasing or decreasing

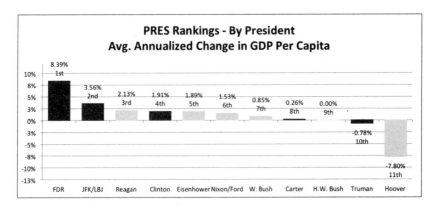

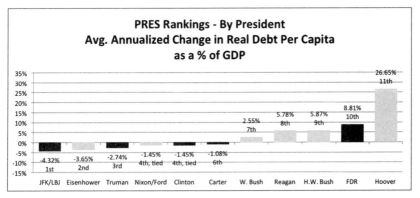

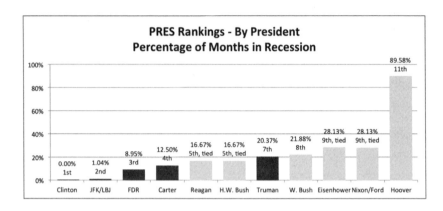

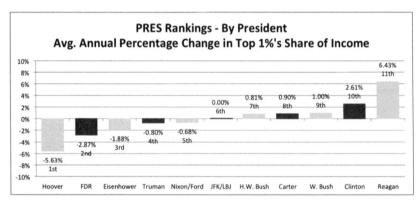

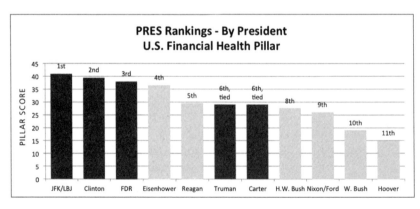

PERSONAL WEALTH PILLAR

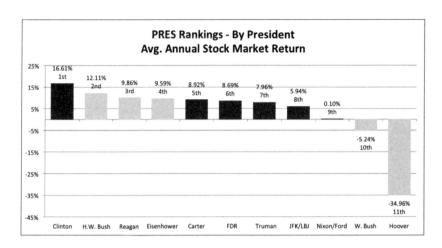

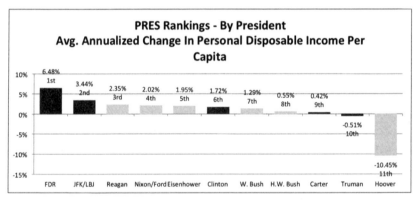

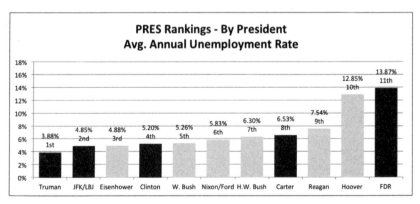

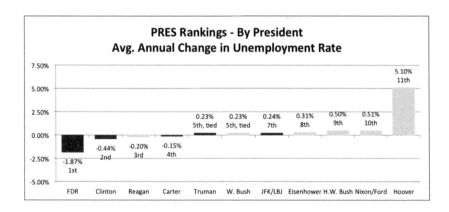

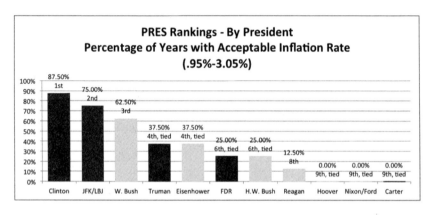

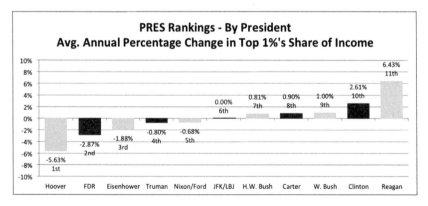

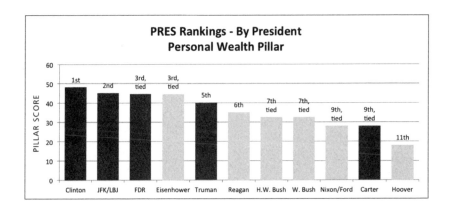

BUSINESS PROSPERITY PILLAR

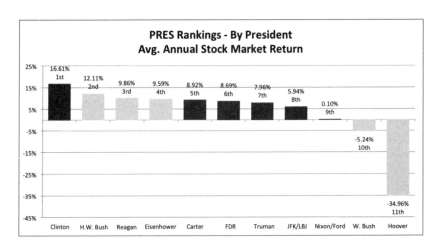

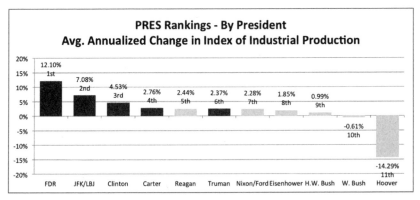

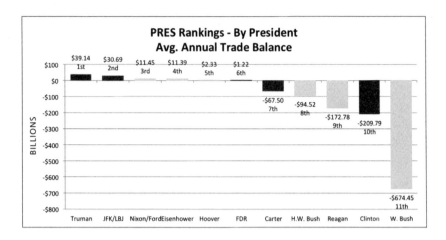

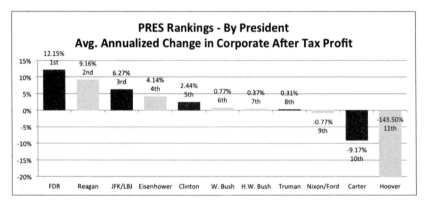

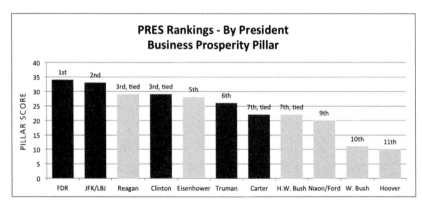

OVERALL: PRESIDENTIAL ECONOMIC STEWARDSHIP SCORE

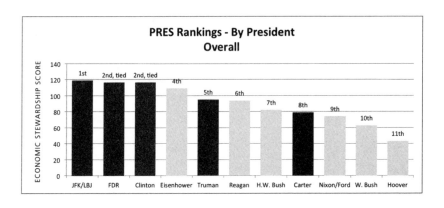

It is abundantly clear which presidents were the best and worst stewards of the U.S economy and your wallet. JFK/LBJ, Bill Clinton, and FDR, all Democrats, were the shining stars, while Nixon/Ford, George W. Bush and Herbert Hoover, all Republicans, trailed the field. Herbert Hoover was by far the worst steward of the U.S. economy, presiding over the Great Depression and ranking last by most measures. The only saving grace for Hoover was that he oversaw a positive trade balance and the income gap narrowed during his tenure as president. George W. Bush was the first president since Hoover to have produced negative stock market returns during his tenure. That indicator, along with the highest trade deficit of any president in our study, anchored him at the bottom, just ahead of Hoover. The Nixon/Ford duo struggled mightily with rising unemployment, high inflation, negligible stock market returns, and some deep recessions, causing them to lag the field just ahead of Bush. The stark contrast in performance between the shining stars and the laggards can best be illustrated by some simple math. If you had $100,000 in your 401(k) account in 1993, at the beginning of Bill

Clinton's eight years in office, and had withdrawn it for retirement when he left office in 2001, you would have had $341,894 to fund your retirement. If you had invested the same $100,000 in your 401(k) account just eight years later, in 2001, when George W. Bush took office, and had withdrawn it for retirement when he left office in 2009, you would have had $64,990 to fund your retirement, a whopping difference of $277,000. Playing this out further, if you had invested $400,000 at those two different time periods – only eight years apart – you would have had better than $1.1 million more at the end of the Clinton presidency than the Bush presidency – what a huge difference that would have made to you and your family during your retirement years. Your golden years might have lived up to their name. Are you convinced yet that it matters who is at the helm of our economy?

As you can see, the rankings are fairly consistent across all three pillars, with our three shining stars dominating the rankings under each pillar. JFK/LBJ, who ranked best overall, also ranked the best under our U.S. Financial Health Pillar, at or near the top in GDP growth, percentage of months in recession, and reduction of national debt. Bill Clinton, who ranked second overall, also ranked the best under the Personal Wealth Pillar, ranking at or near the top in stock market returns, inflation, and reduction in unemployment. FDR proved to be the best president for U.S. business, standing atop the Business Prosperity Pillar, reaping the benefits of a stellar performance in bringing this country out of the Great Depression (with the help of his colleague Marriner Eccles), and presiding over huge increases in industrial production and corporate profits during his tenure.

Harry Truman, another Democrat, finished in the top half of our rankings with an impressive fifth place showing overall, edging out Ronald Reagan for that spot. Truman was helped immensely by low unemployment during his presidency, a positive trade balance after World War II, and a narrowing of the income gap between the bottom 99% and top 1% of income earners. Among the Republicans, only Dwight Eisenhower and Ronald Reagan placed in the top six economic stewards during the 80-year period, with Eisenhower fourth overall and Reagan sixth. Ike had a consistent showing. He finished fourth under the U.S. Financial Health Pillar, tied for third under the Personal Wealth Pillar, and sixth under the Business Prosperity Pillar, with a strong performance as measured by most economic indicators in our PRES Ranking System. His performance was hindered by the three recessions suffered by the country during his presidency. Ronald Reagan also had a respectable and consistent showing – finishing fifth under the U.S. Financial Pillar, sixth under the Personal Wealth Pillar, and in a tie for third (with Clinton) under the Business Prosperity Pillar. His chances to rank near the top dwindled due to his poor performance in increasing the national debt by almost three-fold; plus his struggle with high unemployment, inflation, a significant trade deficit, and especially by a widening income gap (the worst of any president in our study).

George H.W. Bush performed better than his son in steering the U.S. economy; however, his performance was nothing to brag about. Despite a booming stock market during Bush's term, he finished seventh in our overall rankings, finishing near that spot for all indicators. In particular, his performance suffered due to minimal growth in GDP, employment and industrial production, and a rising national debt. Jimmy Carter was the only Democrat in the bottom half of the rankings overall and under each economic pillar. His presidency was marred by extremely high inflation and a significant drop in corporate profits. He ended up with a mediocre eighth place ranking.

Four of the top five spots in our PRES rankings are occupied by Democrats, as are the top three spots under every pillar, even the Business Prosperity Pillar. The bottom three spots are all held by Republicans. Are you surprised by these rankings? Despite the conventional wisdom espoused by much of the media and GOP hyperbole, that the Republican party has been better for business, the economy, or the average American's wallet; the reality is, the opposite is true.

Due to only two full years of data, we do not rank current President Barack Obama's performance as an economic steward. Suffice it to say, the country has struggled mightily with unemployment, debt, and a significant trade deficit during his presidency. It is interesting to note however, that corporate profits have increased dramatically under Obama and that the historical trend of bull markets under Democratic presidents has continued.[liv] The entire story of his economic legacy has yet to be told.

In Chapters 3 through 13, our readers will become acquainted with each of these men to whom we have tied our economic fortunes, what may have influenced them as people and as presidents, and what events and actions may have caused them to succeed or fail as stewards of the U.S. economy and your wallet. For our reader's enlightenment, at the top of the first page of each chapter, we provide a graphic (an example is shown on the next page) that summarizes each President's performance. We include a dollar amount that represents what your 401(k) or other investment account, worth $100,000 at the beginning of the president's term, would have been worth at the end of his term. The differences in that amount among our various economic stewards will surprise you. Also shown are the president's PRES Ranking overall and under each economic pillar (1st through 11th).

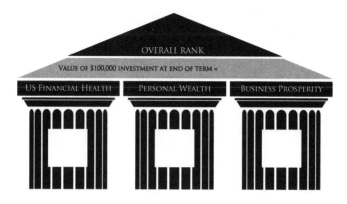

In Chapter 14, we will compare and contrast in more detail what the statistics show for the 40 years of Democratic presidents and 40 years of Republican presidents. It was not a close competition. In politics, such a lopsided result is called a landslide.

★ ★ ★ ★ ★ ★ ★ ★

CHAPTER 2 ENDNOTES

[xlix] Library of Congress. Accessed January 1, 2012. http://memory.loc.gov/ammem/pihtml./pihome.html.

[l] The Free Dictionary by Farlex, "Presidential Powers." Accessed December 13, 2011. http://legal-dictionary.thefreedictionary.com/Presidential+Powers.

[li] Aaron Bernstein, "Are We Better Off Than 4 Years Ago?" *Bloomberg Buisnessweek*, October 25, 2004. Accessed December 13, 2011. Retrieved from http://www.businessweek.com/magazine/content/04_43/b3905101_mz021.htm.

[lii] "The Presidential Puzzle: Political Cycles and the Stock Market," Accessed December 14, 2011. http://personal.anderson.ucla.edu/rossen.valkanov/Politics.pdf and The Journal of Finance, Vol.LVIII, No. 5, October 2003.

[liii] Graham Summers, "Protect Your Portfolio From the Government's Lies," *Global Stock Monitor*, May 5th, 2008. Accessed December 13, 2011. Retrieved from http://www.theglobalstockmonitor.com/archives.php?id=24.

[liv] John Maggs, "Corporate Profits' Big Climb," *Politico*, October 28, 2010. Accessed December 13, 2011. Retrieved from http://www.politico.com/news/stories/1010/44268.html.

CHAPTER 3

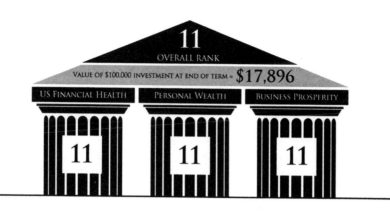

HERBERT HOOVER

WE BEGIN WITH A FAILING PRES RANKING

★ ★ ★ ★ ★ ★ ★ ★ ★ ★ ★ ★

*"Blessed are the young, for they shall
inherit the national debt."* [lv]

– Herbert Hoover

★ ★ ★ ★ ★ ★ ★ ★ ★ ★ ★ ★

Herbert Clark Hoover was born in 1874 in the small town of West Branch, Iowa. Orphaned at age 9 and raised by an uncle who was no more than a stranger, Herbert forged a natural aloofness and became a reticent analytic.[lvi] Although he never finished high school, he was admitted to and graduated with the first class at Stanford University,[lvii] where he majored in geology.[lviii]

Hoover was employed as a mining consultant for 20 years after Stanford.[lix] He, like Marriner Eccles, was a self-made multimillionaire who seemed to understand, at least in his early professional life, the government's important role in protecting the nation's labor force and providing a minimal standard of living to its people. Before he had declared his political status, in 1909, Hoover published *Principles of Mining*, a manual that advocated collective bargaining for workers, fair compensation, and serious attention to mine safety, among other things.[lx] The book helped spread Hoover's reputation as a sagacious businessman. In 1914, Hoover volunteered to organize international relief efforts for Belgium and after World War I he insisted the U.S. provide aid to the defeated Germans and the famine-stricken Bolshevik areas of Russia.[lxi] When asked why the United States was helping the Russians, he retorted: "Twenty million people are starving. Whatever their politics, they shall be fed!"[lxii] His success earned him a global reputation as a man of the people[lxiii] and he returned home to serve as an administrator for Democrat Woodrow Wilson.[lxiv] Unfortunately, Hoover was not a man of the people after he became president, a failure that disappointed Marriner Eccles. Hoover deviated substantially from the PRES Rules during his term in office, and that contributed significantly to the economic disaster over which he would preside.

Progressives of both parties courted Hoover after the war, but ultimately he declared himself a Republican, remarking that he could not become a a member of the Democratic Party whose only member in his hometown of West Branch had been the town drunk.[lxv] Hoover campaigned for Warren G. Harding and was rewarded with the cabinet post of Commerce, a role he competently filled for almost eight years.[lxvi]

The Great Mississippi Flood of 1927 set the stage for Hoover's successful bid for the White House. President Coolidge called upon him to oversee the flood relief effort, propelling him back into the national spotlight. After the flood, many blacks were sent to refugee camps in the South, where thousands were abused by local whites. Federal aid specifically intended for black sharecroppers went to white landowners instead. To cover up the travesty, Hoover made a deal with Robert Moton of the Tuskegee Institute. He promised Moton that black Americans would have unprecedented influence in his administration when he was elected president; in turn, Moton would agree to squelch the stories of abuse and mistreatment of blacks post-flood. Moton cooperated on his end of the bargain; however, Hoover recanted the deal upon his election. This deception led to a backlash in 1932 – one that shifted African-American allegiance to the Democrats for the next eight decades.[lxvii] In the short term, however, Hoover's strategy worked and he won the White House in a landslide.[lxviii]

THE PRESIDENTIAL YEARS

A wave of popular acclaim lifted Herbert Hoover into the White House after a distinguished career as an engineer, businessman, administrator, and Cabinet member. In his acceptance speech for the Republican nomination at his alma mater, Stanford University, he remarked, "We have not yet reached the goal, but given a chance to go forward with the policies of the last eight years, we shall soon with the help of God be in sight of the day poverty will be banished from this nation."[lxix] That statement, four years later, would define the word irony.

Also, in his inaugural address, he claimed that businesses should be allowed to self-govern – a concept we suspect would have somewhat disappointed Marriner Eccles. During the same speech, Hoover remarked, "The election has again confirmed the determination of the American people that regulation of private enterprise and not government ownership or operation is the course rightly to be pursued in our relation to business."[lxx] Famous economist and capitalist Adam Smith[lxxi] would have been proud of Hoover's comments, but Eccles likely would not have been. Hoover's inaugural address foreshadowed one his greatest shortcomings as chief steward of the U.S. economy: failure to adhere to the PRES Rule that, *"The federal government plays a vital role in creating and maintaining a healthy economy."*

In September of 1929, Hoover outlined a highly ambitious endeavor to recruit the best brains in the country to create a landmark study of American society. Their analysis would be the basis for "large national policies looking to the next phase in the nation's development" – a blueprint for the country to move forward.[lxxii] However, Black Monday and the chaos that began 30 days later doomed Hoover's hopes of any orderly command of the future.

You will recall that in Chapter 2 we ranked Hoover's performance as an economic steward the worst of the 11 administrations reviewed. According to our PRES Ranking System, Hoover's performance was the worst under each economic pillar – U.S. Financial Health, Personal Wealth, and Business Prosperity. For virtually all of our indicators, Hoover earned the dubious award of coming in last as the country wallowed through the Great Depression. He presided over a steady decline of the nation's economy during his term, culminating with a loss of more than 12 million jobs and an unemployment rate of 25.1%.[lxxiii] Hoover did little to assist the financial markets as he had unconditional faith that they would magically self-correct, contrary to what Marriner Eccles would have advocated.[lxxiv]

Hoover's troubles began in October of 1929, when in two short days the Dow Jones Industrial Average plummeted, losing 23% of its value.[lxxv] This signaled the beginning of a perfect storm. According to Eccles, the Great Depression resulted primarily from over-speculation and excessive leverage on Wall Street during the Harding/Coolidge years and also because the velocity of money (which, simply put, means that all of the money in circulation needs to be flowing through the system freely at all times) had slowed to a crawl – with too much wealth being concentrated in the hands of too few. [lxxvi] By late 1929, 1% of the population controlled more than 42% of the wealth in the United States.[lxxvii] Unfortunately, today we are re-approaching the same dangerous statistic: namely, that more than 40% of the wealth in the U.S. is held by 1.2% of the population.[lxxviii] *Hoover drastically deviated from our first two PRES Rules – to advance the interests of the common good, not solely the interests of the advantaged few, and to recognize the importance to the U.S. economy of the middle class.* In fact, his economic policies diminished the velocity of the money supply – a key to a strong and vibrant economy, according to Marriner Eccles.

So instead of achieving an economy in which money circulated freely, Eccles believed "a giant suction pump had, by 1929-1930, drawn into a few hands an increasing portion of currently produced wealth. By taking purchasing power out of the hands of mass consumers, the affluent savers denied themselves the kind of effective demand for their products that would justify a reinvestment of their capital accumulations in new plants. In consequence, as in a poker game, where the chips were concentrated in fewer and fewer hands, the other fellows could only stay in the game by borrowing. When their credit ran out, the game stopped."[lxxix] According to Eccles, this defined the Great Depression. The debacle that followed was not a total surprise to Marriner Eccles and others who supported his economic philosophies and principles.

Hoover believed in individualism, and as a Quaker he believed in duty and service as well.[lxxx] Government might indeed step in where voluntarism had manifestly failed, but it was not the government's role to substitute bureaucracy for voluntary cooperation. Doing so, Hoover believed, would mean the corruption of America's political soul. Eccles would have labeled that a mistake – not recognizing *the federal government plays a vital role in creating and maintaining a healthy economy.*[lxxxi]

However, history's indictment of Hoover is somewhat premature. Hoover was not a true conservative in the Harding/Coolidge mold. He had been sympathetic to GOP progressives, supported labor, urged closer business-government cooperation, established government control over the technology of radio while at Commerce, and proposed a multibillion-dollar federal public works fund.[lxxxii] Initially, he was not a passive steward. So why did he ultimately fail so miserably?

Hoover's downfall was of his own making: The great engineer was a paradox. Although he was a solid administrator and humanitarian, he was a feeble politician at best. Because he had never held any public office prior to being elected president of the United States, his own Congress held him in little regard and felt he was undeserving of this great office.[lxxxiii] Consequently, he never worked with his own Republican Congress effectively, and they ran roughshod over him.[lxxxiv] The laissez-faire approach Congress desired won the day, causing the Great Depression to deepen and the economic plight of businesses and labor to worsen. Hoover, as CEO of the economy, was left to take all the blame, as he rightfully should. In other words, Hoover was unable to "*lead as a statesman*" and bring Congress to act, another violation of the PRES Rules. This shortcoming would daunt him throughout his presidency.

Hoover believed in the concept of volunteerism, which many viewed as wishful thinking.[lxxxv] His reluctance to provide direct support to America's unemployed and starving was made especially clear when he vetoed the Garner-Wagner Relief Bill, which would have provided funds for aid and relief to the unemployed.[lxxxvi] This stands in stark contrast to his days as an administrator during the Great War, when he insisted that all of the people be fed, regardless of their nationality or political ideology.[lxxxvii] When he had the opportunity to feed and take care of his own citizens, Hoover failed to act. Again, Hoover deviated drastically from the PRES Rules to *advance the common good and the economic wellbeing of all Americans.* What he did finally do was considered at the time as too little too late.

After Hoover vetoed Garner-Wagner, he did sign the Relief and Construction Act in the summer of 1932, which financed some "self-liquidating" public works projects and lent up to $300 million to the states for relief aid.[lxxxviii] But this transformation, again, came too late to buy Hoover any political capital. Cartoonists caricatured him as a heartless money lover whose obsolete doctrines caused men, women and children to go hungry. The Democrats missed no chance to label the crisis as "Hoover's Depression." Shantytowns full of the unemployed and homeless became known as Hoovervilles, and when people pulled-out their empty trouser pockets, they were called "Hoover Flags."[lxxxix]

By the end of Hoover's fourth year, family incomes had plummeted, unemployment had increased eight-fold, and the country was on a relentless downward spiral.[xc] Hoover made a feeble effort to balance the budget in late '32, hoping that would correct the credit crisis, but that failed also.[xci] His balanced budget tactics came at the wrong time and deprived the economy of what it desperately needed – a stimulus that would have provided a shock to the economy. Herbert Hoover failed to recognize that *through deficit spending during recessionary times, the government could play a vital role in creating and maintaining a healthy economy.*

Eccles believed that the velocity of the money supply was as important as the volume of it and, contrary to that principle, the Revenue Act of 1932, among other things, instituted a two-cent tax on all checks and demand deposits.[xcii] The check tax was yet another contributor to the banking crisis that occurred after the Great Crash. Critics of the policy argued that the tax encouraged hoarding and a return to a cash and gold society and encouraged consumers to withdraw their money from banks to avoid paying the tax. This law added fuel to the fire and resulted in more than 9,000 banks closing during Hoover's tenure.[xciii]

THE PRES RANKINGS

Hoover's economic stewardship places him last in the PRES Ranking System. He finishes last in eight of 12 economic indicators and all three of the economic pillars. He is the only president to have presided over negative GDP growth in all four years of his term. Illustrated below is the performance of this president as an economic steward of the U.S. economy and your grandparents' wallets using our PRES Ranking System, which is described in detail in Chapter 2 of this book and Appendix A.

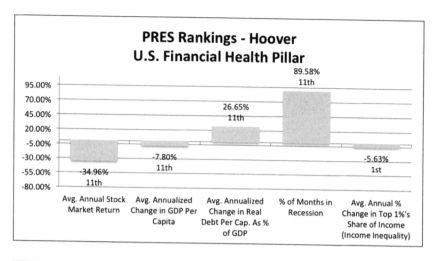

PRES Rankings - Hoover
U.S. Financial Health Pillar

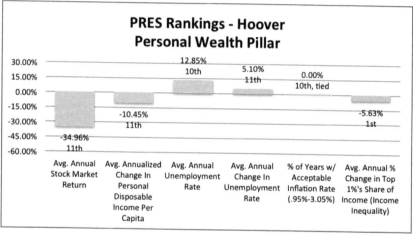

PRES Rankings - Hoover
Personal Wealth Pillar

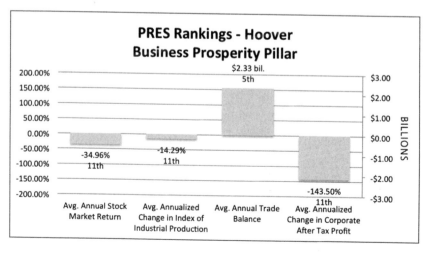

PRES Rankings - Hoover
Business Prosperity Pillar

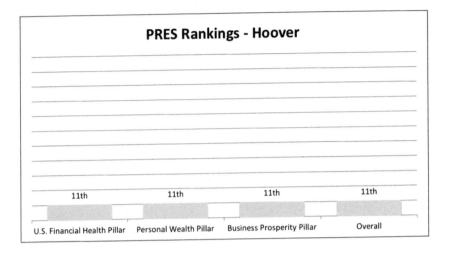

In speeches Eccles made to the banking community in 1932, he conveyed his belief that the political leaders of the world had been utter failures. Before the Utah Bankers Convention in1932, Marriner remarked, "Our difficulties . . . are due, in my opinion, to the failure of financial and political leadership in the world... and particularly in America."[xciv]

Herbert Hoover was a humanitarian and a solid administrator, but he failed to follow the principles that would have made him an effective president – straying far from most of the PRES Rules. By 1932, after four years in office, the most respected man in America had become loathed, his name synonymous with the Great Depression. By the fall of 1932, Hoover had given up on campaigning, and in that election he took a worse beating than the one he had given to Al Smith just four years earlier. Franklin Roosevelt and his brain trust, including his Republican colleague Marriner Eccles, would take over the helm.[xcv]

CHAPTER 3 ENDNOTES

[lv] Notable Quotes. Herbert Hoover as quoted in Francis X Cavanaugh's, *The Truth About the National Debt.* Accessed December 14, 2011. http://www.notable-quotes.com/h/hoover_herbert.html.

[lvi] Herbert Hoover Presidential Library & Museum. Accessed December 14, 2011. http://hoover.archives.gov/info/HooverBio.html.

[lvii] Herbert Hoover Presidential Library and Museum, "Hoover Timeline." Accessed December 12, 2011. http://www.hoover.archives.gov/info/HooverBio.html.

[lviii] The Miller Center of Public Affairs. "American President: A Reference Resource." Accessed December 12, 2011. http://millercenter.org/president/hoover/essays/biography/2.

[lix] Herbert Hoover Presidential Library and Museum, "Hoover Timeline." Accessed December 12, 2011. http://www.hoover.archives.gov/info/HooverTimeLine.html.

[lx] Profiles of the U.S. presidents, "Herbert Hoover – Early Life and Education." Accessed December 12, 2011. http://www.presidentprofiles.com/Grant-Eisenhower/Herbert-Hoover-Early-life-and-education.html.

[lxi] Herbert Hoover: "Presidential Library & Museum." Accessed December 12, 2011. http://www.hoover.archives.gov/exhibits/Hooverstory/gallery02/index.html.

[lxii] The White House, "Herbert Hoover." Accessed December 12, 2011. http://www.whitehouse.gov/about/presidents/herberthoover.

[lxiii] Louis W. Liebovich, *Bylines in Despair: Herbert Hoover, the Great Depression, and the U.S. News Media* (Connecticut: Praeger Publishers, 1994). Accessed December 12, 2011. Retrieved from http://books.google.com/books. Page 15.

[lxiv] United States History, "Herbert Hoover." Accessed December 12, 2011. http://www.u-s-history.com/pages/h1580.html.

[lxv] Donald W. Whisenhunt. Herbert Hoover. Nova Science Publishers, Inc. 2007. Accessed January 11, 2012. http://Books.google.com.

[lxvi] Totally History: Past, Present and Future, "Herbert Hoover." Accessed December 12, 2011. http://totallyhistory.com/herbert-hoover/.

[lxvii] PBS, "Robert Moton and the Colored Advisory Commission." Accessed December 12, 2011. http://www.pbs.org/wgbh/americanexperience/features/general-article/flood-moton-cac/.

[lxviii] 270towin.com, "1928 Election." Accessed December 12, 2011. http://www.270towin.com/1928_Election/.

[lxix] Brian Snowdon and Howard R. Vane, *Modern Macroeconomics: Its Origins, Development and Current State* (Massachusetts: Edward Elgar Publishing, 2005). Accessed December 12, 2011. Retrieved from http://books.google.com/books. Page 11.

[lxx] Yale Law School, Lillian Goldman Law Library. "Inaugural Address of Herbert Hoover." Accessed December 14, 2011. http://www.avalon.law.yale.edu/20th_century/hoover.asp.

[lxxi] Ten Great Economists. "The Federal Reserve Bank of San Francisco." Accessed December 14, 2011. http://www.frbsf.org/publications/education/unfrmd.great/greatbios.html.

CHAPTER 3 ENDNOTES

[lxii] David M. Kennedy for Stanford Magazine, "Don't Blame Hoover." Accessed December 12, 2011. http://www.stanfordalumni.org/news/magazine/1999/janfeb/articles/hoover.html.

[lxiii] The Miller Center of Public Affairs. "American President: A Reference Resource." Accessed December 12, 2011. http://millercenter.org/president/hoover/essays/biography/4.

[lxiv] David Madland and Jacob Pawlak, "A Tale of Two Conservatives: Comparing Bush and Hoover on the Economy." Published June 5, 2008. Accessed December 12, 2011. http://www.americanprogress.org/issues/2008/06/two_conservatives.html.

[lxv] Kimberly Amadeo. "How Dow Drop Compares to 1929 Stock Market Crash." Accessed January 7, 2012. http://useconomy.about.com/b/2011/08/13/how-dow-drop-compares-to-1929-stock-market-crash.html.

[lxvi] L. Dwight Israelsen, "Macroeconomic Analysis of Leading Interwar Authorities: Marriner S. Eccles, Chairman of the Federal Reserve Board." Published May 1, 1985. Accessed December 12, 2011. ebscohost.com.

[lxvii] States Department of Labor—Bureau of Labor Statistics. "Table Aa6-8."

[lxviii] Joseph E. Stiglitz, "Of the 1%, by the 1%, for the 1%." Vanity Fair. Accessed January 7, 2012. www.vanityfair.com/society/features/2011/05/top-one-percent-201105.

[lxix] William Greider, Secrets of the Temple: How the Federal Reserve Runs the Country (New York: Touchstone, 1987). Accessed December 12, 2011. Retrieved from http://books.google.com/books

[lxx] The Miller Center of Public Affairs. "American President: A Reference Resource." Accessed December 12, 2011. http://millercenter.org/president/hoover/essays/biography/2.

[lxxi] Laraine and Steve Blackham for the Standard Examiner, "Marriner Eccles: Balance Budget by Increasing Income." Published September 7, 2011. Accessed December 12, 2011. http://www.standard.net/stories/2011/09/07/marriner-eccles-balance-budget-increasing-income.

[lxxii] David M. Kennedy, Freedom From Fear: the American People in Depression and War, 1929-1945 (New York: Oxford Press, 1999). Accessed December 12, 2011. Retrieved from http://books.google.com/books. Page 11.

[lxxiii] National Park Service, "Herbert Hoover National Historic Site." Accessed December 12, 2011. http://www.nps.gov/nr/travel/presidents/herbert_hoover_nhs.html.

[lxxiv] Theodore Goldsmith Joslin, Hoover off the Record (New York: Doubleday, Doran & Company, 1934). Accessed December 12, 2011. Retrieved from http://books.google.com/books. Page 338.

[lxxv] Margaret Hoover, American Individualism: How a New Generation of Conservatives Can Save the World (New York: Crown Publishing Group, 2011). Accessed December 12, 2011. Retrieved from http://books.google.com/books. Page 18.

[lxxvi] "Hoover Kills Relief Bill," Florence Times, July 12, 1932, 1. Accessed December 12, 2011. Retrieved from http://news.google.com/newspapers?nid=1842&dat=19320712&id=Qg4sAAAAIBAJ&sjid=J7oEAAAAIBAJ&pg=4825,314731.

CHAPTER 3 ENDNOTES

[lxxxvi] National Archives and Records Administration, "Herbert Hoover Biography: U.S. Food Administrator." Accessed December 12, 2011. http://www.ecommcode.com/hoover/hooveronline/hoover_bio/food.htm.

[lxxxviii] CQ Researcher, "Provisions of Emergency Relief and Construction Act." Accessed December 12, 2011.

[lxxxix] The U.S. National Archives and Records Administration, "The Ordeal of Herbert Hoover Part II," *Prologue Magazine*, Vol. 36, No. 2, 2004.

[xc] United State Department of Labor—Bureau of Labor Statistics. "Employment status of the civilian noninstitutional population, 1940 to date."
ftp://ftp.bls.gov/pub/special.requests/lf/aat1.txt
Historical Statistics of the United States, series D-9, p. 126, for data before 1940.

[xci] Paul Krugman. "Fifty Herbert Hoovers." The New York Times. Accessed January 7, 2012. http: // www.nytimes.com/2008/12/29/opinion/29krugman.html.

[xcii] Federal Reserve Bank of New York Circular Series. Accessed December 14, 2011. http://fraser.stlouisfed.org/docs/historical/ny%20circulars/1932_01116.pdf.

[xciii] The Great Depression Bank Crisis. "Business and Industry, Hoover and Domestic Policy." Accessed January 7, 2012. *www.u-s-history.com/pages/h1525.htm.*

[xciv] Sidney Hyman, Marriner S. Eccles, Private Entrepreneur and Public Servant 99 (1976).

[xcv] Ipl2: POTUS (Presidents of the United States), "Herbert Clark Hoover." Accessed December 12, 2011. http://www.ipl.org/div/potus/hchoover.html.

CHAPTER 4

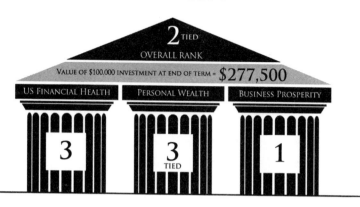

FRANKLIN DELANO ROOSEVELT

IMPRESSIVE ECONOMIC RANKINGS BY A FOUR-TERM PRESIDENT

"The test of our progress is not whether we add more to the abundance of those who have much; it is whether we provide enough for those who have too little." [xcvi]

– FDR's Second Inauguration speech on the U.S. Capitol steps on January 20, 1937

F ranklin Delano Roosevelt was born in upstate New York on January 30, 1882, to wealthy parents. He grew up in an atmosphere of opulence and privilege, and as an only child was doted on by his mother. He had a superb education, attending the Groton School for Boys, Harvard, and Columbia Law School.[xcvii] From his parents, and his Groton headmaster, Endicott Peabody, Franklin learned the importance of giving back to one's community and the value of public service for the greater good. Peabody would preach to Franklin in school that "good Christians strive to help those who were less fortunate than themselves."[xcviii] In addition to Peabody and his parents, Franklin admired his cousin Teddy Roosevelt's zeal for life and charismatic style of oratory, which Franklin adopted.[xcix] Franklin passed the bar in 1907 and became a corporate attorney at one of the most prestigious law firms on Wall Street.[c]

Despite strenuous opposition from his mother, Franklin courted and became engaged to his cousin Eleanor, Teddy Roosevelt's niece.[ci] Married in their early 20s, the two produced six children in the first 10 years of their marriage.[cii]

In 1910, FDR won a seat in the New York State Senate and within three years President Woodrow Wilson had appointed him Assistant Secretary of the Navy. When the United States entered World War I in 1917, FDR demonstrated his abilities as a genuine leader, strong negotiator, and a solid administrator. In 1920 he ran as the vice presidential candidate on the James Cox ticket, but they were badly beaten by the Republican candidate from Ohio, Warren G. Harding.[ciii]

The Roaring Twenties became the Daunting Twenties for Franklin. First, his wife, Eleanor, discovered his affair with her secretary and she immediately sought a divorce.[civ] That initiative was flatly vetoed, however, by Franklin's mother, Sara, who realized a divorce would end her son's political prospects. Because Sara was financially supporting Franklin and Eleanor, her decision was final and the two kept their marriage intact.[cv]

FDR's second crisis occurred when, at the age of 39, he was stricken with polio, which left him paralyzed from the waist down. At that time in our nation's history, absent the tabloid 24/7 news media of today, FDR convinced the general public he was improving. In private he used a wheelchair, but in public he could walk short distances with his braces by swiveling his torso and using a cane.[cvi] Remarkably, this great orator learned to use his head to make gestures while his hands held him upright at the lectern.

By the election in November of 1932, the Great Depression had left millions homeless and unemployed. FDR was the frontrunner within the Democratic Party to run against incumbent President Herbert Hoover. With the help of a coalition he created, that included newspaper mogul William Randolph Hearst and businessman Joseph Kennedy, Roosevelt won the nomination with ease.[cvii] FDR ran his campaign on a simple pledge of hope, coining the phrase, "I pledge you, I pledge myself, to a New Deal for the American people."[cviii] This general theme of hope over fear was simple, and it worked. FDR created the New Deal Coalition – consisting of southern whites, urbanites, blacks, and other minorities – which would hold for the Democratic Party for almost 50 years, fracturing during the civil rights movement and the Vietnam War of the 1960s and finally eroding when Ronald Reagan was elected in 1980.[cix] FDR easily defeated Hoover and started the process of restoring faith to a nation that had lost it, and hope to a nation that feared the worst was on the horizon. As FDR famously observed in his compelling inaugural address: "The only thing we have to fear, is fear itself."[cx]

THE PRESIDENTIAL YEARS

During FDR's first 100 days in office, he used political capital from his landslide win as well as the bully pulpit to rebuild the confidence of a beleaguered public. But FDR was uncertain how to solve the deep economic woes the country faced, as were many experts of the day. In fact, FDR was initially in the "balanced budget" camp with conservatives and some members of his own party, believing that approach would solve the country's problems. FDR began his presidency with the strategy of a balanced budget, which led to a mild recession in late 1933 – precisely the result that Marriner Eccles predicted would occur in a depressed economy. Each day of FDR's first year in office, his brain trust of Henry Morgenthau, Harold Ickes and Rex Tugwell dealt with the human misery created by the Great Depression. They knew better than most people that if the government did not put an end to the distress, then government as they knew it would come to an end through social upheaval.[cxi]

It was not until early 1934, when Eccles introduced to FDR the concepts of deficit spending and government leverage, that Roosevelt embraced these ideas as a means to get the country back on its feet. Eccles believed, as FDR came to believe in time, that "the government had the responsibility to put idle men, money and material back to work..." Eccles went on to say, "as they are put to work, and as private enterprise is stimulated to absorb the unemployed, the budget can and should be brought into balance, to offset the danger of a boom on the upswing, just as an unbalanced budget could counteract a depression on the downswing." Roosevelt came to believe in the Eccles notion that government should use a minimum amount of public money to create a maximum amount of private spending.[cxii]

Marriner Eccles persuaded FDR to take a leap of faith, which involved the exceptional step of borrowing capital from those who had wealth in order to get it into the hands of those who needed it desperately and would spend it. Based on this idea, FDR created temporary but important infrastructure jobs to jumpstart the economy through the "alphabet soup agencies," including the Federal Emergency Relief Administration (FERA), the Works Progress Administration (WPA), the Civilian Conservation Corps (CCC), the Agricultural Adjustment Association (AAA), plus dozens of others.[cxiii]

Recall that in Chapter 1, Marriner Eccles provided his views on what caused the economic collapse known as the Great Depression: "As in a poker game where the chips were concentrated in fewer and fewer hands, the other fellows could stay in the game only by borrowing. When their credit ran out, the game stopped." Eccles instinctively understood that the only viable pathway out of the Depression was through aggressive deficit spending. As prices dropped substantially during the Great Depression because of deflation, the wealthiest individuals in the country (note that the top 1% of the population controlled approximately 40% of the wealth in the United States by 1929) began to hoard capital or delay spending as they could afford to do both.[cxiv] "Savings that find no outlet and accumulate as hoarded funds interrupt the flow of the national income and in this case did result in a depression" commented Eccles in a speech in 1933. One of the basic tenets that keeps a free market economy working concerns the velocity of the money supply. This is one of Eccles' ideas that FDR espoused during his presidency.[cxv]

During the Great Depression, not unlike our world today, large corporations and the super-affluent hoarded money at the top. It took a general economic collapse to show "that too much thrift,"[cxvi] per Eccles, "could... be a source of great danger to the nation as a whole when practiced in excess." He insisted to FDR that the government needed to intervene or the downward spiral of the Depression would accelerate. Government spending increased from 8.0% of gross national product, as GDP was known then, under Hoover in 1932 to 10.2% by 1936. The national debt as a percentage of the GNP had more than doubled under Hoover from 16% to 33.6% in early 1932.[cxvii] However, under FDR, despite all of the investment in the economy over eight years, the national debt held steady at close to 40% as late as the fall of 1941.[cxviii] The reality is that FDR, despite the spending associated with the New Deal, did not significantly increase the national debt as a percentage of GNP because the economy grew substantially during his first eight years in office.

The Great Depression in the United States was due to many factors, but in the view of Eccles, it was primarily due to a collapse of banking and consumer credit. During the four years of Herbert Hoover's tenure, 9,000 banks failed in the United States: in other words, *two out of every five banks closed in the United States in just three years.*[cxix] And unlike today, where savers have Federal Deposit Insurance Corporation (FDIC) coverage to protect them when a bank collapses, depositors at that time lost all their wealth when a bank went down. However, thanks to the creation of the FDIC in 1933 (another Eccles idea), whereas 4,000 banks had failed in the first half of 1933, only nine banks failed in all of 1934. The Banking Act of 1933, which Marriner Eccles championed for Roosevelt, created the FDIC, among other important provisions which are in effect to this day. The Banking Act:[cxx]

- Gave the FDIC authority to provide deposit insurance to member banks.
- Gave the FDIC the authority to regulate and supervise state nonmember banks.

- Extended federal oversight to all commercial banks for the first time.
- Created a giant firewall between commercial and investment banking (the Glass–Steagall Act).
- Prohibited banks from paying interest on checking accounts.
- Allowed national banks to branch statewide.[cxxi]

Under FDR, a system of checks, balances and oversight was created which restored stability and predictability back to a financial system and confidence to a beleaguered public. Fortunately, FDR followed PRES Rule #3, recognizing that *the federal government plays a vital role in creating and maintaining a healthy economy*, including reasonable regulation of institutions vital to the capitalistic system.

Few people realize how severe the Great Depression was and why it took so long to dig out of the hole that Hoover, Coolidge and Harding created. To quantify this: *The Dow Industrial Average of 30 stocks lost 89% of its total value between the fall of 1929 and the summer of 1932.*[cxxii] The problem with a drop of this magnitude is that there is a very disproportionate relationship between the actual market loss and what return is required to make up that loss (to get back to where the market stood before the market drop took place). Consider these examples: When the market falls 10% (in what is considered a typical correction cycle today), it takes an 11% return to get back to where one started. A bear market is usually defined as a drop of 20% from peak to trough, but note it takes a 25% gain to get back to where one started before the decline.[cxxiii] However, in a crash,[cxxiv] which we have had five times over the past 80 years,[cxxv] and in which the market drops 50% or more, it takes a 100% gain to get back to even. And the numbers are more startling as the loss grows larger. As mentioned before, at the start of the Depression, the Dow

Average tumbled an unprecedented 89.2% from July of 1929 to July of 1932. This loss translated into the stock market needing a 945% gain just to get back to even! The return necessary to reacquire the gains that had been lost under Herbert Hoover was a startling 9.5 times greater than the actual loss itself. The Dow Industrial Average lost 29 years of gains in less than three years which explains why it took so long to dig out of the Great Depression.

The notion that many Republicans asserted then and continue to make today was that if FDR had simply left the economy alone, the financial markets would have eventually and magically corrected themselves.[cxxvi] They often talked of a "self-creating force" and thought of capitalism as a natural phenomenon that should never be touched. Eccles strongly disagreed, asserting that the government needed to develop policies that could be implemented quickly and make an immediate impact. "The time element would indefinitely prolong the Depression; such a policy would necessitate the further liquidation of banks, insurance companies, and all credit institutions."[cxxvii] Eccles realized that "this would increase the hoarding of money, decrease its velocity, freezing credit and make for endless deflation."[cxxviii] The business leaders of the 1930s, not unlike many in the 21st century, believed that a system meltdown was unavoidable, but thankfully wiser heads prevailed. Eccles understood that: "Economics is merely the production and distribution of wealth brought about by the application of labor to raw materials . . . and has developed by the application of the human intellect . . . it was subjected at once to man-made rules and regulations, which were changed constantly in accordance with the needs of a dynamic society."[cxxix] *In essence, what man had wrought, man could repair.*

The second New Deal began in 1935 and included a financial safety net called Social Security, which was designed to protect the elderly, poor and the sick. FDR and Eccles never intended Social Security to be the sole source of retirement income for an individual, as too many Americans view it as today, to the contrary, it was designed to augment other sources of income and savings that one would accumulate over the course of a 40-year working career.[cxxx] Unfortunately, due to infighting and hyperbole, Social Security has evolved into a staple benefit that many now call an entitlement: an inaccurate title because the funds are derived from money paid into the trust fund by the owner, unlike welfare and Medicaid, entitlements to which Americans are "entitled" if eligible. Nonetheless, to be clear, Social Security was never intended to be the sole source of retirement income for anyone.

Another highly controversial piece of legislation FDR supported was the Wagner Act, which became a critical event in the history of organized labor in the U.S. It created the National Labor Relations Board, which mediates disputes between unions and corporations, greatly expanded the rights of workers by banning many unfair labor practices, and guaranteed collective bargaining.[cxxxi]

The presidential election of 1936 was another landslide for FDR. The labor unions, energized by the Wagner Act, signed up millions of new members and became a major arm of support for Roosevelt.[cxxxii] There was little key legislation passed in FDR's second term, one notable exception being the Fair Labor Standards Act (FLSA) of 1938, which established a minimum wage of 25 cents per hour.[cxxxiii] When the economy began to deteriorate again in late 1937, Roosevelt asked Congress for $5 billion in relief and public works funding, and that effort created as many as 3.3 million jobs.[cxxxiv] The decision that FDR made in 1937, contrary to what Marriner Eccles had recommended, was to acquiesce to demands from Treasury Secretary Morgenthau to move back to a balanced budget. Eccles wanted to continue to use government leverage and to deficit-spend until the recession had completely ended.[cxxxv]

As a result of this change in strategy, which Morgenthau and the House Republicans vehemently pushed, the economy faltered and slid back into a recession in 1938.[cxxxvi] In response, the business community and the GOP attacked and blamed their fellow Republican Marriner Eccles. They said: "Eccles has sold us a wrong bill of goods…and it's brought us into this mess. What we need is a good capital goods expansion. That alone can do the trick."[cxxxvii] The GOP and the business community argued (incorrectly) that the basis of business confidence is a balanced budget as a means of getting out of the recession. Eccles disagreed. He recognized that the Great Depression began when the budget had been in balance and that spending and an unbalanced budget could help counteract the depression.[cxxxviii] During the recession of 1938, unemployment, which had fallen from 25.1% under Hoover to 14.3% in four years under FDR, jumped back up to 19.0%, slowing the recovery.[cxxxix]

The political wrangling during the Great Depression sounds very similar to today's politically charged climate, in which President Obama and many in the Democratic Party recognize the value of deficit-spending while many others, primarily Republicans, believe that cutting the deficit and balancing the budget will lead the country to greener economic pastures. If our politicians learned from our history and the genius of Marriner Eccles, they would realize the fallacy of budget-balancing during recessionary times and implement carefully crafted government spending programs targeted at the middle class in order to kick-start the private sector and the overall economy.

FDR won an unprecedented third term in 1940. Of course, World War II was the dominant factor in FDR's presidency and the economy from '41 on. At the peak of the war, the unemployment rate dropped to a low of 1.2% in 1944,[cxl] because more than 3.2 million Americans had volunteered or been drafted into the armed services.[cxli]

The war years had a tremendous impact on FDR's physical and emotional well-being, but in 1944 he ran for an unprecedented fourth term and won with Harry Truman at his side. On April 12th of 1945, Roosevelt complained of a terrific pain in his head, collapsed, and died later that day from a massive stroke.[cxlii] The country was stunned and saddened, as our longest serving president and one of our greatest economic stewards died at the age of 63. In Marriner Eccles' words: "I usually found myself in agreement with Roosevelt's social objectives though I often disagreed with his ideas as to the way they could be achieved. But whether I agreed or disagreed . . . I always felt we were working on the same team. I sorely missed him when he was gone."[cxliii]

THE PRES RANKINGS

As described in Chapter 2, Franklin Delano Roosevelt is a shining star in the PRES Ranking System, finishing among the top three spots for each economic pillar. Marriner Eccles admired his employer and colleague because FDR understood when to take bold action and he was smart and pragmatic as well. FDR and Eccles both enjoyed affluence and social privilege, but also shared the bond of being considered traitors to their own ethnic coterie, which they wore as a badge of honor. Franklin and Marriner believed that the creation of a robust, viable middle class was the only answer to solving the unprecedented economic hardships of the day. It was Eccles who taught FDR about the need to correct the disparity between the wealthiest of Americans, who hoarded cash and had far more of it than they would ever need, and the working class, who would spend money and keep the economy moving forward.

Franklin Delano Roosevelt, a pragmatist and a Democrat, hired Marriner Eccles, a Republican and multi-millionaire, to be the architect of many of the New Deal programs. FDR successfully shepherded these programs through Congress, but it was Eccles whose creative mind designed the New Deal landscape. These programs focused on what historians call the Three Rs: Relief (for the unemployed and poor); Recovery (of the economy to normal levels): and Reform (oversight and a reasonable set of regulations for the financial system). These programs worked, as the graphs below illustrate.

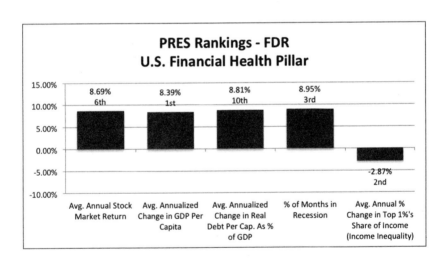

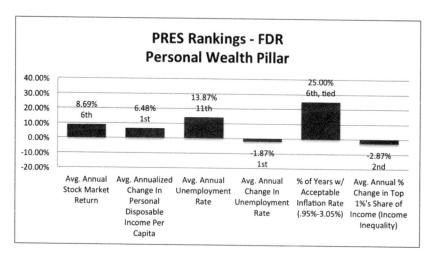

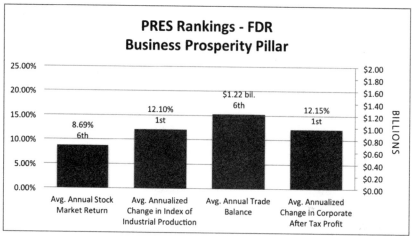

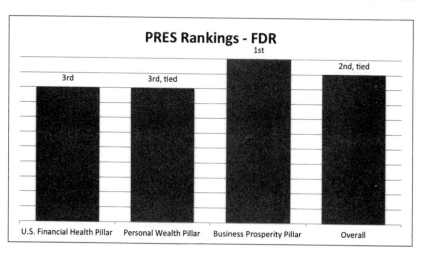

As you can see from the above graphs, FDR scores at the pinnacle of most of our economic indicators. He presided over an economy with the fastest growth and the largest increases in personal disposable income, industrial production, and corporate profits as well. Although unemployment stood at 25.2% during his first year in office, FDR was president during the steepest decline ever in the statistic of unemployment. FDR created an economic climate in which business and government worked cooperatively together and not as antagonists. This environment of *striving for the common good for all citizens, and not just the privileged few*, was another win for FDR, who, perhaps more than any other president in our study, closely followed all of the PRES Rules. He passionately believed, as did his Fed Chair Marriner Eccles, that *the middle class was the engine that drove the economy.* In fact, under FDR, the share of income held by the bottom 99% increased dramatically. This environment worked; indeed it fostered a bullish stock market under relatively low rates of inflation, bringing our country out of the Great Depression, with only one recession during Roosevelt's entire 12-year tenure. Despite his economic prowess, FDR did falter on one of our indicators. A dramatic spike in unemployment during his first year as president, along with the economic debacle he inherited, caused him to have the highest average unemployment rate of any president in our study, at 13.87%. Nonetheless, this weak showing was more than offset by his high ranking under the other indicators of the PRES Ranking System.

CHAPTER 4 ENDNOTES

[xcvi] Works of Franklin D. Roosevelt," The Second Inaugural Address." January 20, 1937. Accessed December 16,2011. http://newdeal.feri.rg/speeches/1937a.htm.

[xcvii] Miller Center of Public Affairs, "American President: A Reference Resource." Accessed December 14, 2011. http://millercenter.org/president/fdroosevelt/essays/biography/2.

[xcviii] Burns, James MacGregor (1956). Roosevelt (Vol. 1). (New York: Easton Press, 1956), 16.

[xcix] Miller Center of Public Affairs, "American President: A Reference Resource." Accessed December 14, 2011. http://millercenter.org/president/fdroosevelt/essays/biography/2.

[c] Franklin Delano Roosevelt Presidential Library and Museum. Accessed December 14, 2011. http://www.fdrlibrary.marist.edu/education/resources/bio_fdr.html.

[ci] Miller Center of Public Affairs, "American President: A Reference Resource." Accessed December 14, 2011. http://millercenter.org/president/fdroosevelt/essays/biography/2.

[cii] Ibid

[ciii] Franklin D. Roosevelt, Presidential Library and Museum. "Biography of Franklin D. Roosevelt." Accessed January 8, 2012. www.fdrlibrary.marist.edu/education/resources/bio_fdr.html.

[civ] Miller Center of Public Affairs, "American President: A Reference Resource." Accessed December 14, 2011. http://millercenter.org/president/fdroosevelt/essays/biography/2.

[cv] Smith, Jean Edward, FDR (New York: Random House. 2007), 160.

[cvi] Miller Center of Public Affairs, "American President: A Reference Resource." Accessed December 14, 2011. http://millercenter.org/president/fdroosevelt/essays/biography/2.

[cvii] Steve Wiegand, "Franklin Delano Roosevelt and the New Deal." Accessed December 14, 2011. http://www.dummies.com/how-to/content/franklin-delano-roosevelt-and-the-new-deal.html.

[cviii] Alex Kingsbury, "Franklin Delano Roosevelt's 'New Deal' Sealed the Deal in 1932," U.S. News, January 17, 2008. Accessed December 14th, 2011. http://www.usnews.com/news/politics/articles/2008/01/17/the-new-deal-sealed-the-deal

[cix] Don Keko, "FDR's New Deal Coalition: 1932-1968," January 12, 2010. Accessed December 14, 2011. http://www.examiner.com/american-history-in-national/fdr-s-new-deal-coalition-1932-1968.

[cx] "Only thing we have to fear is fear itself": FDR's First Inaugural Address. History Matters Website, accessed December 14, 2011.

[cxi] William J. Barber, "FDR's Big Government Legacy," Federal Reserve, Bank of Boston, Summer 1997. Accessed December 15, 2011. http://www.bos.frb.org/economic/nerr/rr1997/summer/barb97_3.htm.

[cxii] "Marriner Stoddard Eccles," Gale Encyclopedia of Biography, Answers.com. 2006. Accessed December 15, 2011. http://www.answers.com/topic/marriner-stoddard-eccles.

[cxiii] Franklin D. Roosevelt. American Heritage Center Museum. New Deal Achievements. Accessed January 8, 2012. www.fdr.heritage.org/new_deal.htm..

CHAPTER 4 ENDNOTES

[cxiv] "The Great Depression Causes and Effects," 2011. Accessed December 15, 2011. http://www.thegreatdepressioncauses.com/.

[cxv] "Marriner Stoddard Eccles," *Gale Encyclopedia of Biography*, Answers.com. 2006. Accessed December 15, 2011. http://www.answers.com/topic/marriner-stoddard-eccles.

[cxvi] Sidney Hyman. "Beckoning Frontiers," Alfred A. Knopf, New York, 1951. Page 37.

[cxvii] "Franklin D. Roosevelt Biography." Accessed December 15, 2011. http://www.paralumun.com/presfranklin.htm.

[cxviii] United States Department of the Treasury. "Historical National Debt Outstanding." June 17, 2011. http://www.treasurydirect.gov/govt/reports/pd/histdebt/histdebt.htm.

[cxix] "Great Depression Bank Crisis: Business and Industry, Hoover and Domestic Policy." Accessed on December 15, 2011. http://www.u-s-history.com/pages/h1525.html.

[cxx] Federal Deposit Insurance Corporation, "The Great Depression: 1929-1939," last modified November 18, 2010. Accessed December 15, 2011. http://www.fdic.gov/about/learn/learning/when/1930s.html.

[cxxi] Ibid

[cxxii] "Stock Market History," Bull Investors Website, last modified November 7th, 2010. Accessed December 15th, 2011. http://www.bullinvestors.com/stock-market-history.

[cxxiii] Jim Jubek, "5 rules for surviving a bear market," January 22, 2008. Accessed December 16, 2011. http://articles.moneycentral.msn.com/Investing/JubaksJournal/5RulesForSurvivingABearMarket.aspx.

[cxxiv] Adam Milton, "Market Crash" *About.com, Day Trading*. Accessed December 16, 2011 http://daytrading.about.com/od/atoc/g/Crash.htm.

[cxxv] Mondo Frazier, "Stock Markets Crashes: Five Stock Mark Downturns Since 1929," November 19, 2008. Accessed December 15, 2011. Novhttp://deathby1000papercuts.com/2008/11/stock-market-crashes-five-stock-market-downturns-since-1929/.

[cxxvi] Brian R. Farmer, *American Conservatism: History, Theory, Practice* (Cambridge Scholars Press, 2005)1.

[cxxvii] "Hearing Before the Committee on Finance, United States Senate, Thirty-Second Congress: Second Session, Pursuant to S. Res. 315. Accessed December 16, 2011. http://fraser.stlouisfed.org/docs/meltzer/ecctes33.pdf.

[cxxviii] Ibid

[cxxix] Edward J. Dodson, *The Discovery of First Principles," (Volume 3, Chapter 2, Part 4)*. Accessed December 16, 2011. http://www.cooperativeindividualism.org/dodson-edward_discovery-of-first-principles-2.4.html.

[cxxx] Just Facts. "Social Security," 2011. Accessed December 16, 2011. http://www.justfacts.com/socialsecurity.asp.

[cxxxi] Miller Center of Public Affairs, "American President: A Reference Resource." Accessed December 16, 2011. http://millercenter.org/president/fdroosevelt/essays/biography/4.

CHAPTER 4 ENDNOTES

[cxxxii] Miller Center of Public Affairs, "American President: A Reference Resource." Accessed December 16, 2011. http://millercenter.org/president/fdroosevelt/essays/biography/8.

[cxxxiii] "Fair Labor Standards Act." Accessed December 16, 2011. http://www.u-s-history.com/pages/h1701.html.

[cxxxiv] Burns, James MacGregor (1956). Roosevelt (Vol. 1). (New York: Easton Press, 1956), 320.

[cxxxv] Miller Center of Public Affairs, "American President: A Reference Resource." Accessed December 16, 2011. http://millercenter.org/president/fdroosevelt/essays/biography/4.

[cxxxvi] Ibid

[cxxxvii] Marriner Eccles, *Beckoning Frontiers: Public and Personal Recollections* (New York: Alfred A. Knopf Inc., 1951) 301.

[cxxxviii] Sidney Hyman, Marriner S. Eccles: Private Entreprener and Public Servent (California: Stanford. 1976), 96.

[cxxxix] Scott Lily, "Pumping Life Back in to the U.S. Economy," January 2009. Accessed December 16, 2011. http://www.americanprogress.org/issues/2009/01/pdf/lilly_stimulus.pdf.

[cxl] "United States Unemployment Rates," 2007. Accessed December 16, 2011. http://www.infoplease.com/ipa/A0104719.html.

[cxli] "Wars and Battles, 1939-1945" *World War II*. Accessed December 16, 2011. http://www.u-s-history.com/pages/h1661.html.

[cxlii] Miller Center of Public Affairs, "American President: A Reference Resource." Accessed December 16, 2011. http://millercenter.org/president/fdroosevelt/essays/biography/6.

[cxliii] Marriner Eccles, *Beckoning Frontiers: Public and Personal Recollections* (New York: Alfred A. Knopf Inc., 1951) 401.

CHAPTER 5

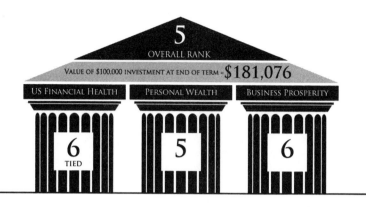

HARRY S. TRUMAN

THE FAIR DEAL PRESIDENT
CREATES ABOVE-AVERAGE RESULTS

★ ★ ★ ★ ★ ★ ★ ★ ★ ★ ★ ★

*"It is amazing what you can accomplish if
you do not care who gets the credit."* [cxliv]

– Harry S. Truman in an interview with *Life Magazine* in 1948

★ ★ ★ ★ ★ ★ ★ ★ ★ ★ ★ ★

H arry S. Truman, the 33rd president of the United States, succeeded Franklin Delano Roosevelt on April 12, 1945. Truman was born in Lamar, Missouri, a small farming town near Kansas City. [cxlv] His middle name is unique in that it stands for absolutely nothing. His parents gave him the middle initial "S" to appease both grandfathers, Anderson Shipp Truman and Solomon Young. [cxlvi]

As a young boy, Harry's favorite interests were reading and history[cxlvii]. Like Roosevelt, Truman was close to his mother, Martha Ellen, and solicited political as well as personal advice from her throughout his lifetime, including his time in the oval office. She died in Truman's third year[cxlviii] in the White House.

In June of 1919, Truman married Bess Wallace[cxlix], his childhood sweetheart. Their only child, Mary Margaret[cl], was born four years later. From 1919 to 1922, Harry ran a haberdashery[cli] in Kansas City. His store failed in the Harding recession of 1922, but through persistence, Truman avoided personal bankruptcy and paid off his share of the store's debts[clii]. Harry was a man of integrity who believed in taking responsibility for his mistakes. Later, as president of the United States, he memorialized this behavior by having a placard on his desk that read: "The Buck Stops Here![cliii]"

Truman started his political career at the relatively late age of 38, when he was elected town judge in Independence, Missouri.[cliv] He built a reputation as an honest and skilled administrator and went on to serve two terms as a county judge.[clv] The Democratic leader in Kansas City, Tommy Pendergast,[clvi] took note of Truman and helped him win a United States Senate seat in 1934[clvii] in what was then a solidly Democratic Missouri.

Truman's integrity and analytical skills won over his constituents and colleagues in the Senate.[clviii] Harry became a workhorse in the Senate compared with others who were mere "show horses." During his second Senate term, he gained national recognition for leading a shrewd but fair investigation into corporate fraud and waste perpetrated upon the U.S. military[clix]. Fed Chair Marriner Eccles likely would have approved of Truman's solid work, as he detested the flagrant war profiteering that took place both during and after the war. Roosevelt selected Truman to run as his vice presidential nominee on the Democratic ticket in the 1944 election,[clx] which propelled FDR into an unprecedented fourth term.

THE PRESIDENTIAL YEARS

Truman, largely left out of FDR's programs and plans, was unprepared to deal with the daunting responsibilities that enveloped his life when Franklin died of a stroke three months into his fourth term. Truman told reporters the day after FDR had died: "I felt like the moon, the stars, and all the planets had fallen upon me."[clxi] However, Truman moved forward, and Marriner Eccles was impressed by the manner in which he took over the helm. Although Harry had little to no foreign policy experience, he was a capable administrator, a skilled politician, and he defined the word tenacity. Upon assuming his new role, Truman requested that all of FDR's cabinet remain,[clxii] including Eccles, conveying to them that he was "open to their advice."[clxiii] However, he made it clear that he was the one making the decisions and "they were to support him or be fired."[clxiv]

After VE (Victory in Europe) Day on May 7, 1945, Truman learned that the test of the first atomic bomb had been successful.[clxv] The next day, Truman sent an ultimatum to the Japanese emperor to surrender or face "utter devastation."[clxvi] At the time, the national debt was hovering at an epic 116% of GDP, and the nation's solvency was on the brink. That fact, coupled with the joint chiefs projecting that 500,000 Americans would be killed if an invasion of mainland Japan were to take place,[clxvii] led Truman (when Japanese officials refused to even respond to his ultimatum), to authorize dropping the atomic bomb on the cities of Hiroshima and Nagasaki.[clxviii] This was one of the most controversial decisions ever made by any president, but it did result in the Japanese surrendering unconditionally days later on August 14th, 1945.[clxix]

The transition from a wartime to a peacetime economy was tumultuous. After the war was over, Marriner Eccles remarked, "Every economic group . . . wanted the benefits of inflation for itself to be paid for by a different group. The farmer wanted a floor for his prices but not a ceiling . . . The real estate people wanted easy credit. Labor always wanted price controls, but vigorously resisted wage controls. The bankers wanted higher interest rates, but they did not want the federal banking agencies to have any other powers over the expansion of credit."[clxx]

When a resurgence of lynchings rocked the South in 1946,[clxxi] Truman called for drastic changes in civil rights. Despite overwhelming opposition, he reached out to African Americans in a manner that was historic for any president. Though Truman's views on race were similar to those of most white Americans of his time, he understood that the U.S. Constitution guaranteed rights to all Americans.[clxxii] Like Marriner Eccles, Truman was a pragmatist, and he realized that African Americans represented a large voting bloc. So for reasons both noble and political, Truman moved forward on the race issue. For example, he issued an executive order to integrate the military.[clxxiii] Truman's positions on race relations paved the way for the equal rights legislation of the 1960s.[clxxiv]

After the war, Truman faced a burdening national debt, a renewal of labor conflicts, severe shortages in housing as the soldiers returned, and shortages in consumer products.[clxxv] There was also widespread inflation as increasing demand for goods and services pushed prices higher.[clxxvi] A wave of strikes hit major industries,[clxxvii] and Truman's response to most of them was viewed as ineffective.[clxxviii] In the spring of 1946, a national strike by railroad workers brought passenger and freight lines to a virtual standstill across the country.[clxxix] Truman acted boldly by seizing control of the railways and threatening to draft the striking workers into the Army.[clxxx] The strike was settled on his terms, but it cost him politically, as his solution was perceived as completely pro-management and anti-labor.[clxxxi]

Adding further to the country's national debt was Truman's decision to invest in Greece and Turkey and other countries in Eastern Europe through what was called the Truman Doctrine.[clxxxii] The Truman Doctrine was a repudiation of Soviet communist aggression.[clxxxiii] It proclaimed America's willingness to provide military aid to those countries resisting communism. Truman also supported the Marshall Plan,[clxxxiv] which sought to rebuild the economies and nations of Europe in the hope that communism could not thrive in the midst of prosperity. Most Americans do not realize that it was the United States that rebuilt Germany, the former Nazi empire, and most of Western Europe from the ashes of the war. All of this spending kept our debt-to-GDP ratio at record highs through the 1940s and well into the early '50s. But, it was the right thing to do, and Eccles was proud of the leadership provided by Truman in this regard.

Truman also believed, as did Marriner Eccles, that *the federal government plays a vital role in creating and maintaining a healthy economy.* It is our contention that much of his success as steward of the nation's economy can be attributed to his belief in adhering to that PRES Rule. In his State of the Union address to the nation in 1950, Truman proclaimed "the policies I am recommending to Congress are designed to reduce the deficit and bring about a budgetary balance as rapidly as we can safely do so. These policies are threefold,"[clxxxv] he said:

- To hold expenditures to the lowest level consistent with

the national interest.

- To encourage and stimulate business expansion, which will result in more revenue.
- To make a number of changes in the tax laws, which will bring in net additional revenue and at the same time improve the equity of our tax system.[clxxxvi]

Truman clearly believed that the federal government could use income and estate taxes as useful tools to create and maintain a healthy economy.

Although Truman cooperated closely with Republican leaders on foreign policy, he fought them tooth-and-nail on almost all domestic spending issues.[clxxxvii] He was determined to persevere with FDR's legacy and to create his own as well. He failed to prevent tax cuts or the removal of price controls.[clxxxviii] The power of the labor unions was diminished by the Taft–Hartley Act,[clxxxix] which was enacted by a GOP Congress override of a Truman veto.[cxc] *Truman fiercely defended policies and legislation that supported the middle class, adhering vehemently to the PRES Rule that the middle class is the engine that drives the economy.*

After Truman's surprising win in the 1948 election, he tried to create his own identity independent of FDR by putting forward what he dubbed "The Fair Deal."[cxci] The Fair Deal included proposals for expanded public housing, increased aid for public education, a higher minimum wage, federal civil rights protections, and what was the first attempt at national health insurance.[cxcii] Truman's proposed programs *exemplified his adherence to our PRES Rules, particularly the importance of the nation's middle class to the nation's economic health and the need to promote legislation which advanced the common good, not solely the advantaged few.* Due to conservative opposition in Congress from Republicans and southern Democrats alike, most Fair Deal proposals either failed to gain momentum or passed in weakened form.[cxciii] Like Marriner Eccles, Harry Truman and some of his domestic proposals were light-years ahead of their time, but Truman succeeded in laying the groundwork for a domestic agenda for decades to come.

THE PRES RANKINGS

In his almost eight years in the White House, Harry Truman fought hard for the things in which he believed. Despite numerous setbacks, he achieved above-average economic success, placing him fifth overall under the PRES Ranking System. Truman finished in a tie for sixth under the U.S. Financial Health Pillar, fifth under the Personal Wealth Pillar, and sixth under the Business Prosperity Pillar. He held the economy together after the war and by the time he left office, America had turned the corner toward economic prosperity and full employment. People were working, and the massive post-war labor struggles were a thing of the past. His economic performance under our PRES Ranking System is graphically illustrated below.

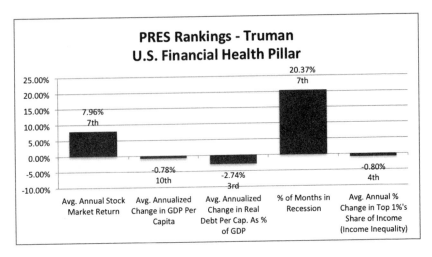

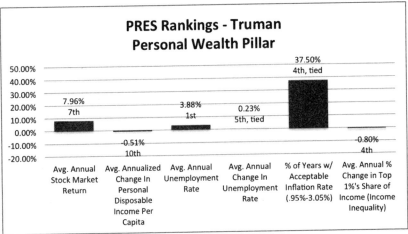

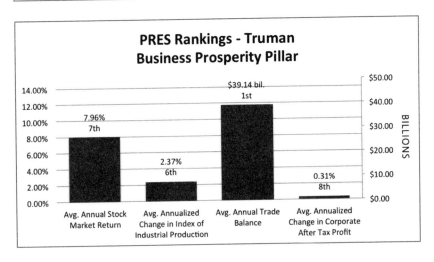

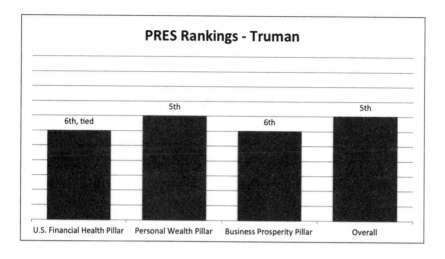

As you can see, Truman scored at the top of our presidential rankings under two indicators, with an average unemployment rate of 3.88% and a positive trade balance of more than $39 billion. He also received high marks for lowering the nation's debt as a percentage of GDP, reducing income inequality between the "bottom 99%" and the "top 1%," and keeping inflation under control. These lofty rankings were helped by the impact of WWII and by his impressive post-war stewardship, which included strict adherence to our PRES Rules.

Conversely, Truman's ranking among the 11 presidential administrations in our study was hurt by his presiding over a negligible increase in corporate profits during his term, a slight decrease in the average personal disposable income of Americans, and positive but below average stock market results.

Truman left Washington at the end of his presidency with feelings of relief. "No one knows what responsibility the presidency puts on a man,"[cxciv] he wrote in a letter in early 1953, adding, "It bears down on a country boy."[cxcv]

CHAPTER 5 ENDNOTES

cxliv Royal Air Force Museum: National Cold War Exhibition, "Biography of Harry Truman." Accessed December 16, 2011. http://www.nationalcoldwarexhibition.org/explore/biography. cfm?name=Truman,%20Harry

cxlv Miller Center of Public Affairs, "American President: Harry S. Truman (1884-1972)." Accessed December 16, 2011. http://millercenter.org/president/truman

cxlvi National Archives' Truman Presidential Museum and Library, "Use of the Period After the 'S' in Harry S. Truman's Name." Accessed December 13, 2011. http://www.trumanlibrary.org/speriod.htm

cxlvii National Archives' Truman Presidential Museum and Library, "Truman's School Years." Accessed December 16, 2011. http://www.trumanlibrary.org/whistlestop/trumanfile/schlyears.htm

cxlviii Ellensburg Daily Record, "Martha Truman Buried on Knoll in Kansas City." Accessed December 13, 2011. http://news.google.com/newspapers?id=a4sKAAAAIBAJ&sjid=6EsDAAAAIBAJ&pg=6120,4 147432&dq=martha+truman&hl=en

cxlix Miller Center of Public Affairs, "Bess Truman." Accessed December 16, 2011. http://millercenter. org/president/truman/essays/firstlady

cl National Archives' Truman Presidential Museum and Library, "Biographical Sketch: Margaret Truman Daniel." Accessed December 16, 2011. http://www.trumanlibrary.org/mtd-bio.htm

cli The Miller Center of Public Affairs, "Domestic Affairs." Accessed December 16, 2011. http://millercenter.org/president/truman/essays/biography/2

clii National Archives' Truman Presidential Museum and Library, "Biographical Sketch: Harry S. Truman, 33rd President of the United States." Accessed December 16, 2011. http://www.trumanli-brary.org/hst-bio.htm

cliii National Archives' Truman Presidential Museum and Library, " 'The Buck Stops Here' Desk Sign." Accessed December 16, 2011. http://www.trumanlibrary.org/buckstop.htm

cliv The White House, "Harry S. Truman." Accessed December 14, 2011. http://www.whitehouse.gov/ about/presidents/harrystruman

clv National Archives' Truman Presidential Museum and Library, "County Judge." Accessed December 16, 2011. http://www.trumanlibrary.org/lifetimes/county.htm

clvi National Archives' Truman Presidential Museum and Library, "Truman Trivia Collection." Accessed December 16, 2011. http://www.trumanlibrary.org/trivia/penderga.htm

clvii United States Senate, "Harry S. Truman, 34th Vice President (1945)." Accessed December 14, 2011. http://www.senate.gov/artandhistory/history/common/generic/VP_Harry_Truman.htm

clviii United States Senate, "Harry S. Truman, 34th Vice President (1945)." Accessed December 16, 2011. http://www.senate.gov/artandhistory/history/common/generic/VP_Harry_Truman.htm

clix Biography, "Harry S. Truman." Accessed December 16, 2011. http://www.biography.com/people/ harry-s-truman-9511121?page=2

clx United States Senate, "Henry Agard Wallace, 33rd Vice President (1941-1945)." Accessed December 16, 2011. http://www.senate.gov/artandhistory/history/common/generic/VP_Henry_ Wallace.htm

CHAPTER 5 ENDNOTES

clxi The White House, "Harry S. Truman." Accessed December 16, 2011. http://www.whitehouse.gov/about/presidents/harrystruman

clxii The Miller Center of Public Affairs, "Domestic Affairs." Accessed December 16, 2011. http://millercenter.org/president/truman/essays/biography/4

clxiii Heritage Institute, "Leadership – Taking Responsibility." Accessed December 16, 2011. http://heritageinstitute.com/leadership/responsibility.htm

clxiv Heritage Institute, "Leadership – Taking Responsibility." Accessed December 16, 2011. http://heritageinstitute.com/leadership/responsibility.htm

clxv The Miller Center of Public Affairs, "American President: A Reference Resource." Accessed December 16, 2011. http://millercenter.org/president/truman/essays/biography/5

clxvi The Churchill Centre and Museum at the Churchill War Rooms, London, "Churchill as War Leader." Accessed December 16, 2011. http://www.winstonchurchill.org/learn/biography/the-war-leader/churchill-as-war-leader

clxvii National Park Service, "The Archeology of the Atomic Bomb." Accessed December 16, 2011. http://www.nps.gov/history/history/online_books/swcrc/37/chap2.htm

clxviii The Miller Center of Public Affairs, "American President: A Reference Resource." Accessed December 16, 2011. http://millercenter.org/president/truman/essays/biography/5

clxix Central Intelligence Agency, "The Final Months of the War With Japan." Accessed December 16, 2011. https://www.cia.gov/library/center-for-the-study-of-intelligence/csi-publications/books-and-monographs/the-final-months-of-the-war-with-japan-signals-intelligence-u-s-invasion-planning-and-the-a-bomb-decision/csi9810001.html

clxx Marriner Eccles, *Beckoning Frontiers: Public and Personal Recollections* (New York: Alfred A. Knopf Inc., 1951) 408.

clxxi PBS, "American Experience: Domestic Policy." Accessed December 16, 2011. http://www.pbs.org/wgbh/americanexperience/features/general-article/truman-domestic/

clxxii PBS, "American Experience: Domestic Policy." Accessed December 16, 2011. http://www.pbs.org/wgbh/americanexperience/features/general-article/truman-domestic/

clxxiii Library of Congress, "President Harry Truman Wipes Out Military Segregation." Accessed December 14, 2011. http://www.loc.gov/exhibits/odyssey/educate/truman.html

clxxiv PBS, "American Experience: Domestic Policy." Accessed December 16, 2011. http://www.pbs.org/wgbh/americanexperience/features/general-article/truman-domestic/

clxxv The Miller Center of Public Affairs, "American President: A Reference Resource." Accessed December 16, 2011. http://millercenter.org/president/truman/essays/biography/print

clxxvi The Miller Center of Public Affairs, "Domestic Affairs." Accessed December 16, 2011. http://millercenter.org/president/truman/essays/biography/4

clxxvii The Miller Center of Public Affairs, "Domestic Affairs." Accessed December 16, 2011. http://millercenter.org/president/truman/essays/biography/4

CHAPTER 5 ENDNOTES

[clxxviii] The Miller Center of Public Affairs, "Domestic Affairs." Accessed December 16, 2011. http://millercenter.org/president/truman/essays/biography/4

[clxxix] The Economic Populist, "The Great Strike Wave of 1946." Accessed December 16, 2011. http://www.economicpopulist.org/content/great-strike-wave-1946

[clxxx] The Economic Populist, "The Great Strike Wave of 1946." Accessed December 16, 2011. http://www.economicpopulist.org/content/great-strike-wave-1946

[clxxxi] The Economic Populist, "The Great Strike Wave of 1946." Accessed December 16, 2011. http://www.economicpopulist.org/content/great-strike-wave-1946

[clxxxii] Ourdocuments.gov, "Truman Doctrine (1947)." Accessed December 14, 2011. http://ourdocuments.gov/doc.php?flash=true&doc=81

[clxxxiii] National Archives' Truman Presidential Museum and Library, "The Truman Doctrine Study Collection." Accessed December 14, 2011. http://www.trumanlibrary.org/whistlestop/study_collections/doctrine/large/index.php

[clxxxiv] Harry S. Truman Library and Museum, "Marshall Plan." Accessed December 14, 2011. http://truman.doit.missouri.edu/whistlestop/BERLIN_A/MARSHALL.HTM

[clxxxv] The American Presidency Project, "Special Message to the Congress on Tax Policy." Accessed December 16, 2011. http://www.presidency.ucsb.edu/ws/?pid=13545#axzz1giajD2ux

[clxxxvi] The American Presidency Project, "Special Message to the Congress on Tax Policy." Accessed December 16, 2011. http://www.presidency.ucsb.edu/ws/?pid=13545#axzz1giajD2ux

[clxxxvii] Encyclopedia.com, "Harry S Truman." Accessed December 16, 2011. http://www.encyclopedia.com/topic/Harry_S_Truman.aspx

[clxxxviii] The American Presidency Project, "Message to the Congresson the State of the Union and on the Budget for 1947." Accessed December 16, 2011. http://www.presidency.ucsb.edu/ws/index.php?pid=12467#axzz1giajD2ux

[clxxxix] The Miller Center of Public Affairs, "On the Veto of the Taft-Hartley Bill (June 20, 1947)." Accessed December 16, 2011. http://millercenter.org/president/speeches/detail/3344

[cxc] The Miller Center of Public Affairs, "On the Veto of the Taft-Hartley Bill (June 20, 1947)." Accessed December 16, 2011. http://millercenter.org/president/speeches/detail/3344

[cxci] Miller Center of Public Affairs, "Truman Announces Fair Deal Program – January 5, 1947." Accessed December 14, 2011. http://millercenter.org/president/events/01_05

[cxcii] Miller Center of Public Affairs, "Truman Announces Fair Deal Program – January 5, 1947." Accessed December 14, 2011. http://millercenter.org/president/events/01_05

[cxciii] The Miller Center of Public Affairs, "American President: A Reference Resource." Accessed December 16, 2011. http://millercenter.org/president/events/01_05.

[cxciv] Harry S. Truman Library, "Letters, Literature, and the President." Accessed December 16, 2011. http://www.krohm.com/tewsp/lm/lm6.htm

[cxcv] Harry S. Truman Library, "Letters, Literature, and the President." Accessed December 16, 2011. http://www.krohm.com/tewsp/lm/lm6.htm

4
OVERALL RANK

VALUE OF $100,000 INVESTMENT AT END OF TERM = **$208,047**

US FINANCIAL HEALTH | PERSONAL WEALTH | BUSINESS PROSPERITY

4 | 3 TIED | 5

DWIGHT D. EISENHOWER

A HERO IN WAR; A MODERATE IN IDEOLOGY

*"I despise people who go to the gutter
on either the right or the left and hurl rocks
at those in the center."* cxcvi

– Dwight D. Eisenhower, in an interview for *The New Yorker*

Prior to his election as the 34th president of the United States, Dwight David Eisenhower had established himself as one of the most respected and admired leaders in American history. A five-star general; president of Columbia University; the first Supreme Commander of NATO [cxcvii] – Eisenhower's accomplishments stood unrivaled. This remarkable leader came from very humble beginnings, like so many great Americans. Growing up poor in rural Kansas,[cxcviii] Eisenhower developed self-reliance and a strong work ethic. As a military officer, he learned that cooperation worked better than adversarial tactics[cxcix] in unleashing the potential in his men. With these values, along with a commitment to pragmatism over ideology, President Dwight D. Eisenhower led the country through a period of relative economic prosperity, coming in fourth under the PRES Ranking System – the highest rank of any Republican president.

Eisenhower was known for his practicality, enduring optimism and affable disposition. Born in Denison, Texas, on October 14, 1890, he would take the nickname given to all the Eisenhower boys – Ike.[cc] Encouraged to consider the military, he originally was motivated to attend West Point because the tuition was free, but upon taking the Cadet Oath his views changed and he decided to make the military his career.[cci] An average student by West Point's standards, he would go on to graduate as valedictorian in a class at the Command and General Staff School at Fort Leavenworth, Kansas[ccii] – a school for the Army's top young officers.

In 1916, shortly after reporting to duty, Ike married the love of his life, Mamie Geneva Doud of Denver, Colorado. After losing their firstborn to scarlet fever,[cciii] they had their only other child, a son named John, in 1922. The presidential retreat near Frederick, Maryland – Camp David – is named after one of John's children.

[cciv] John Eisenhower, age 89 at the writing of this book, is the oldest living child of any U.S. president today.[ccv]

Eisenhower volunteered to participate as a Tank Corps observer in the War Department's First Transcontinental Convoy in 1919,[ccvi] which traveled from Baltimore to San Francisco along the old Lincoln Highway. This was no easy task, considering the underdeveloped state of the road system in the country at that time – the convoy's average speed was a mere six miles per hour and it took 61 days to cross the U.S.[ccvii] The memory of this frustrating exercise would be the catalyst for the Interstate Highway Act that was promoted by Ike and passed during his presidency.[ccviii]

By 1926, Ike had established himself as the brightest, most capable member of the Army officer corps and his meteoric rise began. He worked for some of the greatest military minds of the 20th century, including Generals John Pershing, Douglas MacArthur and George Marshall.[ccix] Marshall promoted Eisenhower to major general and made him commanding general of the European Theater.[ccx] Eisenhower went toe-to-toe with Nazi General Erwin Rommel in North Africa, made direct invasions of Sicily and Italy, and was responsible for the masterful invasion of Nazi-occupied Western Europe, which commenced on June 6, 1944, commonly referred to as D-Day.[ccxi]

After the war, Eisenhower's political capital skyrocketed. He was paraded through Western European cities as a hero, and after two years as Army chief of staff, he accepted a post as president of Columbia University,[ccxii] where he worked for three years before being appointed the first supreme commander of NATO in 1950. [ccxiii] Dwight Eisenhower's military accomplishments and reputation made him a strong presidential candidate in the 1952 election for either political party. Declaring as a Republican, Ike became the GOP standard bearer[ccxiv] because he was considered the most electable candidate at the time. With Richard Nixon as his running mate, Eisenhower won a landslide victory against Adlai Stevenson and John Sparkman,[ccxv] and the Republicans took back the White House after a 20-year absence.[ccxvi]

THE PRESIDENTIAL YEARS

Within months of taking office, Eisenhower was faced with his first recession – one that lasted 10 months.[ccxvii] Fearful that unemployment would make his first term his last, he set out to ensure that wouldn't happen. He created his own version of an FDR stimulus through the Federal Highway Act,[ccxviii] which involved massive infrastructure investment in a new, state of the art interstate highway system.[ccxix] Drawing on his personal experience with the Transcontinental Convoy some 34 years earlier, and his ride along the German autobahn at the end of the war,[ccxx] Eisenhower championed the Federal Highway Act of 1956.[ccxxi] He commented on the highway bill in his 1956 State of the Union address. "More than any single action by the government since the end of the war, this one will change the face of America. Its impact on the American economy – the jobs it will produce in manufacturing and construction, the rural areas it will open up – is beyond calculation."[ccxxii] Eisenhower insisted that the program not add to the national debt; therefore, the new highway system was predominantly paid for with new taxes on gasoline and diesel fuel.[ccxxiii] President Eisenhower's ability to work with a Democratic Congress on such a momentous piece of legislation is a testament *to his adherence to the PRES principle that a president should lead as a statesman – not as a partisan.*

Over the eight years of Eisenhower's tenure as CEO of the country, he preached a doctrine that he called "dynamic conservatism,"[ccxxiv] which today would be labeled as progressivism. Ike advocated balanced federal budgets, although he would accomplish that only in three of his eight years in office.[ccxxv] Eisenhower believed, as Eccles did, that the nation's prosperity was a function of creating a cooperative environment between government, business and labor. He continued with the New and Fair Deal programs of FDR and Truman, but slowed their growth, except for Social Security, which he boldly expanded.[ccxxvi] In fact, he created a new Cabinet-level agency, the Department of Health, Education and Welfare,[ccxxvii] to support it. Eisenhower extended Social Security benefits to an additional 10 million workers,[ccxxviii] most of who were the working poor of that day – much like President Obama strived for with the Patient Care and Affordable Health Care Act of 2010.

Ike's approach to the economy focused on balance. He supported policies of growth and investment, but worked for a balanced budget as the economy grew, which was clearly in line with the PRES Rules. Eisenhower refused to cut taxes on the affluent,[ccxxix] realizing that would only increase the national debt, despite chiding from House Republicans to do so. *This was in line with the PRES Rules that the middle class is the engine that drives the economy and the president should strive for the common good – not solely the advantaged few.* Eisenhower realized that the federal government can and should play a vital role in protecting and stabilizing the national economy.[ccxxx] His approach created relative growth and prosperity over his term, despite some turmoil along the way. Eisenhower's long-term economic success is, however, overshadowed by the fact that he presided over three recessions, more than any other president in our 80-year analysis.

In the 1956 election, Eisenhower faced Democrat Adlai Stevenson once again, and in this second round won by an even greater margin.[ccxxxi] Eisenhower, like Herbert Hoover, had never been elected to national office before he was president and he was not a politician by profession,[ccxxxii] and like Hoover he struggled with Congress at times. Ike had a Republican Congress during his first two years in office, but after that he was compelled to work with the likes of Senate Majority Leader Lyndon Johnson and Speaker of the House Sam Rayburn,[ccxxxiii] both formidable Democrats. Eisenhower did not surround the Oval Office with political operatives like Karl Rove[ccxxxiv] or James Carville,[ccxxxv] who could solve problems with political skill; instead he worked through his own cronies and subordinates to deal with Congress, often achieving results that were short of his goals. This lack of political acumen became a significant weakness for Ike over time.

THE PRES RANKINGS

President Eisenhower ranks fourth overall in our rankings, finishing fourth in the U.S. Financial Health Pillar, tied for third with FDR in the Personal Wealth Pillar, and fifth in the Business Prosperity Pillar. Those rankings are higher than the rankings of any other Republican president in our 80-year study, except for Ronald Reagan, who finished a notch ahead of Ike in the Business Prosperity Pillar. President Eisenhower's consistent and exemplary performance as steward of the nation's economy is graphically illustrated below.

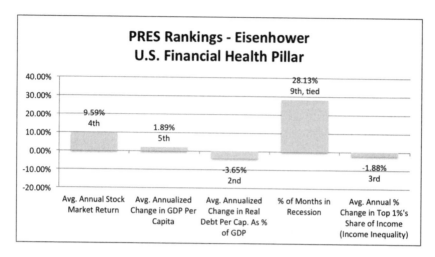

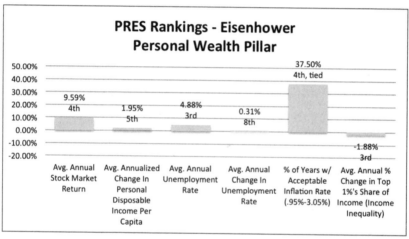

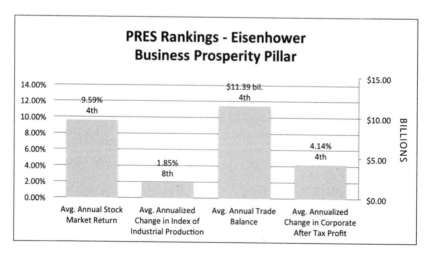

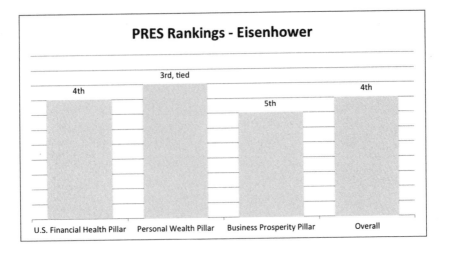

As you can see, Ike ranked consistently among the top five performers as measured by the economic indicators utilized in our PRES Ranking System. Most impressively, he ranked: (1) a close second to JFK/LBJ in his ability to reduce the country's debt as a percentage of GDP, reducing it an average of 3.65% per year; (2) third in his ability to maintain relatively low unemployment, averaging 4.88% during his term; and (3) third in his ability to narrow the income gap between the top 1% and the bottom 99%, reducing the gap an average of 1.88% per year.

Some economists have criticized President Eisenhower's efforts to rein in inflation as too rigid, yet low inflation combined with relative growth in personal disposable income of nearly 2% per year during his eight years led to an increase in personal wealth for middle-income Americans. Again, Ike's governing philosophy and the economic results created by his philosophy support the *benefits of following the PRES Rules, primarily those relating to the importance of the middle class and advancing the common good.*

Although Ike's overall performance was impressive, he did falter in a few categories, preventing him from ascending into the top three of our overall rankings. As graphically illustrated above, he presided over too many months of recession, three separate recessions in over eight years, a significant growth in unemployment, and a lagging industrial production index.

In 1953, in an address dubbed the "Chance for Peace Speech,"[ccxxxvi] Eisenhower warned about the emergence of the "military-industrial complex" in the United States.[ccxxxvii] Paradoxically, Eisenhower, a five-star general, and Marriner Eccles, a retired Fed chairman, both loathed war. Eisenhower said prior to his departure to become a private citizen, "I hate war as only a soldier who has lived it can, only as one who has seen its brutality, its futility, its stupidity."[ccxxxviii] He added, "Every gun that is made, every warship launched, every rocket fired signifies, in the final sense, a theft from those who hunger and are not fed, those who are cold and are not clothed. This world in arms is not spending money alone. It is spending the sweat of its laborers, the genius of its scientists, and the hopes of its children... Under the cloud of threatening war, it is humanity hanging from a cross of iron... Is there no other way the world may live?"[ccxxxix] In Ike's farewell address to the nation in January 1960, he stated, "We must avoid the impulse to live only for today, plundering for our own ease and convenience the precious resources of tomorrow. We cannot mortgage the material assets of our grandchildren without risking the loss also of their political and spiritual heritage. We want democracy to survive for all generations to come, not to become the insolvent phantom of tomorrow."[ccxl]

CHAPTER 6 ENDNOTES

cxcvi U.S. HistorySite.com Accessed December 16, 2011. http://ushistorysite.com/eisenhower-quotes.php

cxcvii The White House, "Dwight D. Eisenhower." Accessed December 15, 2011. http://www.whitehouse.gov/about/presidents/dwightdeisenhower

cxcviii The White House, "Dwight D. Eisenhower." Accessed December 15, 2011. http://www.whitehouse.gov/about/presidents/dwightdeisenhower

cxcix The U.S. Army Center of Military History, "Dwight David Eisenhower." Accessed December 15, 2011. http://www.history.army.mil/brochures/Ike/ike.htm

cc Miller Center of Public Affairs, "American President: Dwight D. Eisenhower (1890-1969)." Accessed December 15, 2011. http://millercenter.org/president/eisenhower

cci Miller Center of Public Affairs, "American President: A Reference Source." Accessed December 15, 2011. http://millercenter.org/president/eisenhower/essays/biography/1

ccii Command and General Staff College, "Watershed at Leavenworth: Dwight D. Eisenhower and the Command and General Staff School." Accessed December 16, 2011. http://www.cgsc.edu/carl/resources/csi/bender/bender.asp

cciii National Achieves and Records Administration's The Dwight D. Eisenhower Library and Museum, "Mamie Doud Eisenhower." Accessed December 16, 2011. http://www.eisenhower.utexas.edu/all_about_ike/chronologies.html#mde

cciv The White House, "Camp David." Accessed December 16, 2011. http://www.whitehouse.gov/about/camp-david

ccv The Examiner, "The Eisenhowers at the National Portrait Gallery." Accessed December 16, 2011. http://www.examiner.com/cultural-events-in-washington-dc/the-eisenhowers-at-the-national-portrait-gallery

ccvi National Achieves and Records Administration's The Dwight D. Eisenhower Library and Museum, "The 1919 Transcontinental Motor Convoy." Accessed December 16, 2011. http://www.eisenhower.archives.gov/research/online_documents/1919_convoy.html

ccvii National Achieves: Prologue Magazine, "Ike's Interstates at 50: Anniversary of the Highway System Recalls Eisenhower's Role as Catalyst." Accessed December 16, 2011. http://www.archives.gov/publications/prologue/2006/summer/interstates.html

ccviii National Achieves: Prologue Magazine, "Ike's Interstates at 50: Anniversary of the Highway System Recalls Eisenhower's Role as Catalyst." Accessed December 16, 2011. http://www.archives.gov/publications/prologue/2006/summer/interstates.html

ccix The White House, "Dwight D. Eisenhower." Accessed December 16, 2011. http://georgewbush-whitehouse.archives.gov/history/presidents/de34.html

ccx Korean War 60th Anniversary, "Biographies: Dwight David 'Ike' Eisenhower." Accessed December 16, 2011. http://koreanwar.defense.gov/bio_eisenhower.html

ccxi Rutgers Eagleton Institute of Politics, "American Political History." Accessed December 16, 2011. http://www.eagleton.rutgers.edu/research/americanhistory/ap_ww2-pacific.php

CHAPTER 6 ENDNOTES

[ccxii] Columbia University Libraries: University Achieves, "Columbia University President Profiles." Accessed December 16, 2011. http://library.columbia.edu/indiv/uarchives/presidents.html

[ccxiii] The U.S. Army Center of Military History, "Dwight David Eisenhower." Accessed December 15, 2011. http://www.history.army.mil/brochures/Ike/ike.htm

[ccxiv] Miller Center of Public Affairs, "American President: A Reference Source." Accessed December 15, 2011. http://millercenter.org/president/eisenhower/essays/biography/3

[ccxv] Nation Park Service U.S. Department of the Interior, "The Ike Blog." Accessed December 16, 2011. http://www.nps.gov/eise/parknews/ike-blog.htm

[ccxvi] U.S. Embassy, "Outline of U.S. History." Accessed December 16, 2011. http://www.usembassy-mexico.gov/bbf/le/historytln.pdf

[ccxvii] The Dwight D. Eisenhower Library, "Dwight D. Eisenhower Library." Accessed December 16, 2011. http://www.eisenhower.archives.gov/research/finding_aids/pdf/Jacoby_Neil_Papers.pdf

[ccxviii] National Atlas, "Federal-aid Highway Act of 1956: Creating the Interstate System." Accessed December 16, 2011. http://nationalatlas.gov/articles/transportation/a_highway.html#three

[ccxix] The U.S. Department of Transportation Federal Highway Administration, "Why President Dwight D. Eisenhower Understood We Needed the Interstate System." Accessed December 16, 2011. http://www.fhwa.dot.gov/interstate/brainiacs/eisenhowerinterstate.htm

[ccxx] Illinois Department of Transportation, "Today's Interstate Highway System: The Eisenhower System of Interstate and Defense Highways." Accessed December 16, 2011. http://www.dot.il.gov/il50/ike_system.html

[ccxxi] The U.S. Department of Transportation Federal Highway Administration, "Why President Dwight D. Eisenhower Understood We Needed the Interstate System." Accessed December 16, 2011. http://www.fhwa.dot.gov/interstate/brainiacs/eisenhowerinterstate.htm

[ccxxii] The U.S. Department of Transportation Federal Highway Administration, "Happy 40th Anniversary: National System of Interstate and Defense Highways." December 16, 2011. http://www.fhwa.dot.gov/infrastructure/40thannv.cfm

[ccxxiii] The U.S. Department of Transportation Federal Highway Administration, "Previous Interstate Facts of the Day." Accessed December 16, 2011. http://www.fhwa.dot.gov/interstate/previousfacts.cfm

[ccxxiv] The U.S. Department of Labor, "MDTA: The Origins of the Manpower Development and Training Act of 1962." Accessed December 16, 2011. http://www.dol.gov/oasam/programs/history/mono-mdtatext.htm

[ccxxv] Miller Center of Public Affairs, "American President: A Reference Resource." Accessed December 16, 2011. http://millercenter.org/president/eisenhower/essays/biography/print

[ccxxvi] Social Security Online History Pages, "Eisenhower's Statements on Social Security." Accessed December 16, 2011. http://www.ssa.gov/history/ikestmts.html

[ccxxvii] The U.S. Department of Health and Human Services, "Reorganization Plan 1 of 1953." Accessed December 16, 2011. http://www.fda.gov/RegulatoryInformation/Legislation/ucm148720.htm

CHAPTER 6 ENDNOTES

ccxxviii Social Security Online History Pages, "Special Collections: 1950s." Accessed December 16, 2011. http://www.ssa.gov/history/1950.html

ccxxix National Park Service: Eisenhower National Historic Site, "Ike's Top 5 Presidential Accomplishments." Accessed December 16, 2011. http://www.nps.gov/features/eise/jrranger/5accompX.htm

ccxxx U.S. Small Business Administration, "The Role of Small Business in Economic Development of The United States: From the End of the Korean War (1953) to Present." Accessed December 16, 2011. http://www.sba.gov/advocacy/7540/12143

ccxxxi The U.S. Department of Transportation Federal Highway Administration, "The Man Who Changed America, Part II." Accessed December 16, 2011. http://www.fhwa.dot.gov/publications/publicroads/03may/05.cfm

ccxxxii The White House, "Dwight D. Eisenhower." Accessed December 16, 2011. http://www.whitehouse.gov/about/presidents/dwightdeisenhower

ccxxxiii United States Senate, "Lyndon Baines Johnson, 37th Vice President (1961-1963)." Accessed December 16, 2011. http://www.senate.gov/artandhistory/history/common/generic/VP_Lyndon_Johnson.htm

ccxxxiv Karl Rove, "Biography." Accessed December 16, 2011. http://www.rove.com/bio

ccxxxv The Office of James Carville, "The Winning Streak." Accessed December 16, 2011. http://www.carville.info/

ccxxxvi Miller Center of Public Affairs, "Change for Peace (April 16, 1953)." Accessed December 16, 2011. http://millercenter.org/president/speeches/detail/3357

ccxxxvii Miller Center of Public Affairs, "Key Events in the Presidency of Dwight D. Eisenhower." Accessed December 16, 2011. http://millercenter.org/president/keyevents/eisenhower

ccxxxviii PBS: American Experience, "Dwight D. Eisenhower." Accessed December 16, 2011. http://www.pbs.org/wgbh/americanexperience/features/biography/bulge-eisenhower/

ccxxxix Miller Center of Public Affairs, "Change for Peace (April 16, 1953)." Accessed December 16, 2011. http://millercenter.org/president/speeches/detail/3357

ccxl U.S. Government Printing Office, "The Congressional Record." Accessed December 16, 2011. http://www.gpo.gov/fdsys/pkg/CREC-1995-05-12/html/CREC-1995-05-12-pt1-PgS6643-5.htm

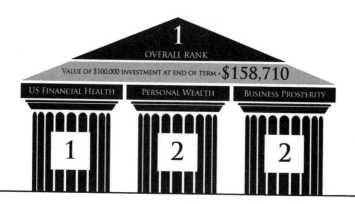

Value of $100,000 investment at end of term = $158,710

US FINANCIAL HEALTH	PERSONAL WEALTH	BUSINESS PROSPERITY
1	2	2

OVERALL RANK: 1

JOHN F. KENNEDY
AND
LYNDON B. JOHNSON

OVERCOMING ADVERSITY
TO TOP OUR RANKINGS

★ ★ ★ ★ ★ ★ ★ ★ ★ ★ ★ ★

"A man may die, nations may rise and fall,
but an idea lives on." ccxli

– John F. Kennedy

★ ★ ★ ★ ★ ★ ★ ★ ★ ★ ★ ★

"The presidency has made every man who occupied it, no matter how small, bigger than he was; and no matter how big, not big enough for its demands." [ccxlii]

– Lyndon Baines Johnson

⋆　⋆　⋆　⋆　⋆　⋆　⋆　⋆　⋆　⋆　⋆　⋆

D espite serving as president just shy of three years, John Fitzgerald Kennedy is widely regarded as one of our country's most beloved leaders. Born on May 29, 1917, in Brookline, Massachusetts, to a well-to-do Irish-Catholic family, John Kennedy was the second of nine children.[ccxliii] The family patriarch, Joe Kennedy Sr., had turned the modest wealth of the Kennedy and Fitzgerald families into a fortune by skillfully playing the stock market, bootlegging through the dry '20s, and becoming an entrepreneur in Hollywood.[ccxliv] Joe Kennedy threw his power and resources behind his children's careers: it was no secret that he wanted to see one of his boys in the White House. That dream was realized in 1960 when John F. Kennedy and running mate Lyndon Baines Johnson defeated Richard Nixon and Henry Cabot Lodge by the closest popular vote margin in U.S. history.[ccxlv] Unfortunately, tragedy cut short JFK's presidential legacy. On November 22, 1963, John Kennedy was assassinated as his motorcade passed through downtown Dallas. The American public was stunned by the tragedy and the circumstances surrounding the alleged killer, Lee Harvey Oswald. Dallas nightclub owner, Jack Ruby, shot and killed Oswald as he was being transferred from Dallas police headquarters to the Dallas County Jail. The event was captured live on national television. Coincidentally, Oswald died in the very same hospital where Kennedy had died from his mortal gunshot wounds delivered by Oswald two days earlier. JFK's assassination left generations to ponder how the course of history might have been different had he lived a full life and had two terms in the White House. But the nation's adoration for Kennedy had as much to do with the substance of his vision for the country as it did with the conviction with which he delivered the message. He was sorely missed by millions at his death.

Lyndon Baines Johnson was sworn in as president aboard Air Force One within two hours after Kennedy's death.[ccxlvi] Five days after Kennedy's assassination, LBJ spoke to a joint session of Congress and seized on Kennedy's inaugural plea to "let us begin anew." His request to Congress was "let us continue."[ccxlvii] Over the next year, Johnson endorsed JFK's programs as he announced his own. He pushed for passage of Kennedy's tax cuts, promoted a new civil rights bill with real teeth, and launched his "War on Poverty."[ccxlviii] LBJ ran against Republican Barry Goldwater in 1964 and won in a landslide with the largest popular vote margin in American history: 61.1%. Goldwater won only his home state of Arizona and five states in the Deep South.[ccxlix]

Kennedy and Johnson had no real liking for each other; in fact the only thing they had in common was their affiliation with the Democratic Party. JFK was raised in an upscale neighborhood outside of Boston, whereas Johnson grew up dirt poor in the small farming community of Stonewall, Texas. Johnson once exclaimed that, "When I was young, poverty was so common we didn't know it even had a name."[ccl] This likely explains why LBJ sought to eradicate poverty through his creation of the Great Society when he became president. During the summers, JFK and his family would go to their summer home in Hyannis Port on Cape Cod where they enjoyed swimming, sailing, and touch football. In sharp contrast, Lyndon Johnson lived a "no frills" lifestyle. He worked as a student teacher to put himself through Southwest Texas State Teachers College.[cclі cclіі]

Kennedy and Johnson had starkly different personalities. Kennedy was very affable and almost always jovial; LBJ was serious and could be depressive. LBJ was also known by Washington insiders as one of the most ruthless politicians of his day. A workaholic who put in 15-hour days, LBJ would arm-twist his fellow Democrats into submission through his infamous "Johnson Treatment," consisting of "supplication, accusation, cajolery, exuberance, scorn, tears, complaint and the hint of thinly veiled threats."[ccliii] Though crass, his style made him an effective politician. Johnson was not particularly fond of economics and finance. In fact, LBJ once declared, "Making a speech on economics is a lot like pissing down your leg. It seems hot to you, but it never does to anyone else."[ccliv] Despite the big differences in personality and leadership style, both men supported a similar legislative agenda, one designed to build upon and expand FDR's New Deal legacy in order to create a more viable and enduring middle class and to build a safety net for the working poor.[cclv] These are values expressed in our PRES Rule #2 and would prove very beneficial in their stewardship of the nation's economy.

THE PRESIDENTIAL YEARS

Kennedy's first three months in office were marred by disaster. The Bay of Pigs invasion in mid-April of 1961 was an unsuccessful action by a CIA-trained force of Cuban exiles to invade Cuba with support from the United States in an attempt to overthrow the government of Fidel Castro. The invasion lasted three days and was an utter debacle, which severely embarrassed the Kennedy administration.[cclvi] Kennedy remarked days later: "There's an old saying that victory has a hundred fathers and defeat is an orphan."[cclvii] Kennedy was so irate about the advice he had received from the CIA and the Joint Chiefs of the Staff, he remarked he would "splinter the CIA in a thousand pieces and scatter it to the wind."[cclviii] Kennedy said to his journalist crony Ben Bradlee, "The first advice I'm going to give my successor is to watch the generals and to avoid feeling that because they were military men their opinions on military matters were worth a damn."[cclix] This experience was critically important for Kennedy, as it would come into play again 18 months later during the Cuban missile crisis.

Kennedy's selection of LBJ as his running mate is a good example of how politics makes for strange bedfellows. Kennedy picked LBJ because he knew that without him, the South would be lost and the election with it. Ultimately, 1960 was one of the closest elections in U.S. history, but at the end of the day, JFK defeated Nixon by 35/100 of 1% of the popular vote and 84 electoral votes.[cclx] Even though Democrats controlled both the House and Senate during his presidency, JFK had a difficult time advancing his domestic agenda. In what he proclaimed to be the New Frontier, Kennedy made a commitment on the campaign trail to end racial discrimination in the South, provide federal funding for education, health care and rural economic development, and to end the recession that he inherited from Eisenhower.[cclxi]   In a speech about his New Frontier, JFK proclaimed, "the pioneers of old gave up their safety, their comfort and sometimes their own lives to build a new world here in the West. Their motto was not 'every man for himself' but 'all for the common cause.'"[cclxii] *Kennedy strongly adhered to the PRES Rule of striving for the common good of all citizens and not solely the advantaged few.* JFK's agenda fought for the rights of all people. He did not try and push his party's agenda; instead he worked toward bettering conditions around the entire globe.

Most of JFK's legislative attempts to achieve these goals languished in Congress; however, LBJ used Kennedy's death as a catalyst to turn those objectives into reality with the advent of what he called the Great Society. Together Kennedy and Johnson played key roles in the creation and expansion of NASA, the Housing Act of 1961,[cclxiii] the 24th Amendment to the U.S. Constitution (which prohibits both Congress and the states from conditioning the right to vote in federal elections on payment of a poll tax or other types of tax), the Civil Rights Act of 1964, the Voting Rights Act of 1965, as well as Medicare and Medicaid. These programs were essentially designed to broaden the middle class and fight the war Johnson had declared on poverty. *Like Kennedy, Johnson strongly believed in the values espoused by the PRES Rules regarding the importance of the middle class and the advancement of the common good rather than the interests of the advantaged few.*

Marriner Eccles agreed with the notion of broadening the middle class; in his autobiography, Marriner, a businessman and a Republican, asserts: "Government can and should insist on minimum standards of decency in the mode and conditions of life for its people. Within the limits of the nation's resources, it can and should insist on a minimum income for its families; a minimum age for schooling and employment; a maximum age for retirement; decent and safe conditions of work; increasing benefits for labor as productivity increases; adequate protection and security for the aged and unemployed; and adequate educational, health, and recreational facilities. These standards of honesty and decency can and should be set by the government."[cclxiv] Marriner went on to add that government, under capitalism, should not compete with private activity, but that it could put idle men and capital to work. Johnson and Kennedy would both have likely agreed with Eccles' remarks as they demonstrated their recognition of PRES Rule #3, that *the federal government plays a vital role in creating and maintaining a healthy economy.* Their records as chief stewards of the nation's economy made that abundantly clear.

It is generally accepted among political scientists that the Civil Rights Act of 1964 broke the bonds connecting southern Democrats (the Dixiecrats) to their own party. Dixiecrats, or the States' Rights Democratic Party, felt that it was not the federal government's role to end racial discrimination. LBJ understood the consequences of what would happen in the South if he moved forward with the legislation; nonetheless, he stood behind the Civil Rights Act because it was the right thing to do. LBJ was decades ahead of his time in that he realized the futility of cultural bigotry and understood that the only way to end it was for the federal government to act and to act in a compelling manner. After he signed the Civil Rights Act into law, he is reported to have told his press secretary, Bill Moyers, "We have lost the South for a generation,"[cclxv] anticipating the coming backlash from southern whites against Johnson's Democratic Party. He was correct – the Deep South has belonged to the GOP ever since. *Consistent with PRES Rule #5, LBJ led as a statesman, not as a partisan* who would take action purely to benefit his re-election chances or to advance his party's political fortunes.

THE PRES RANKINGS

As mentioned in Chapter 2, JFK and LBJ together were ranked first overall in the PRES Ranking System. Their two administrations demonstrated consistency, predictability and stability (CPS), coming in first in the U.S. Financial Health Pillar and second under each of the other two economic pillars – Business Prosperity and Personal Wealth.

We have graphically illustrated below the top-ranking economic performance of JFK/LBJ in our PRES Rankings.

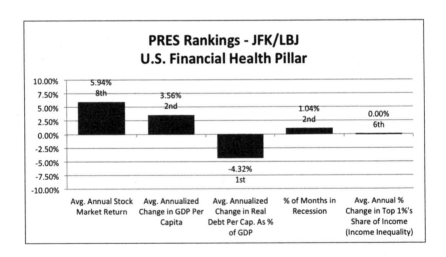

126

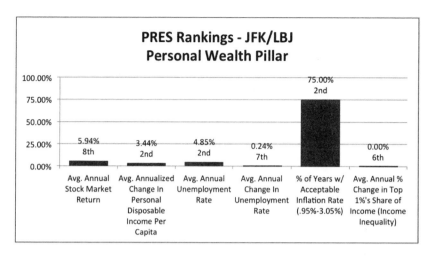

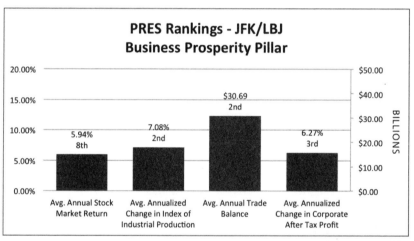

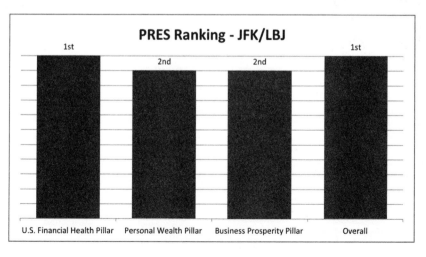

Kennedy and Johnson saw success in the U.S. Financial and Business Prosperity Pillars because of strong growth in industrial output, which provided millions of high-wage manufacturing jobs and steady increases in the overall size of the economy. The average annualized change in real GDP per capita from 1961 to 1969 was a robust 3.56%, second only to Roosevelt. JFK inherited the tail end of Eisenhower's third recession, and by JFK's inauguration in 1961, business bankruptcies reached their highest levels since the 1930s, farm incomes had declined 25% since 1951, and 5.5 million Americans were looking for work. Kennedy's economic response to this was a combined effort of lowering taxes modestly, protecting the unemployed, increasing the minimum wage, and focusing on the business and housing sectors to stimulate the economy.

JFK and his team – dubbed the Best and the Brightest – believed that such measures would initiate an economic boom that would last late into the 1960s, and they were right. JFK's strategy worked – there was only one month of recession as he entered the Oval Office, and that was the only month of recession during that entire eight-year period.[cclxvi] Both presidents maintained a positive trade balance of more than $30 billion per year and finished second for both average annualized change in industrial production and third in after-tax corporate profits. JFK and LBJ reduced the real debt per capita more than any other administration over the course of our 80-year analysis. The average annualized change in real debt per capita as a percentage of GDP was -4.32%. The stock market performed modestly through the Kennedy/Johnson years with an average annual compound return of 5.94%.

Regarding the Personal Wealth Pillar, JFK and LBJ benefited from rising wages and low unemployment. They edged out Dwight Eisenhower to take the second-best rating for unemployment, with an average unemployment rate from 1961 to 1969 of just 4.85%. Furthermore, average disposable income, adjusted for inflation, rose at the second fastest rate of the 20th century during the same time period. By the end of the decade, the average American worker had an inflation-adjusted disposable income that was higher than we enjoyed in 2011.[cclxvii]

John F. Kennedy and Lyndon Baines Johnson presided over a tumultuous period in American politics and world history. The Cold War, riots, racial tension, protests, the assassinations of Bobby Kennedy and Martin Luther King: American culture seemed to be tearing apart at the seams at the end of LBJ's first term in office. Nonetheless, during this period of cultural upheaval, when the country was striving toward the goal of creating equality for all American citizens, the U. S. economy was undergoing one of its most prolific periods of economic growth in our 80-year cycle. Kennedy and Johnson go down in history with the best overall PRES Rankings in our study.

CHAPTER 7 ENDNOTES

ccxli John F. Kennedy Presidential Library and Museum, "John F. Kennedy Quotations." Accessed December 20, 2011. http://www.jfklibrary.org/Research/Ready-Reference/JFK-Quotations.aspx

ccxlii Smithsonian Institution, traveling Exhibition Service. "The American Presidency." Accessed December 20, 2011. http://www.sites.si.edu/exhibitions/archived_exhibitions/presidency/main.htm.

ccxliii John F. Kennedy Presidential Library and Museum, "Life of John F. Kennedy." Accessed December 10, 2011. http://www.jfklibrary.org/JFK/Life-of-John-F-Kennedy.aspx.

ccxliv CNN Money, "Joseph P. Kennedy: A portrait of the founder (Fortune Classics, 1963)." Accessed December 10, 2011. http://features.blogs.fortune.cnn.com/2011/04/10/joseph-p-kennedy-a-portrait-of-the-founder/.

ccxlv infoplease, "The Closest Presidential Races." Accessed December 10, 2011. http://www.info-please.com/spot/closerace1.html.

ccxlvi Debbie Levy, Lyndon B. Johnson (Minneapolis: Lerner Publications Company, 2003) 72.

ccxlvii Lyndon Baines Johnson Library and Museum, "Address Before a Joint Session of the Congress, November 27, 1963." Accessed December 10, 2011. http://www.lbjlibrary.org/collections/selected-speeches/november-1963-1964/11-27-1963.html.

ccxlviii Lyndon Baines Johnson Library and Museum, "President Lyndon B. Johnson's Biography." Accessed December 10, 2011. http://www.lbjlib.utexas.edu/johnson/archives.hom/biographys.hom/lbj_bio.asp#Top.

ccxlix The American Presidency Project, "Election of 1964." Accessed December 10, 2011. http://www.presidency.ucsb.edu/showelection.php?year=1964.

ccl Robert Dallek, Lone Star Rising: Lyndon Johnson and His Times, 1908-1960 (New York: Oxford University Press, 1991) 13.

ccli John F. Kennedy Presidential Library and Museum, "Life of John F. Kennedy." Accessed December 12, 2011. http://www.jfklibrary.org/JFK/Life-of-John-F-Kennedy.aspx?p=2.

cclii Miller Center of Public Affairs, "American President: A Reference Resource." Accessed December 12, 2011. http://millercenter.org/president/lbjohnson/essays/biography/2.

ccliii Character Above All, "Lyndon B. Johnson." Accessed December 12, 2011. http://www.pbs.org/newshour/character/essays/johnson.html.

ccliv Robert A. Caro, The Years of Lyndon Johnson: Master of the Senate (New York: Alfred A. Knopf, 2002) 416.

cclv U.S. History Pre-Columbian to the New Millennium, "56b. Kennedy's New Frontier." Accessed December 12, 2010. http://www.ushistory.org/us/56b.asp.

cclvi John F. Kennedy Presidential Library and Museum, "The Bay of Pigs." Accessed December 12, 2011. http://www.jfklibrary.org/JFK/JFK-in-History/The-Bay-of-Pigs.aspx.

cclvii The American Presidency Project, "John F. Kennedy." Accessed December 12, 2011. http://www.presidency.ucsb.edu/ws/index.php?pid=8077&st=defeat&st1=#axzz1gLCA41pH.

CHAPTER 7 ENDNOTES

[cclviii] Gus Russo, *Live by the Sword: The Secret War Against Castro and the Death of JFK* (Baltimore: Bancroft Press, 1998) 24.

[cclix] Robert F. Kennedy, *Thirteen Days: A Memoir of the Cuban Missile Crisis* (New York: W.W. Norton & Company Inc., 1999) 5.

[cclx] http://www.archives.gov/federal-register/electoral-college/scores.html .

[cclxi] John F. Kennedy Presidential Library and Museum, "Acceptance of Democratic Nomination for President." Accessed January 4, 2012. http://www.jfklibrary.org/Asset-Viewer/AS08q5oYz0S-FUZg9uOi4iw.aspx

[cclxii] Miller Center of Public Affairs, "Acceptance of the Democratic Party Nomination (July 15, 1960)." Accessed December 12, 2011. http://millercenter.org/president/speeches/detail/3362.

[cclxiii] The American Presidency Project, "John F. Kennedy." Accessed December 12, 2011. http://www.presidency.ucsb.edu/ws/index.php?pid=8216#axzz1gLCA41pH.

[cclxiv] Marriner Stoddard Eccles, *Beckoning Frontiers: Public and Personal Recollections* (Alfred A. Knopf Inc., 1951) 81

[cclxv] Alan Greenspan, *The Age of Turbulence: Adventures in a New World* (New York: Penguin Press, 2007) 246.

[cclxvi] The National Bureau of Economic Research, "US Business Cycle Expansions and Contractions." Accessed January 5, 2012.   http://www.nber.org/cycles/#announcements

[cclxvii] Business Library, "Presidents, profits, productivity & poverty: a great divide between the pre- & post-Reagan U.S. economy?" Accessed December 13, 2011. http://findarticles.com/p/articles/mi_m0CYZ/is_3_31/ai_n6205471/pg_8/.

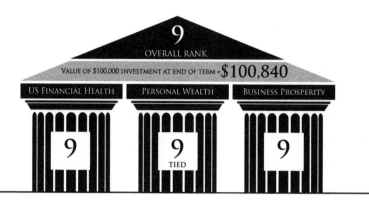

9
OVERALL RANK

VALUE OF $100,000 INVESTMENT AT END OF TERM = $100,840

US FINANCIAL HEALTH | PERSONAL WEALTH | BUSINESS PROSPERITY

9

9
TIED

9

RICHARD MILHOUS NIXON
AND
GERALD RUDOLPH FORD

ECONOMIC STRUGGLES AMID FOREIGN POLICY TRIUMPHS

★ ★ ★ ★ ★ ★ ★ ★ ★ ★ ★ ★

"People react to fear, not love –
they don't teach that in Sunday school, but it's true."

– Richard M. Nixon [cclxviii]

★ ★ ★ ★ ★ ★ ★ ★ ★ ★ ★ ★

"Truth is the glue that holds government together.
Compromise is the oil that makes governments go."

– Gerald R. Ford [cclxix]

Richard M. Nixon was born January 9, 1913, in Yorba Linda, California, to a relatively poor Quaker family. An exceptional student, he was accepted at Harvard but decided to stay close to home and attend a small liberal arts college in Southern California named Whittier College in order to help run the family grocery store. Despite working demanding hours, Dick still managed to graduate near the top of his class. He earned a scholarship to Duke Law School where he graduated in 1937. After a brief stint in corporate law, Richard went on to have an extraordinary political career with the GOP, serving as a member of the House of Representatives, the U.S. Senate, as vice president to Dwight Eisenhower, and ultimately as the 37th president of the United States. [cclxx]

As a congressman, Nixon earned the reputation of being an avid anti-communist. He learned that he could intimidate voters and win campaigns by tainting his opponents as "pink" or too liberal, even going so far as accusing them or their spouses of being communists. He successfully did this to Helen Douglas in the U.S. Senate race of 1950, turning a close race into a rout. [cclxxi]

During his tenure as a U. S. Senator, Nixon portended some of his vulnerabilities that would later surface when he became chief steward of the nation's economy – his tendency to deviate from the PRES Rules regarding the importance of the middle class and the advancement of the common good. Consistent with that vulnerability, Nixon supported the Taft-Hartley Act, which limited the powers of labor unions and repealed much of the 1935 Wagner Act, which had protected collective bargaining rights.[cclxxii]

When the Republican establishment recruited Dwight Eisenhower to run for president, he had no strong preference for a running mate. Nixon was eventually chosen for his youth, his stance against Communism, and his hailing from the electoral-vote-rich state of California. As vice president from 1953 to 1961, he was given substantial responsibility, particularly regarding national security.[cclxxiii] As the GOP candidate in the 1960 presidential campaign Nixon was poised to win, so his close loss to JFK came as a shock to most of his Republican colleagues. That loss was attributed to JFK's ability to use the new medium of television to his great advantage; many viewers were struck by the stark contrast between the two men and their appearances in the first nationally televised presidential debate in 1960. While Kennedy looked youthful and energetic on live camera, Nixon appeared fatigued, perspiring on his upper lip, and had a visible 5 o'clock shadow. Nixon narrowly lost to Kennedy in one of the closest popular votes the country has ever seen – just over three tenths of 1%, or approximately 118,000 votes.[cclxxiv]

THE PRESIDENTIAL YEARS

After losing the California gubernatorial race two years later, Nixon said he was finished with politics and from that point until the 1968 campaign, he virtually disappeared from the national scene. He returned to the political stage in 1968 as the GOP candidate for president, believing that the Democrats were torn in half over

Vietnam, and he painted his opponent, Hubert Humphrey, as a surrogate of Lyndon Johnson. Nixon promised the country "peace with honor," insisting that he had a "secret plan" to achieve that goal.[cclxxv] With Robert Kennedy's assassination in June of 1968 and George Corley Wallace Jr. of Alabama on the ballot in many states peeling off southern Democrats who likely would have voted for Humphrey, Nixon won the election – appealing to what he called the "silent majority" of Americans who disapproved of the counter-culture movement and high crime rates in urban areas.[cclxxvi]

Nixon had several notable political achievements as president, including ending the Vietnam War after escalating it, easing tensions with China, ushering in a new era of environmentalism, and negotiating some treaties with the Soviets, including SALT I and the Anti-Ballistic Missile Treaty.[cclxxvii] Nixon has been criticized for being more concerned with foreign policy issues than domestic ones, but of course Nixon is ultimately remembered as the only sitting U. S. president to resign his office, the result of his role in the Watergate scandal and cover-up.

Gerald Ford's ascent to the presidency is one of the most unusual paths ever taken in American history, in that he is the only person to have held the offices of both vice president and president without being elected to either.[cclxxviii] He attended the University of Michigan and Yale Law School. A natural leader, he was handsome, affable and athletic. He was an All-American football player at Michigan. After serving in the U. S. Navy in WWII, Ford began his political career.

He represented Michigan's Fifth District in the House for nearly a quarter of a century, eventually serving as House Minority Leader. In 1973, his political fortunes changed dramatically.[cclxxix] Nixon, invoking the 25th Amendment to the Constitution, appointed him vice president, with congressional approval, after former Vice President Spiro Agnew was forced to resign amidst a money laundering and tax evasion scandal.[cclxxx] One year later, President Nixon, facing certain impeachment, resigned in the wake of revelations about his role in Watergate, in which Republican operatives were caught breaking into the Democratic National Committee headquarters in the Watergate Towers during the summer of 1972. After Nixon's resignation, Gerald Ford became the 38th president of the United States. He had the shortest tenure of any president in our study. He is most remembered for pardoning President Nixon – a decision so unpopular at the time it ultimately was one of the causes for his loss to Jimmy Carter in 1976.[cclxxxi]

Nixon governed far to the left of what would be considered a contemporary Republican candidate of today. Although he is often portrayed as the consummate ideologue, the reality was that Richard Nixon was the consummate politician. Politics were first, foremost and everything to Nixon. For instance, although Nixon had no real interest in the first Earth Day or the environmental movement, he recognized that he could take advantage of voter sentiment surrounding Earth Day in 1970 to acquire votes for his upcoming re-election bid. So he seized the opportunity to get in front of the environmental movement anyway. Surprisingly, it was also Nixon, a Republican, who established the Environmental Protection Agency (EPA) and worked to pass the National Environmental Policy Act and the Clean Air Act, all of which are condemned by most contemporary Republicans. Nixon also recommended and signed into law the Occupational Health and Safety Act (OSHA) in 1970.[cclxxxii] It's almost impossible to imagine a contemporary Republican supporting any of these measures, all of which imposed a broad new set of rules and regulations to protect the health, safety and the welfare of the American people. And all of this was pushed through during a relatively dismal economic period when inflation, unemployment, and the national debt were increasing to highly uncomfortable levels.

Nixon was a strong advocate for balanced budgets. But unlike current Republicans, he favored balancing the budget using both tax increases and spending cuts. Nixon signed into law The Tax Reform Act of 1969 which was notable for creating the Alternative Minimum Tax (AMT). While the AMT closed tax loopholes for many affluent taxpayers, it also reduced the top marginal income tax rate on earned income from 70% to 50%.[cclxxxiii] Nixon created more balance in the tax code, evidence that he was *adhering to the PRES Rule of striving for the common good and not just the advantaged few.* However, like many strategies that Nixon employed, it was shortsighted. He never considered indexing the AMT for inflation, so over time, it began to impact the upper end of the middle class, who were never supposed to be targeted by the tax at all. Nixon's intent was noble, but his implementation was weak, illustrating some deviation from the PRES Rule prescribing *bold action after careful and innovative thought.*

Inflation plagued the U.S. economy during the Nixon years for several reasons. First, the end of the Vietnam conflict brought home returning soldiers in 1973 and 1974, and that had an impact on inflation analogous to the end of World War II.[cclxxxiv] Second and more importantly, the Arab oil embargo had a significant impact on the U.S. economy.[cclxxxv] The embargo was instigated by the Arab League and OPEC, who became furious over Nixon's decision to provide weapons and supplies to Israel during the 1972 Yom Kippur

War against Syria and Egypt. OPEC reacted by raising the price of oil by 70% to a whopping $5.11 per barrel. In response, Nixon doubled down on his strategy and gave an additional $3.7 billion in aid and grants to Israel. In a much more egregious retaliation, OPEC refused to sell crude oil to the United States entirely, calling the United States a "hostile country."[cclxxxvi] Israel ultimately won the Yom Kippur War and the Arabs blamed the United States and our pro-Israeli policy for their defeat.[cclxxxvii]

The Arab Oil embargo began a massive transfer of wealth from the middle class of the United States to the oil-producing countries in OPEC, including Venezuela and Iran, which has lasted four decades. It also made our nation acutely aware, for the first time, of its reliance on foreign oil. The price of oil quadrupled over a few weeks, capping out at $12 per barrel by Halloween of 1973. This oil price-shock, in tandem with the Watergate scandal, exacerbated the 1973–1974 stock market crash in which investors saw their money and the Dow and S&P drop some 46% from its peak to trough on Nixon's watch.[cclxxxviii]

Nixon's response to all of this was relatively modest. He imposed wage and price controls on two separate occasions, a power that Congress temporarily granted him. However, government price controls worsened the crisis in the United States, which limited the price of "old oil" (that which had been already discovered) while allowing newly discovered oil to be sold at a much higher price. This resulted in a withdrawal of the old oil from the market and the creation of artificial scarcity. Nixon's price controls discouraged development of more-efficient fuels or technologies, which was a mistake as well. This had a dramatic impact on the U.S. economy in the short run, and it made the country acutely aware that something needed to be done about our nation's nonexistent energy policy.[cclxxxix]

Gerald Ford described himself as "a moderate in domestic affairs, a conservative in fiscal affairs, and a dyed-in-the-wool internationalist in foreign affairs," and for the most part he stayed true to his self-description.[ccxc] By the time Ford took the helm at the White House in August of 1974, inflation had become worse. To deal with the dilemma, Ford first advocated a one-year, 5% income tax increase, or surcharge, on corporations and the wealthy.[ccxci] Ford reversed his strategy one year later, as the unemployment rate persisted at very high levels; he then worked with Congress to temporarily cut all income taxes. Although Ford advocated spending cuts to accompany the tax cuts, by the time the bill emerged from Congress, the spending cuts were removed and the tax cuts increased, exacerbating the 1975 budget deficit. Ford's concern for fiscal conservatism was hindered by the fact that the government ran budget deficits for the two years while he was in office, although to be fair, he did veto a number of bills he believed would unnecessarily add to the national debt. However, on the plus side for Gerald Ford, the economy began to recover during the Ford presidency after Nixon had resigned and been pardoned, with both unemployment and inflation dropping significantly.[ccxcii]

THE PRES RANKINGS

So how did Nixon and Ford perform under the PRES Ranking System? These two Republicans together rank ninth overall out of the 11 administrations we have reviewed. Nixon and Ford, as stewards of our economy, performed consistently but poorly across all three economic pillars, ranking them ninth in both the U.S. Financial Health Pillar and the Business Prosperity Pillar, and tied for ninth (with Jimmy Carter) in the Personal Wealth Pillar. Their dismal economic performance under our PRES Rankings is graphically illustrated below.

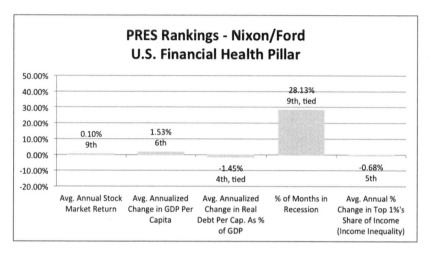

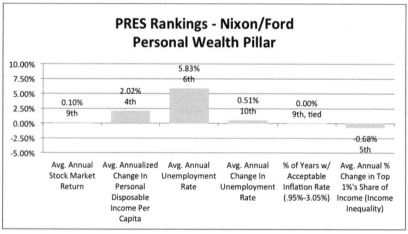

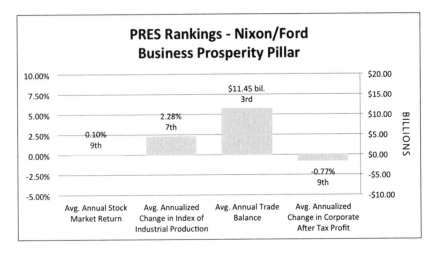

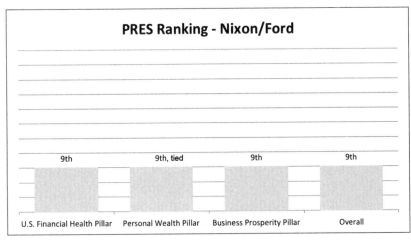

As for the U.S. Financial Health Pillar, the average annual stock market returns during this eight-year period were abysmally low, at just +.10% of one percent, third worst overall, in fact. With a total of 27 months of recession over their combined eight-year term, Nixon and Ford presided over the second-longest period of recession in our study, behind only that of Herbert Hoover. Somewhat surprisingly, Nixon and Ford share this unenviable position with fellow Republican Dwight Eisenhower, who ranked fourth overall on the

PRES Ranking System, having had three separate recessions during his eight-year tenure. With regard to average annualized change in both GDP per capita and real debt per capita as a percentage of GDP, Nixon and Ford ranked closer to the middle of the pack at 1.53% and -1.45% respectively. On a positive note, the income gap between the top 1% and bottom 99% actually narrowed under the Nixon/Ford administration, by an average of .68% per year, placing them a respectable fifth in our rankings.

Most Americans did not do well economically after eight years of Nixon and Ford at the helm, and this is borne out by the data we have collected for the Personal Wealth Pillar. This opened up a window of opportunity for Jimmy Carter in 1976. Stock market returns were weak, averaging only +.10% per year over eight consecutive years; inflation was relatively high, outside the acceptable range for every year during their eight-year term; and unemployment rates were moderate, averaging 5.83% per year, but that increased steadily during the Nixon/Ford years. Despite these bleak results, average disposable income increased 2.02% per year and the income gap narrowed as described above.

American businesses didn't fare well under Nixon and Ford either. By and large, publicly traded companies that make up the Dow and the S&P 500 saw the .10% average annual growth rate in the market as a drag on performance. This factor, combined with the poor financial condition of the average American consumer, goes a long way to explain the .77% average annualized drop in corporate after-tax profits during the Nixon/Ford years. One minor bright spot for Nixon and Ford was their third best overall rating in the average annual trade balance category, at $11.45 billion, but at the same time the Index of Industrial Production grew slowly, at an average annual rate of 2.28%, fifth-worst overall.

Richard Nixon did make some significant strides in international relations for the country. However, his domestic policy decisions and the decisions that led to the Arab oil embargo appear careless and shortsighted from an economic perspective, clearly a violation of the PRES Rule that advocates *bold action after careful and innovative thought.* It can be argued that the Arab Oil embargo and the subsequent war in Iraq have cost the citizens of the United States trillions of dollars in wealth over the past four decades, largely borne by the middle class. *This does not adhere to the PRES Rules recognizing the importance of the middle class and the advancement of the common good to a healthy economy.* As a result, Nixon and his successor Ford find themselves near the bottom of all of our rankings.

CHAPTER 8 ENDNOTES

ccxlviii William Safire, *Before the Fall: An Inside View of the Pre-Watergate White House* (New York: Doubleday, 2005) 8.

ccxlix Douglas Lynne, *Contemporary United States (1968 to the Present)* (New York: Weigl Publishers Inc.) 15.

cclx The Richard Nixon Foundation. Accessed December 13, 2011. http://nixonfoundation.org/president-richard-nixon/.

cclxi Los Angeles Times, " 'Pink Right Down to Her Underwear': Politics: The 1950 Senate campaign of Richard Nixon against Helen Douglas reached an unequaled low. Comparison is unfair to John Van de Kamp." Accessed December 13, 2011. http://articles.latimes.com/1990-04-09/local/me-664_1_helen-gahagan-douglas.

cclxii History News Network, "How Did the Taft-Hartley Act Come About?" Accessed December 13, 2011. http://hnn.us/articles/1036.html.

cclxiii United States Senate, "Richard M. Nixon, 36th Vice President (1953-1961)." Accessed December 13, 2011. http://www.senate.gov/artandhistory/history/common/generic/VP_Richard_Nixon.htm.

cclxiv http://www.archives.gov/federal-register/electoral-college/scores.html.

cclxv Bruce O. Solheim, *The Vietnam War Era: A Personal Journey* (Westport: Praeger Publishers, 2006) 91.

cclxvi Robert Mason, *Richard Nixon and the Quest for a New Majority* (Chapel Hill: University of North Carolina Press) 64.

cclxvii U.S. Department of State, "Treaty Between the United States of America and the Union of Soviet Socialist Republics on the Limitation of Anti-Ballistic Missile Systems." Accessed January 6, 2012. http://www.state.gov/www/global/arms/treaties/abm/abm2.html

cclxviii The White House, "Gerald R. Ford." Accessed December 14, 2011. http://www.whitehouse.gov/about/presidents/geraldford.

cclxix Gerald R. Ford Presidential Library & Museum, "Gerald R. Ford Biography." Accessed December 14, 2011. http://www.ford.utexas.edu/grf/fordbiop.asp.

cclxx United States Senate, "Spiro T. Agnew, 39th Vice President (1969-1973)." Accessed December 14, 2011. http://www.senate.gov/artandhistory/history/common/generic/VP_Spiro_Agnew.htm.

cclxxi "President Gerald R. Ford's Proclamation 4311, Granting a Pardon to Richard Nixon." Accessed December 14, 2011. http://www.ford.utexas.edu/library/speeches/740061.htm.

cclxxii Miller Center of Public Affairs, "American President: A Reference Resource." Accessed December 14, 2011. http://millercenter.org/president/nixon/essays/biography/4.

cclxxiii Tax Policy Center, Urban Institute and Brookings Institute. Accessed January 10, 2012. http://www.taxpolicycenter.org/legislation/1960.cfm.

CHAPTER 8 ENDNOTES

cclxxiv Harold D. Clarke, Marianne C. Stewart & Gary Zuk, *Economic Decline and Political Change: Canada, Great Britain, and the United States* (Pittsburgh: University of Pittsburgh Press, 1989) 113. See http://books.google.com/books?id=Xdqwbh4g0zUC&pg=PA113&dq=world+war+ii+vietnam+war+effect+on+us+inflation&hl=en&sa=X&ei=VkELT6mVFpHhggf_qOCiAg&ved=0CEoQ6AEwBA#v=onepage&q=world%20war%20ii%20vietnam%20war%20effect%20on%20us%20inflation&f=false

cclxxv Tugwell Franklin, *The Energy Crisis and the American Political Economy: Politics and Markets in the Management of Natural Resources* (Stanford: Stanford University Press, 1988) 97.

cclxxvi George Lenczowski, *American Presidents and the Middle East* (Durham: Duke University Press, 1990)130.

cclxxvii Columbia International Affairs Online, "Détente and Confrontation: The 1973 Israeli-Arab October War." Accessed January 9, 2012. http://www.ciaonet.org/access/boa01/index.html

cclxxviii Michael Hill, *Cannibal Capitalism: How Big Business and the Feds are Ruining America* (Hoboken: John Wiley & Sons, Inc., 2012) 83.

cclxxix Commanding Heights, "Nixon Tries Price Controls." Accessed December 15, 2011. http://www.pbs.org/wgbh/commandingheights/shared/minitextlo/ess_nixongold.html.

ccxc The White House, "Gerald R. Ford." Accessed December 15, 2011. http://www.whitehouse.gov/about/presidents/geraldford.

ccxci Miller Center of Public Affairs, "American President: A Reference Resource." Accessed December 15, 2011. http://millercenter.org/president/keyevents/ford.

ccxcii Miller Center of Public Affairs, "American President: A Reference Resource." Accessed December 15, 2011. http://millercenter.org/president/ford/essays/biography/4.

CHAPTER 9

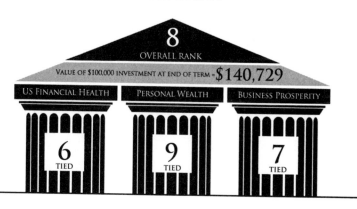

JAMES EARL CARTER, JR.

BAD FOR THE ECONOMY, GOOD FOR HUMANITY

"I say to you quite frankly that the time for racial discrimination is over."

– Jimmy Carter at his gubernatorial inauguration [ccxciii]

J ames Earl Carter Jr., known to the world as Jimmy Carter, was raised with a diverse set of values and a unique devotion to his faith. Jimmy was born on October 1, 1924 in Plains, Georgia, a small town near Macon. His father, James Earl

Sr., was a farmer and businessman. Jimmy inherited a strong work ethic from his father, who was also a politician in the Georgia state legislature.ccxciv Jimmy's father demanded a lot from his son, whom he nicknamed "Hot Shot." In his memoir, *An Hour Before Daylight*, Jimmy reflected: "As a child, my greatest ambition was to be valuable around the farm and to please my father. He was the center of my life and the focus of my admiration." However, James Sr., like many in the Deep South at that time, was a cultural bigot who did not care for those of a different heritage, especially blacks.

Jimmy was also influenced greatly by his mother Lillian, who countered her husband's strong beliefs on race. She was an avid sports fan who was color-blind, refusing to abide by the social code of segregation that dominated Georgia in the 1940s and '50s. This diverse array of values from his parents would serve Jimmy well in the political arena, allowing him to see various perspectives on significant issues, especially those involving race.ccxcv

After graduating from the U.S. Naval Academy, Jimmy married Rosalynn Smith in July of 1946. Carter, who has a rather droll sense of humor, like the authors of this book do, once said about his wife: "I have often wanted to drown my troubles, but I can't seem to get my wife to go swimming." Jimmy originally had intentions of becoming a submariner and making the Navy a career. However, he resigned his naval commission and returned to Georgia after his father's untimely death in 1953. Jimmy and Rosalynn assumed responsibility for operating the family peanut farm, which they were able to do profitably for over a decade.ccxcvi

Throughout his life, Jimmy Carter has been a believer in volunteering and giving back to his community. In Plains, he served in various nonprofit organizations and on boards, parlaying his name recognition into election to the Georgia State Senate in 1962. Four years later, he ran for governor but lost, causing him to disappear from the political limelight much like Nixon did after his loss of the California statehouse in 1962.[ccxcvii] In 1970, Carter tried again and won. In his inaugural address he said unequivocally: "The time for racial discrimination is over."[ccxcviii] As governor he opened up state jobs to blacks, reorganized the confusing maze of state agencies, and introduced tighter budgeting procedures.[ccxcix] These efforts brought him into the national spotlight, and he was featured on the cover of *Time* magazine in May of 1971 as a symbol of good government and the New South.

In 1974, long before any other nominees had declared they were running, Carter announced his candidacy for the Democratic nomination for president. Carter's strategy was bold and unique – he reached a region before another candidate could extend influence there. Before any other candidates had even announced they were in the race, Jimmy Carter had traveled a remarkable 50,000 miles, visited 37 states, and delivered more than 200 speeches. Carter won the Democratic nomination in July and the general election in November of 1976 – edging out incumbent Gerald R. Ford by just 2% of the popular vote. The kid from Plains nicknamed "Hot Shot" was now the most powerful leader in the free world.[ccc]

THE PRESIDENTIAL YEARS

President Carter considered himself a man of the people. On Inauguration Day, he walked down Pennsylvania Avenue hand-in-hand with First Lady Rosalynn rather than take the safer and more traditional ride in the presidential limousine.[ccci] He continued this down-to-earth image through his presidency, adopting an informal style of dress and speech in public appearances, holding frequent press conferences, and having fireside chats like FDR. However, Carter's White House years, unlike his inauguration, were tumultuous. He had modest accomplishments followed by significant political setbacks.[cccii]   Like Herbert Hoover,[ccciii] Carter struggled to get along effectively with a Congress controlled by his own party. He struggled *to adhere to that important PRES Rule of leading as a statesman*, demonstrating an inability to garner political support and enthusiasm for his ideas, including the significant congressional support needed to enact his policies.[ccciv]

International affairs were an ongoing problem that dogged Carter as well. They took a disastrous turn in late 1979, when Iranian students took over the U.S. embassy during the Iranian revolution, taking 52 U.S. citizens hostage.[cccv] Carter's response was to boycott the 1980 Olympics in Moscow.[cccvi] His failed attempt to rescue the hostages further hindered his popularity with the American people. [cccvii] Ironically, the hostages were released the day Ronald Reagan was inaugurated in January of 1981.[cccviii]

On the domestic front, Carter had two extraordinary dilemmas. Clearly he had inherited an economic mess from his predecessors Nixon and Ford.[cccix] In addition, through the late 1970s, hundreds of thousands of women entered the workforce, which made it more challenging to keep inflation and unemployment in check. In an effort to better address the economic problems and other challenges faced by the country, Carter tried to reorganize the federal government to make it more effective and more responsive to the needs of citizens. He instructed a project team created within the Office of Management and Budget to implement a zero-based budgeting plan,[cccx] remove unnecessary regulations, put in sunset laws to cancel archaic programs, and eliminate duplication.[cccxi] In addition,

Carter established a program of voluntary wage and price controls. [cccxii] However, neither of these strategies worked effectively, and by the end of the 1970s the nation was suffering from unprecedented inflation and very high unemployment. [cccxiii] Carter's actions demonstrated his belief in *PRES Rule #3, which recognizes that the federal government plays a vital role in creating and maintaining a healthy economy.* Carter's prescribed actions were not the desired remedy to the problem.

Carter had some modest accomplishments in domestic affairs. He established the Department of Energy in response to the energy crisis and the Arab oil embargo. He created the Department of Education and passed some important environmental legislation. [cccxiv] One of Carter's most notable accomplishments which is often overlooked is that he deregulated the airline industry in 1978, removing government control over fares, routes, and the entry of new airlines into the marketplace. This allowed more passengers to fly, prices dropped and routes opened up exponentially. These actions were clearly in line with *the PRES Rule to strive for the common good of all citizens.* Understanding the government's role in protecting the public, Carter did not diminish the FAA's regulatory powers over airline safety. [cccxv] This fact is significant and stands in sharp contrast to how George W. Bush handled the deregulation of the financial industry, when Bush removed many of the regulations that would keep the public safe. In Chapter 13, we will further discuss how deregulation of the financial industry under Bush proved disastrous to the U.S. economy. Despite Carter's good intentions, a problematic economy and the Iranian hostage crisis doomed his re-election bid in 1980.

THE PRES RANKINGS

Jimmy Carter's economic performance during his four years in the White House was disappointing. He ranks eighth among the 11 presidential administrations studied during this 80-year period. Among the three economic pillars, Carter tied for sixth with Truman in the U.S. Financial Health Pillar, tied for ninth with Nixon/Ford in the Personal Wealth Pillar, and tied for seventh with George H.W. Bush in the Business Prosperity Pillar. We graphically illustrate below Carter's below average performance as an economic steward under our PRES Ranking System.

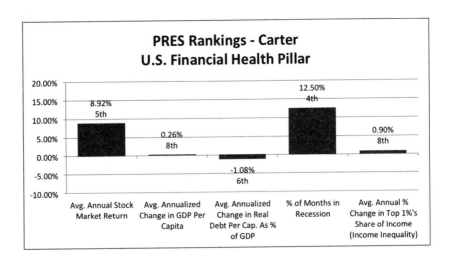

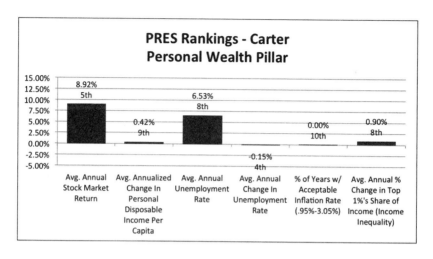

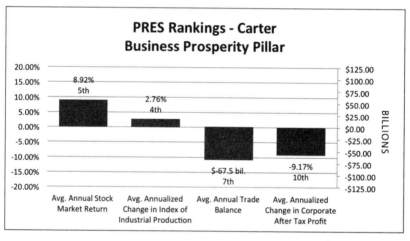

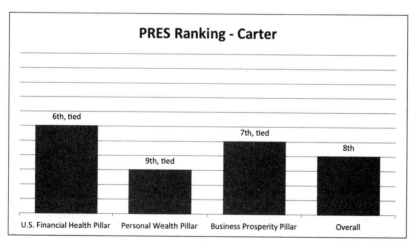

The economic nemesis that haunted Carter and caused him to finish so poorly was rampant inflation that his administration could not get under control. The inflation rate started at 6% in 1977, soaring to more than 13% by early 1980.[cccxvii] Oil and gas prices intensified the problem, as OPEC used the "oil weapon" during his last two years in office. The price per barrel of oil was $14.95 in 1978, but by early 1980 it had climbed to $37.42[cccxviii] (which is the equivalent of more than $102.26 per barrel in today's dollars). Carter never got inflation in check, and one might argue that this was because of his lack of leadership with the Federal Reserve. Carter changed his Federal Reserve chair a record three times during his tenure, finally appointing Paul Volker in August of 1979.[cccxix] By then, as was the case with Herbert Hoover in 1931,[cccxx] it was deemed as having been too little too late. By the time Volker was able to get inflation in check, it was well into Ronald Reagan's first term.

Carter also finished near the bottom of the PRES Rankings in several other important categories. He finished second-to-last in Average Annualized Change in Corporate Profits, third-to-last in Average Annualized Change in Disposable Income per Capita, and in the bottom half of Average Annualized Change in GDP and Average Unemployment Rate. The economy experienced negligible national growth during his term as well. Carter was the only president in our study to experience what economists call stagflation – a combination of high inflation and sluggish economic growth.[cccxxi] To make matters worse, the income gap between the bottom 99% and top 1% widened considerably during this time period, growing at an average rate of .90% per year, or approximately 3.60% during his four-year term.

Significantly, Carter produced the worst score of any U.S. president on what is called the Misery Index (MI), which is the simple combination of unemployment and inflation.[cccxxii] Carter scores an average of 16.26 on this scale; compare that to Dwight Eisenhower who had the lowest score of 6.25. Carter attacked Gerald Ford during the presidential campaign of 1976, when the Misery Index stood at 13.27, claiming throughout the campaign that "No man responsible for giving the country a misery index this high has the right to even ask to be president."[cccxxiii] The MI hit an all-time high of 21.98 in the summer of 1980; ironically, Carter's own words became the self-fulfilling prophecy of his own political demise.

Despite the malaise the economy suffered under Carter, there were a few bright spots during his presidency, albeit not many. Carter reduced the national debt and was steward over a stock market that produced some solid gains, particularly in the tech sector. In fact, if one had invested $100,000 in January of 1977, his or her account would have appreciated to $159,009.80 in an S&P 500 Indexed account by January of 1980, and the same amount of capital would have appreciated to $319,922.86 in the tech-heavy NASDAQ index. [cccxxiv] Carter kept the country out of recession for all but six months during his term, and presided over an increase in industrial production of 2.76% per year.

Jimmy Carter's presidency was a paradox consisting of great volatility, little consistency, and even less predictability during his four years in the Oval Office. Carter's rankings are poor because he did not lead the nation effectively, deviating dramatically from PRES Rule #5's prescription for economic success – *to lead as a statesman*. He failed to deliver the economic results expected by the American electorate and lost the 1980 presidential election in a landslide to

Ronald Reagan,[cccxxv] who inherited the difficult challenge of revitalizing a wounded economy.

CHAPTER 9 ENDNOTES

ccxciii Jimmy Carter Library and Museum, Inaugural Address, January 12, 1971 Page 1-2. Accessed December 18, 2011. http://www.jimmycarterlibrary.gov/documents/inaugural_address.pdf.

ccxciv The New Georgia Encyclopedia, History and Archaeology, Carter Family, Accessed December 13, 2011 http://www.georgiaencyclopedia.org/nge/Article.jsp?id=h-2735

ccxcv Miller Center of Public Affairs, Essays on Jimmy Carter and His Administration, A Life in Brief, Accessed December 10, 2011 http://millercenter.org/president/carter/essays/biography/1

ccxcvi Miller Center of Public Affairs, Essays on Jimmy Carter and His Administration, Life Before the Presidency, Accessed December 10, 2011 http://millercenter.org/president/carter/essays/biography/2

ccxcvii Miller Center of Public Affairs, Essays on Richard Nixon and His Administration, Life Before the Presidency, Accessed December 10, 2011 http://millercenter.org/president/nixon/essays/biography/2

ccxcviii Jimmy Carter Library and Museum, Inaugural Address, January 12, 1971, Accessed December 12, 2011, http://www.jimmycarterlibrary.gov/documents/inaugural_address.pdf http://www.jimmycarter-library.gov/documents/inaugural_address.pdf

ccxcix Academy of Achievement, A President of Peace, Revised on July12, 2010 10:51 PST, Accessed December 12, 2011 http://www.achievement.org/autodoc/page/car0bio-1

ccc Miller Center of Public Affairs, Essays on Jimmy Carter and His Administration, Campaigns And Elections, Accessed December 13, 2011 http://millercenter.org/president/carter/essays/biography/3

ccci Academy of Achievement, A President of Peace, Revised on July 12, 2010 10:51 PST, Accessed December 12, 2011 http://www.achievement.org/autodoc/page/car0bio-1

cccii Miller Center, Essays on Jimmy Carter and His Administration, A Life in Brief, Accessed December 12, 2011 http://millercenter.org/president/carter/essays/biography/1

ccciii The White House, Presidents, Herbert Hoover, Accessed December 13, 2011 http://www.white-house.gov/about/presidents/herberthoover

ccciv Miller Center, Essays on Jimmy Carter and His Administration, Accessed December 13, 2011 http://millercenter.org/president/carter/essays/biography/9

cccv Public Broadcast Service, General Article: The Iranian Hostage Crisis, Accessed December 13, 2011 http://www.pbs.org/wgbh/americanexperience/features/general-article/carter-hostage-crisis/

cccvi Miller Center, Key Events, Accessed December 13, 2011 http://millercenter.org/president/keyevents/carter

cccvii Miller Center, Essays on Jimmy Carter and His Administration, Foreign Affairs, Accessed December 13, 2011 http://millercenter.org/president/carter/essays/biography/5

cccviii The Presidential Timeline of the Twentieth Century, Accessed December 13, 2011 http://www.presidentialtimeline.org/html/timeline.php?id=39

cccix The White House, Gerald Ford, Accessed December 13, 2011 http://www.whitehouse.gov/about/presidents/geraldford

CHAPTER 9 ENDNOTES

cccx Jimmy Carter: "Zero-Base Budgeting for the Fiscal Year 1979 Budget Memorandum to the Heads of Executive Departments and Agencies," February 14, 1977. Online by Gerhard Peters and John T. Woolley, *The American Presidency Project*. Accessed December 14, 2011 http://www.presidency. ucsb.edu/ws/?pid=7910

cccxi John R. Dempsey, "Carter Reorganization: A Midterm Appraisal" 74, posted on Public Management Forum, Carl Steinberg, Editor. Accessed December 17, 2011. http://www.jstor.org/ stable/3110382

cccxii Jimmy Carter: "The President's News Conference," February 23, 1977. Online by Gerhard Peters and John T. Woolley, *The American Presidency Project*. Accessed December 14, 2011 http://www.presidency.ucsb.edu/ws/?pid=6887

cccxiii US Department of Labor, Bureau of Labor Statistics http://www.dlt.ri.gov/lmi/pdf/cpi.pdf

cccxiv Miller Center, Accessed December 14, 2011 http://millercenter.org/president/carter/essays/ biography/4

cccxv Jimmy Carter: "Airline Industry Regulation Message to the Congress.," March 4, 1977. Online by Gerhard Peters and John T. Woolley, *The American Presidency Project*. Accessed December 14, 2011 http://www.presidency.ucsb.edu/ws/?pid=7113

cccxvi New York Times, Mark Landler and Sheryl Gay Stolberg, Accessed December 15, 2011 http://www.nytimes.com/2008/09/20/business/worldbusiness/20iht-prexy.4.16321064. html?pagewanted=all

cccxvii US Department of Labor, Bureau of Labor Statistics, Accessed December 15, 2011 http://www. dlt.ri.gov/lmi/pdf/cpi.pdf

cccxviii U.S. Department of Energy, Energy Information Administration, Monthly Energy Review, March 2011, Washington, D.C., Table 9.1. Accessed December 15, 2011 cta.ornl.gov/data/tedb30/Spread-sheets/Table10_03.xls

cccxix Federal Reserve Bank of New York, Accessed December 15, 2011 http://www.ny.frb.org/about-thefed/PVolckerbio.html

cccxx The White House, President Herbert Hoover, Accessed December 16, 2011 http://www.white-house.gov/about/presidents/herberthoover

cccxxi Jimmy Carter: "Atlanta, Georgia, Remarks Before a Joint Session of the Georgia General Assembly," February 20, 1979. Online by Gerhard Peters and John T. Woolley, *The American Presidency Project*. Accessed December 16, 2011 http://www.presidency.ucsb.edu/ws/?pid=31936

cccxxii David Gergen, *Eyewitness to Power: The Essence of Leadership Nixon to Clinton* (New York: Simon & Schuster, 2000) 154.

cccxxiii Ronald Regan, *An American Life* (New York: Simon and Schuster, 1990) 220.

cccxxiv Compiled based upon "Presidential Stock Market Returns Data" spreadsheet in Appendix A.

cccxxv Miller Center, President Reagan, Campaigns and Elections, Accessed December 16, 2011 http://millercenter.org/president/reagan/essays/biography/3

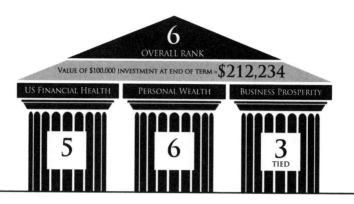

6

OVERALL RANK

VALUE OF $100,000 INVESTMENT AT END OF TERM = $212,234

US FINANCIAL HEALTH | PERSONAL WEALTH | BUSINESS PROSPERITY

5 | 6 | 3
TIED

RONALD REAGAN

THE GREAT COMMUNICATOR INTRODUCES
TRICKLE-DOWN ECONOMICS

"If you will forgive me. . .
someone has likened government to a baby. . .
an alimentary canal with an appetite at one end
and no sense of responsibility at the other."

– Ronald Reagan [cccxxvi]

T aking office in 1981 and presiding over a country with a wounded psyche, Ronald Reagan is widely credited with meeting his self-prescribed goal of "making the American people believe in themselves again."[cccxxvii]

Ronald Wilson Reagan was born on February 6, 1911, in Tampico, Illinois,[cccxxviii] a small village located west of Chicago. His father, Jack, was a salesman who constantly was searching for a good job,[cccxxix] and the family (including young Ronnie and his brother, Neil) eventually settled in Dixon, Illinois.[cccxxx] Reagan would spend most of his formative years there.

Like many of the presidents reviewed in this book, Ron had a very special bond with his mother, Nelle, who nurtured and encouraged her sons. His parents were both Democrats,[cccxxxi] a party affiliation that young Reagan would adopt for half of his life. During high school, Ron was very active in sports and other activities,[cccxxxii] in sharp contrast to his indifference in the classroom, where he typically achieved mediocre grades.[cccxxxiii] Dutch,[cccxxxiv] as he was known to his friends, graduated in 1928 from Dixon High School, where he played football and basketball, acted in theater, and was the student body president.[cccxxxvi]

Dutch became the first member of his family to attend college when he enrolled at Eureka College in Illinois.[cccxxxvii] He graduated in 1932 with a degree in economics[cccxxxviii] and embarked on a career in radio, ultimately becoming an announcer for the Chicago Cubs and Big Ten football.[cccxxxix] What Ron lacked in broadcasting experience, he made up for with his imagination and resonant voice.

Standing six-foot-one, with wavy brown hair, blue eyes, and a gregarious personality, Reagan projected a Hollywood look. He took advantage of these attributes on a visit to Los Angeles while covering the Chicago Cubs spring training camp and signed with an agent.[cccxl] Ron subsequently appeared in 52 films between 1937 and 1957.[cccxli] He is probably best remembered for his portrayal of the terminally ill Notre Dame football player, George Gipp, in the film *Knute Rockne – All American*.[cccxlii] In one somber scene, Gipp tells Coach Rockne:

"Someday, when things are tough, maybe you can ask the boys to go in there and win one for the Gipper."[cccxliii] Reagan would use that line often during his political career to rally followers, earning the nickname Gipper from reporters who covered him.[cccxliv] Reagan's knowledge of filmmaking and the art of staging a scene would prove invaluable throughout his political career.

In the late 1930s, young Ron married a Hollywood actress, Jane Wyman,[cccxlv] but they divorced in 1948.[cccxlvi] Four years later, Ron married another actress, Nancy Davis,[cccxlvii] who also happened to be a Republican, and embarked with her on an amazing lifelong journey and partnership.

As his acting career began to wane, Reagan looked at alternate career paths, and chose politics. Reagan, a liberal Democrat until he was in his 40s, had been a great admirer of FDR[cccxlviii] and a proponent of the New Deal programs that employed both his father and older brother during the 1930s.[cccxlix] Although Reagan never lost his admiration for FDR, he became an ardent conservative and switched his party allegiance to the GOP in 1962.[cccl] Reagan's ideological evolution was due to a variety of factors including his increased wealth and tax burden,[cccli] his wife Nancy's influence, conflicts with union leaders while serving as president of the Screen Actors Guild,[ccclii] and his changing views of the government's role in people's lives. In a surprising about face, Ron had come to believe that programs such as the New Deal stifled economic growth and individual freedom.[cccliii]

Like Barack Obama in his speech at the Democratic National Convention in 2004, Ronald Reagan broke onto the political stage with a riveting televised speech supporting Barry Goldwater just prior to the 1964 election.[cccliv] Reagan was elected governor of California in 1966 and again in 1970.[ccclv] He was a successful governor who balanced the state's budget with a strategy that included a record tax increase.[ccclvi] He also enacted educational and welfare reform and property tax relief.[ccclvii]

THE PRESIDENTIAL YEARS

Building on his success as a two-term governor, Ronald Reagan set his sights on the White House. At 69, he realized he would be the oldest man ever elected to the Oval Office[ccclviii] and the 1980 election would be his last chance at the White House brass ring. His optimistic message of hope embodied in the phrase *"America is a shining city on the hill"*[tcclix] resonated with the American electorate, and he won a sweeping victory over Jimmy Carter. Reagan had a very specific set of policy goals:

- *Revitalize the economy.*
- *Reduce federal income tax rates, especially on the most affluent.*
- *Balance the federal budget.*
- *Reduce the size and scope of the federal government.*
- *Restore power to the states.*
- *Build a stronger national defense.*

Campaigning on a platform of sending "the welfare bums back to work,"[ccclx] Reagan clearly wanted to dismantle LBJ's Great Society. [ccclxi] He strongly advocated the Republican ideals of less government regulation,[ccclxii] and in foreign affairs Reagan vowed to strengthen the nation's military and to confront the Soviet Union with tenacious vigor.[ccclxiii] In essence, Reagan as our CEO decided to invest enough capital to spend the Soviets into submission. Ultimately, this strategy was a stimulus bill that would cost the United States hundreds of billions of dollars, but it worked. In one of the most famous speeches Ronald Reagan or any United States president has ever given, he stood at the hated Berlin Wall in June of 1987 and beseeched Soviet leader Mikhail Gorbachev: "If you seek peace, if you seek prosperity for the Soviet Union and Eastern Europe, if you seek liberalization, come here to this gate! Mr. Gorbachev, open this gate! Mr. Gorbachev, tear down this wall!"[ccclxiv] *This was a good example of Reagan taking bold action after careful and innovative thought (PRES Rule #4).* Within 29 months after this speech, the Berlin Wall had been razed.[ccclxv]

While getting into his presidential limousine on a cold March afternoon in Washington in 1981, fewer than 70 days into his first term,[ccclxvi] Ronald Reagan nearly lost the opportunity to implement any of his ideas. A 22-caliber bullet shot by erotomaniac and would-be assassin John Hinckley narrowly missed Reagan's heart.[ccclxvii] Despite the severity of his wound, Reagan managed to walk into the emergency room,[ccclxviii] collapsing once inside. His performance in the hospital and his comment to his doctors, "I hope you're all Republicans,"[ccclxix] as he was being wheeled into the operating room were seen as humorous and courageous. Few people know that while Reagan was recovering in the hospital, Speaker of the House Tip O'Neill visited him.[ccclxx] Upon entering his room, Tip grasped Ronald's hands and the two men recited the Lord's Prayer in unison.[ccclxxi] This remarkable event was an affirmation of Reagan and O'Neill's kinship, friendship, and statesmanship in that moment. Reagan and O'Neill may not have agreed on much in the way of politics, but despite that fact, both men had great respect and admiration for one another, and both were patriots who loved the United States. Reagan and O'Neill, much like Eccles and Roosevelt, a Republican and a Democrat, were colleagues; and although politically they were miles apart, they were smart enough to put pettiness, politics, and ideology aside to do what was right for the country: and at the end of the day, they could still have a beer together. This dynamic speaks volumes about why so much was accomplished by these four great men during their respective periods in office. Reagan and Roosevelt adhered to the principle of putting country first, a fundamental philosophy of both PRES Rules #5 and #1, that require leading as a statesman and not as a partisan, and advancing the interests of the common good and not solely the advantaged few. This story of kinship, despite political differences, is a tremendous testament to statesmanship, a value which is so desperately needed in our country today.

After his recovery, Reagan's popularity with the American electorate soared to 73%.[ccclxxii] Ronald Reagan had inherited an economic mess from Jimmy Carter, not unlike the ones that Roosevelt inherited from Hoover and Obama inherited from George W. Bush. However, Ronald Reagan did not make excuses. He acted boldly. During his first months in office, unemployment stood at 7.5%[ccclxxiii] and inflation was at 12.5%,[ccclxxiv] so the Misery Index (the sum of the two), was a staggering 20.[ccclxxv ccclxxvi] Reagan decided to implement policies based on the economic theories of Art Laffer,[ccclxxvii] who was a proponent of supply-side economics. Laffer advocated the laissez-faire philosophy of seeking to stimulate the economy with large across-the-board tax cuts.[ccclxxviii] Reagan promoted such tax cuts, presuming they would stimulate the economy enough to expand the aggregate tax base and offset the revenue lost due to these reduced rates – a theory called the "Laffer Curve."[ccclxxix] *By implementing these policies, Reagan demonstrated his recognition of the role of government in the economy, as prescribed by PRES Rule #3: The government can play a unique and vital role in creating and maintaining a healthy economy.* However, "trickle down" economics[ccclxxx] – called "Reaganomics" – was untested, and it was then and is today a subject of great debate. Supporters point to some key economic indicators as evidence of its success[ccclxxxi] while critics point to substantial increases in the budget deficit and the national debt as its inherent failure.[ccclxxxii] Although the nation's economy improved under Reagan based on many measurements, it also worsened based on some macroeconomic measures:[ccclxxxiii] the budget deficit, which stood at $994 billion when Reagan entered office in 1981, tripled to almost $2.87 trillion when he left eight years later.[ccclxxxiv] Moreover, the country's national debt increased significantly, and the income gap widened dramatically.

After his hospital recovery, Reagan won passage of the Economic Recovery Tax Act (ERTA),[ccclxxxv] which featured the largest phased-in tax cuts in U.S. history,[ccclxxxvi] smaller-than-advertised spending cuts, and a substantial military buildup. Reagan's close rapport with Democratic Speaker Tip O'Neill and his ability to work with a Democratic House and a GOP Senate were paramount in achieving passage of this monumental bill.[ccclxxxvii] The Reaganomics theory, that was put to the test with the passage of ERTA, proposed that economic growth would occur when marginal tax rates were low enough to spur investment, which would lead to increased economic activity, more jobs, and higher wages.[ccclxxxviii]

Reagan's critics observed that this theory of trickle-down economics was no different than what a prior generation had called the horse-and-sparrow theory.[ccclxxxix] In 1896, Democratic presidential candidate William Jennings Bryant refuted the theory of "trickle-down" economics that held that "if you feed a horse enough oats, some will fall down upon the road for the sparrows."[cccxc] Bryant argued, "The Democratic idea is that if you legislate to make the masses prosperous – their prosperity will find its way up and through every class that rests upon it."[cccxci]   The belief that tax policies made for the wealthy trickle down to the poor and middle class does not coincide with PRES Rules #1 and #2. Bryant's philosophy advocated for the common good of all citizens and recognized that the middle class is the engine that drives the nation's economy. Many economists have disagreed with Reagan's theory of trickle-down economics because they believed that a viable middle class was essential to create the demand for the goods and services which business owners create, and not the other way around. In his autobiography, *Beckoning Frontiers*,[cccxcii] Marriner Eccles tenaciously contends: "I saw at this time that men with great economic power had an undue influence in making the rules of the economic game, in shaping the actions of government that enforced those rules and in conditioning the attitude taken by people as a whole toward those rules…"[cccxciii] Eccles goes on to state emphatically, "After I had lost faith in all of my business heroes, I concluded that I, and everyone else in the country, had an equal right to share in the process by which economic rules are made and changed."[cccxciv]   Here Eccles defines his version of economic pluralism. Marriner Eccles, a wealthy successful banker and businessman, a man who may have been the Warren Buffet of his day, changed his life's path and decided that it was in the best interest of the nation that he be a stalwart champion for the middle class.

Critics argue that Reagan's policies really benefited the wealthy more than those living in poverty and in Middle America. Our PRES rankings seem to bear that out, as the income gap between the bottom 99% and top 1% widened three times more under Reagan than any other president in our 80-year study. The poor, minorities and college students viewed Reagan as harsh and indifferent to their plight. These views were solidified when Reagan froze the minimum wage at $3.35 an hour during his eight year tenure, slashed federal assistance to local governments by 60%, cut the budget for public housing and Section 8 rent subsidies, and eliminated Community Development Block Grants. Adhering to his campaign promise of "sending the welfare bums back to work,"[cccxcv] Reagan cut Medicaid, food stamps, federal education programs, as well as Nixon's EPA.[cccxcvi] Tip O'Neill stood firm on the programs of Social Security and Medicare[cccxcvii] – Reagan did not touch those; in fact Reagan and O'Neill agreed to raise taxes to keep Social Security solvent in 1983.[cccxcviii]

The reality is, Reagan's first effort at implementing Reaganomics, ERTA or the Economic Recovery Tax Act of 1981, was a bridge too far and it failed.[cccxcix] The program backfired so much it resulted in massive budget deficits and weakened the economy, which plunged into what is referred to as the first "double-dip" recession[cd] in our nation's history. Unemployment soared to a post-Great Depression record of 10.8% by December of 1982;[cdi] in fact as late as August of 1983, when unemployment stood at 9.5%, Reagan did not believe he would be re-elected for a second term.

As a result of the severe recession, a shortfall in tax revenue spurred concern over the budget deficit.[cdii] The Tax Equity and Fiscal Responsibility Act, or TEFRA, sponsored by House Democrat Pete Stark of California, was written to reduce the budget gap through the closure of tax loopholes and the tougher enforcement of tax rules.[cdiii] TEFRA, introduced by a Democrat and signed into law by Republican President Ronald Reagan in September of 1982,[cdiv] was the largest peacetime tax increase in our nation's history.[cdv] Despite that fact, it was the shot in the arm the economy and the equity markets needed. Both began to expand almost immediately after TEFRA's passage. It is important to note that TEFRA raised taxes by $37.5 billion per year,[cdvi] which was almost 1% of the nation's GDP at the time. This important course correction worked, and the stock market reacted positively, creating an expansion that would continue for more than five years. *This is a solid example again where Reagan implemented the PRES Rule of taking bold action after careful and innovative thought.* Among other things, TEFRA involved rolling back tax cuts from ERTA,[cdvii] filling in loopholes, and enforcing regulations more strictly. *Reagan used government policies to spur economic recovery, recognizing the PRES Rule that government can be a useful tool in maintaining a vibrant and healthy economy.*

Ronald Reagan's ability to adapt, after having made an overreach one year before, illustrates that he was willing to do whatever it took to see his economic vision take hold. He may have resisted calls for tax increases, but ultimately he supported and signed many of them into effect because it was the right thing to do to keep the economy moving forward. This strategy of compromise worked. *Unbeknown to many, Ronald Reagan signed nine tax bills into law during his tenure,[cdviii] seven of which raised taxes.[cdix] ERTA had been an overreach and TEFRA became the remedy.* The course correction that followed the passage of TEFRA created the catalyst for a boom in the stock market, unprecedented since the 1933-1937 surge under FDR. Reagan would receive the credit as the economy expanded, as he deservedly should as CEO of the economy. But the reality is the passage of TEFRA likely made Ronald Reagan the two-term president he would become. To Reagan's credit, he was able to reach across the aisle and work with two Democrats in Congress – Pete Stark and Tip O'Neill – to pass TEFRA and attain the best result for the country. *This clearly shows that Ronald Reagan modeled the PRES Rule of leading as a statesman and not as a partisan.*

The economic turnaround was dramatic from that point forward. Unemployment, which is a lagging economic indicator, had been more than 10% during most of Reagan's first term, but it began to abate by the autumn of 1983.[cdx]   In July it broke below 10% and by November of 1984 it had fallen to 7.4%![cdxi]   Reagan won his re-election bid against Walter Mondale by a landslide because it was clear the economy was on the mend.[cdxii]   Even after Reagan was reelected in a landslide over Mondale, it took two long years, until the end of 1986, for the unemployment rate to fall below 7%.

THE PRES RANKINGS

As discussed in Chapter 2, Reagan finished in the middle-of-the-pack of our PRES Rankings, landing in sixth place overall. He finished fifth under the U.S. Financial Health Pillar, sixth under the Personal Wealth Pillar, and an impressive third under our Business Prosperity Pillar, in a tie with Bill Clinton.   Even though Ronald Reagan signed TEFRA into law, resulting in the single largest peacetime tax increase in American history, he remains best known for his tax cuts and trickle-down theory of economics. His performance as economic steward under our PRES Rankings is illustrated in the graphs below.

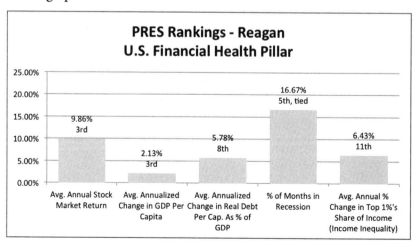

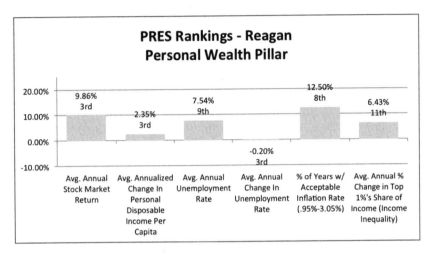

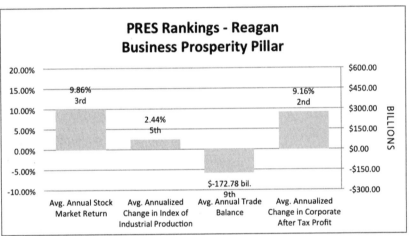

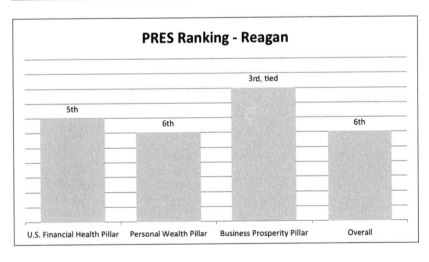

Reagan finished in the top three of many of our economic indicators, with average corporate profits and personal disposable income increasing considerably and GDP growing steadily during the final six years he was in office, growing overall at an annual rate of 2.13%. In addition, the stock market reacted in the affirmative to Reagan's policies with an average annual return of 9.86% over eight years. With impressive showings under many indicators, why did Reagan finish sixth in our rankings? We must look at the whole picture, as Reagan fared very poorly under several key indicators. He finished last under our indicator that measures income inequality, with the gap between the bottom 99% and top 1% widening dramatically under Reagan's trickle-down economic policies, widening at a rate of 6.43% per year. Not much "trickling down" occurred during his eight years as the country's CEO.

Reagan also had poor showings under some other indicators: fighting high unemployment and inflation during his presidency, accumulating significant debt to pay for his policies, and presiding over a large trade deficit of nearly $173 billion per year. It is historically interesting to note that unemployment peaked at 10.8% in December 1982 – higher than any time since the Great Depression,[cdxiii] but then it dropped during the rest of Reagan's presidency. Sixteen million jobs were created under Reagan's tenure, most of which were in his second term.[cdxiv] Nonetheless, Reagan deserves credit for the enormous economic recovery of the 1980s.

Ronald Reagan left office in January of 1989 with one of the highest approval ratings of any president in history (62%),[cdxv] handing over the Oval Office to his vice president, George H.W. Bush. After suffering from Alzheimer's disease for many years, Ronald Reagan died on June 5, 2004.[cdxvi] His death brought forth an outpouring of bipartisan and global affection.

CHAPTER 10 ENDNOTES

cccxxvi The Ronald Reagan Presidential Foundation & Library, "Remarks before a Joint Session of the Canadian Parliament, Ottawa." Accessed January 11, 2012. http://www.reaganfoundation.org/reagan-quotes-detail.aspx?tx=2104

cccxxvii Miller Center of Public Affairs, "Ronald Reagan: A Life in Brief." December 16, 2011. http://millercenter.org/president/reagan/essays/biography/1

cccxxviii The White House, "Ronald Reagan." Accessed December 17, 2011. http://www.whitehouse.gov/about/presidents/ronaldreagan

cccxxix Miller Center of Public Affairs, "Ronald Reagan: Life Before the Presidency." Accessed December 17, 2011. http://millercenter.org/president/reagan/essays/biography/2

cccxxx Ibid

cccxxxi Ibid

cccxxxii The Ronald Reagan Presidential Foundation & Library, "1924, Dixon High School." Accessed January 11, 2012. http://www.reaganfoundation.org/life-and-times.aspx

cccxxxiii Miller Center of Public Affairs, "Reagan Before Politics." Accessed December 18, 2011. http://millercenter.org/president/reagan/essays/biography/print

cccxxxiv Miller Center of Public Affairs, "American President: Ronald Reagan (1911-2004)." Accessed December 17, 2011. http://millercenter.org/president/reagan

cccxxxv Miller Center of Public Affairs, "Ronald Reagan: Youth and College Years." Accessed December 17, 2011. http://millercenter.org/president/reagan/essays/biography/2

cccxxxvi The University of Texas at Austin, "Ronald Reagan's Pre-Presidential Time Line, 1911-1980." Accessed December 17, 2011. http://www.reagan.utexas.edu/archives/reference/prepreschrono.html

cccxxxvii Eureka College, "The Moment of Discovery: The Reagan Brothers." Accessed December 17, 2011. http://www.eureka.edu/discover/reaganinflu.htm

cccxxxviii Ibid

cccxxxix Miller Center of Public Affairs, "American President: Biography of Ronald Wilson Reagan." Accessed December 17, 2011. http://millercenter.org/president/reagan/essays/biography/print

cccxl Lee Edwards, *The Essential Ronald Reagan: A Profile in Courage, Justice and Wisdom* (Lanham: Rowman & Littlefield Publishers, Inc.) 21-22.

cccxli Miller Center of Public Affairs, "American President: Radio, Film, and Television Career." Accessed December 17, 2011. http://millercenter.org/president/reagan/essays/biography/print

cccxlii Ibid

cccxliii MSNBC, "The Legacy of Ronald Reagan: Phrases That Defined a Career." Accessed December 17, 2011. http://www.msnbc.msn.com/id/3638320/ns/us_news-the_legacy_of_ronald_reagan/t/phrases-defined-career/#.Tu0sSzWvKSo

CHAPTER 10 ENDNOTES

cccxliv Ibid

cccxlv Miller Center of Public Affairs, "American President: Radio, Film, and Television Career." Accessed December 17, 2011. http://millercenter.org/president/reagan/essays/biography/print

cccxlvi Ibid

cccxlvii Ibid

cccxlviii The Washington Examiner, "Ronald Reagan at 100: A true believer who caught destiny's eye." Accessed December 18, 2011. http://washingtonexaminer.com/politics/2011/01/ronald-reagan-true-believer-who-caught-destinys-eye

cccxlix Miller Center of Public Affairs, "Shifting Politics: Union and Anti-Communist Leader." Accessed December 18, 2011. http://millercenter.org/president/reagan/essays/biography/2

cccl Miller Center of Public Affairs, "Political Aspirations and Success." Accessed December 18, 2011. http://millercenter.org/president/reagan/essays/biography/1

cccli Ibid

ccclii Screen Actors Guild, "Ronald Reagan." December 18, 2011. http://www.sag.org/ronald-reagan

cccliii Miller Center of Public Affairs, "Political Aspirations and Success." Accessed December 18, 2011. http://millercenter.org/president/reagan/essays/biography/1

cccliv Miller Center of Public Affairs, " 'A Time for Choosing' (October 27, 1964)." Accessed December 18, 2011. http://millercenter.org/president/speeches/detail/3405

ccclv The White House, "Ronald Reagan." Accessed December 17, 2011. http://www.white-house.gov/about/presidents/ronaldreagan

ccclvi Miller Center of Public Affairs, "Political Aspirations and Success." Accessed December 18, 2011. http://millercenter.org/president/reagan/essays/biography/1

ccclvii Miller Center of Public Affairs, "Governor of the Golden State." Accessed December 18, 2011. http://millercenter.org/president/reagan/essays/biography/2

ccclviii USA Today, "Ronald Reagan Case Study." Accessed December 18, 2011. http://www.usatoday.com/educate/casestudies/K-12Reagan.pdf

ccclix Gary Scott Smith, Faith and the Presidency: From George Washington to George W. Bush (New York: Oxford University Press) 325.

ccclx UC Berkley, "Ronald Reagan launched political career using the Berkley campus as a target." Accessed December 18, 2011. http://berkeley.edu/news/media/releases/2004/06/08_reagan.shtml

ccclxi CBS News, "Ronald Reagan Revealed. Accessed December 18, 2011. http://www.cbsnews.com/8301-500803_162-2822710-500803.html

CHAPTER 10 ENDNOTES

ccclxii Miller Center of Public Affairs, "Domestic Affairs." December 18, 2011. http://millercenter.org/president/reagan/essays/biography/4

ccclxiii U.S. Government Printing Office, "Ronald Reagan 1911-2004." Accessed December 18, 2011. http://www.gpo.gov/fdsys/pkg/CDOC-108hdoc227/pdf/CDOC-108hdoc227.pdf

ccclxiv The Ronald Reagan Presidential Foundation and Library, "Berlin Wall." Accessed December 18, 2011. http://www.reaganfoundation.org/berlin-wall.aspx

ccclxv Miller Center of Public Affairs, "Address from the Brandenburg Gate (Berlin Wall) (June 12, 1987)." Accessed December 18, 2011. http://millercenter.org/president/speeches/detail/3415

ccclxvi Miller Center of Public Affairs, "Reagan Officials on the March 30, 1981 Assassination Attempt." Accessed December 17, 2011. http://millercenter.org/academic/oralhistory/news/2007_0330

ccclxvii Los Angeles Times, "Former President Reagan Dies at 93." Accessed December 18, 2011. http://www.latimes.com/news/obituaries/la-reagan,1,4780792.story?page=6&coll=la-news-obituaries&ctrack=1&cset=true

ccclxviii CBS News, "The Reagan Shooting: A Closer Call Than We Knew." Accessed December 17, 2011. http://www.cbsnews.com/stories/2011/03/27/sunday/main20047616.shtml

ccclxix Ibid

ccclxx University of Southern California, "'Branching Out: Policy Leadership and Legislative Relations Under Reagan's Policy." Accessed December 18, 2011. http://www.usc.edu/schools/price/events/reagan/news/policy_panel.html

ccclxxi The Churchill Centre and Museum at the Churchill War Rooms, London, "Finest Hour, The Journals of Winston Churchill." Accessed December 18, 2011. http://www.winstonchurchill.org/images/finesthour/Vol.01%20No.137.pdf

ccclxxii ABC News, "Reagan's Ratings: 'Great Communicator's' Appeal Is Greater in Retrospect." Accessed December 18, 2011. http://abcnews.go.com/sections/us/Polls/reagan_ratings_poll_040607.html

ccclxxiii The Bureau of Labor Statistics, "Employment and Unemployment in the First Half of 1981." Accessed December 18, 2011. http://www.bls.gov/opub/mlr/1981/08/art1full.pdf

ccclxxiv U.S. Agency for International Development, "Reagan and the Economy." Accessed December 18, 2011. http://pdf.usaid.gov/pdf_docs/PNABD484.pdf

ccclxxv United States Department of Labor, Bureau of Labor Statistics, "Labor Force Statistics from the Current Population Survey." Accessed January 11, 2012. http://data.bls.gov/timeseries/lns14000000.

ccclxxvi U.S. Social Security Administration, "Consumer Price Index for Urban Wage Earners and Clerical Workers."Accessed January 12, 2012. http://www.ssa.gov/oact/STATS/cpiw.html.

ccclxxvii The Heritage Foundation, "The Laffer Curve: Past, Present, and Future." Accessed December 18, 2011. http://www.heritage.org/research/reports/2004/06/the-laffer-curve-past-present-and-future

CHAPTER 10 ENDNOTES

[ccclxxviii] Ibid

[ccclxxix] Ibid

[ccclxxx] Rodney P. Carlisle & J. Geoffrey Golson, *The Reagan era from the Iran crisis to Kosovo* (Santa Barbara: ABC-CLIO, Inc., 2008) 25.

[ccclxxxi] Lawrence University, "The science and/or art of election forecasting." Accessed December 18, 2011. http://www.lawrence.edu/news/pubs/lt/fall04/forecasting.shtml

[ccclxxxii] Ibid

[ccclxxxiii] Princeton, "Partisan Politics and the U.S. Income Distribution." Accessed December 18, 2011. http://www.princeton.edu/~bartels/income.pdf

[ccclxxxiv] Northern University: College of Computer and Information Science, "Honesty Campaign." Accessed December 18, 2011. http://fiji4.ccs.neu.edu/~zerg/lemurcgi/ISU_data/TREC/cd-data/vol1/ap/ap890119

[ccclxxxv] The Heritage Foundation, "Golden Years – Lee Edwards." Accessed December 18, 2011. http://www.reagansheritage.org/html/reagan_edwards12.shtml

[ccclxxxvi] CNN Money, "Taxes: What People Forget about Reagan." Accessed December 18, 2011. http://money.cnn.com/2010/09/08/news/economy/reagan_years_taxes/index.htm

[ccclxxxvii] Miller Center of Public Affairs, "Domestic Affairs." Accessed December 18, 2011. http://millercenter.org/president/reagan/essays/biography/4

[ccclxxxviii] Ibid

[ccclxxxix] Nicholas Wapshott, *Keynes Hayek: The Clash That Defined Modern Economics* (New York: W.W. Norton & Company, Inc., 2011) 263.

[cccxc] Ibid

[cccxci] Ibid

[cccxcii] Marriner S. Eccles, *Beckoning Frontiers: Public and Personal Recollections* (New York: Alfred A. Knopf, 1951).

[cccxciii] Robert B. Reich, *"Aftershock: The Next Economy and America's Future,"* (published by Alfred A. Knopf Inc.) Accessed December 18, 2011. http://www.powells.com/biblio?show=HARDCOVER:NEW:9780307592811:25.00&page=excerpt

[cccxciv] Ibid

[cccxcv] UC Berkeley, "Ronald Reagan launched political career using using the Berkley campus as a target." Accessed December 18, 2011. http://berkeley.edu/news/media/releases/2004/06/08_reagan.shtml

[cccxcvi] PBS, "Domestic Politics." Accessed December 18, 2011. http://www.pbs.org/wgbh/americanexperience/features/general-article/nixon-domestic/

CHAPTER 10 ENDNOTES

[cccxcvii] Ibid

[cccxcviii] The White House, "Press Briefing by Press Secretary Jay Carney, 7/12/2011." Accessed December 18, 2011. http://www.whitehouse.gov/the-press-office/2011/07/12/press-briefing-press-secretary-jay-carney-7122011

[cccxcix] Alan M. Rugman & Gavin Boyd, *Alliance Capitalism for the New American Economy* (Northampton: Edward Elgar Publishing, Inc.) 109.

[cd] The Moderate Voice, "The Church of Ronald Reagan." Accessed December 18, 2011. http://themoderatevoice.com/17221/the-church-of-ronald-reagan/

[cdi] The New York Times, "Federal Reserve (The Fed)." Accessed December 18, 2011. http://topics.nytimes.com/top/reference/timestopics/organizations/f/federal_reserve_system/index.html

[cdii] Bureau of Labor Statistics, "The Nation's Unemployment Situation Worsens in the First Half of 1982." Accessed December 18, 2011. http://bls.gov/opub/mlr/1982/08/art1full.pdf

[cdiii] UC Berkeley, "Starve the Beast or Explode the Deficit?: The Effects of Tax Cuts of Government Spending." Accessed December 18, 2011. http://elsa.berkeley.edu/~cromer/draft507.pdf
[cdiv] Miller Center of Public Affairs, "Presidents and Tax Policy." Accessed December 18, 2011. http://millercenter.org/newsroom/news/tax2010#reagan

[cdv] Bruce R. Bartlett, *The New American Economy: The Failure of Reaganomics and a New Way Forward* (New York: Palgrave Macmillan, 2009) 152.

[cdvi] ABC News, "The Note, 6/26/09: Caps and Tradeoffs: Energy Bill Takes Political Temperature." Accessed December 18, 2011. http://abcnews.go.com/blogs/politics/2009/06/caps-and-tradeoffs-energy-bill-takes-political-temperature/

[cdvii] Citizens for Tax Justice, "CTJ's Presidential Election Tax Policy Scorecard." Accessed December 18, 2011. http://www.ctj.org/html/taxvotes.htm

[cdviii] Miller Center of Public Affairs, "Key Events in the Presidency of Ronald Reagan." Accessed December 18, 2011. http://millercenter.org/president/keyevents/reagan

[cdix] U.S. Department of the Treasury, OTA Paper 81, "Revenue Effects of Major Tax Bills." Accessed January 12, 2012. http://www.treasury.gov/resource-center/tax-policy/tax-analysis/Documents/ota81.pdf

[cdx] Congressional Budget Office, "CBO Testimony." Accessed December 18, 2011. http://www.cbo.gov/ftpdocs/76xx/doc7636/91doc70.pdf

[cdxi] USA Today, "Obama's Reagan Parallels Are Falling Away." Accessed December 18, 2011. http://www.usatoday.com/news/opinion/forum/2011-07-04-obama-reagan-reelection_n.htm

[cdxii] NPR, "Assessing Ronald Reagan at 100." Accessed December 18, 2011. http://www.npr.org/blogs/itsallpolitics/2011/02/06/133448787/assessing-ronald-reagan-at-100

[cdxiii] U.S. News and World Report, "Is Unemployment the Worst Since the Great Depression?" Accessed December 18, 2011. http://money.usnews.com/money/business-economy/articles/2009/08/27/is-unemployment-the-worst-since-the-great-depression

CHAPTER 10 ENDNOTES

[cdxiv] The House of Representatives, "The Reagan Prosperity." Accessed December 18, 2011. http://www.house.gov/jec/growth/prosper/prosper.htm

[cdxv] CBS News, "A Look Back At the Polls." Accessed December 18, 2011. http://www.cbsnews.com/stories/2004/06/07/opinion/polls/main621632.shtml

[cdxvi] Miller Center of Public Affairs, "Reagan After the Presidency." Accessed December 18, 2011. http://millercenter.org/president/reagan/essays/biography/1

CHAPTER 11

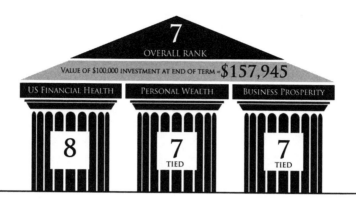

GEORGE H.W. BUSH

COMMANDER-IN-CHIEF OF THE MILITARY BUT NOT THE ECONOMY

★ ★ ★ ★ ★ ★ ★ ★ ★ ★ ★ ★

"Read my lips: No new taxes."

– George H.W. Bush,
RNC acceptance speech,
August 18, 1988 [cdxvii]

★ ★ ★ ★ ★ ★ ★ ★ ★ ★ ★ ★

Born June 12, 1924, George H.W. Bush, our 41st president, was the son of Dorothy Walker Bush and Prescott Bush, a well-connected U.S. senator and businessman from Connecticut. Growing up in Milton,

Massachusetts, and Greenwich, Connecticut, young Bush was drawn to his family's tradition of public service, a desire that guided his childhood and adult life.[cdxviii]

At the age of 18, after the Japanese bombed Pearl Harbor, George Bush joined the U.S Navy, becoming the youngest naval aviator of his day. As a member of Air Group 51's Torpedo Squadron aboard the *USS San Jacinto*, Bush acquired the nickname "Skin" due to his lanky physique. Bush flew 58 military sorties, including a near tragic one on September 2, 1944. While bombing Japanese installations over the Pacific Ocean, Bush's plane was hit by anti-aircraft fire. While his plane plummeted into the Pacific, Bush parachuted out and survived four hours in a small raft until a nearby U.S. submarine rescued him. During his military career, Bush received the Distinguished Flying Cross, three Air Medals, and the Presidential Unit Citation. George Bush was honorably discharged in September 1945.[cdxix]

Just prior to his discharge, Bush married Barbara Pierce,[cdxx] a descendant of President Franklin Pierce.[cdxxi] You will read about the life, political career, and economic performance of one of their six children, George W. Bush, our 43rd president, in Chapter 13 of this book. George, Sr. and his wife, Barbara, are the longest-married presidential couple in U.S. history, 67 years and counting as of the publishing of this book.

Bush balanced being a father, husband and student while attending Yale University and graduated Phi Beta Kappa in 1948[cdxxii] with a bachelor of arts in economics. He also excelled in athletics, playing first base and captaining Yale's baseball team. After graduation, Bush moved his family to West Texas and ventured into the oil business. George co-founded the Zapata Petroleum Company and served as president of its subsidiary, Zapata Off-Shore Company.[cdxxiii] The subsidiary was profitable, becoming independent in 1958, when

Bush moved it from Midland to Houston. He continued to oversee this lucrative venture until he was 40, when his ambitions shifted to the political arena.[cdxxiv] By this time, George Bush had become a millionaire.[cdxxv]

Over the next 14 years, George Bush would have a very diverse and accomplished political career. He bounced back from two unsuccessful bids for the U.S. Senate to become a member of the House of Representatives where he served two terms. His political prowess, in tandem with his family's connections, opened many doors. Richard Nixon and Gerald Ford appointed him to a series of high-level positions, including ambassador to the United Nations, chairman of the Republican National Committee, chief of the U.S. Liaison Office in China, and director of the CIA.[cdxxvi]

In 1980, an ambitious George H.W. Bush campaigned for the Republican nomination for president, losing out to former California Governor Ronald Reagan.[cdxxvii] Ironically, Reagan would select Bush, one of his greatest critics and the man who had called his trickle-down economic theory "voodoo economics," as his running mate. [cdxxviii] Together, the two would win the 1980 presidential election in a landslide over a beleaguered and weak Jimmy Carter.[cdxxix]

THE PRESIDENTIAL YEARS

After serving as vice president to President Reagan for two terms, Bush decided it was time to put his hat in the ring to run for president once again. As the GOP nominee, he started his campaign by making an awkward selection for his running mate in Dan Quayle, a young, inexperienced Senator from Indiana.[cdxxx] As late as June of 1988, his Democratic opponent, Michael Dukakis, had a substantial lead.^{cdxxxi} A GOP political operative named Lee Atwater was hired to change that. Negative politics have always been a fact of life in America; however, in 1988, Lee Atwater took negative politics to a new and very disturbing level. Atwater ran television ads accusing Dukakis of being soft on crime,[cdxxxii] accusing Dukakis' wife, Kitty of having burned an American flag during Vietnam,[cdxxxiii] and accusing Dukakis of being mentally ill – all of which were utterly untrue. [cdxxxiv] Atwater is quoted as saying about Dukakis: "I am gonna strip the bark off the little bastard and make Willie Horton his running mate." This was the beginning of a troublesome new era in political gamesmanship and trickery that has persisted now for more than 20 years in the United States.[cdxxxv] George Bush could have stepped up to the plate and stopped this when he knew it was untrue, but he chose to look the other way. In this instance, Bush did not adhere to the PRES Rule of leading as a statesman and not as a partisan.

George H.W. Bush is primarily remembered for his foreign policy accomplishments. The highlight of his presidency and zenith of his popularity came in early 1991 with the stunning success of Operation Desert Storm. Bush created a military coalition of international forces led by General Norman Schwarzkopf that drove the Iraqi army out of Kuwait. The execution of the land battle that routed the Iraqi army took all of five days, which was remarkable in and of itself and which demonstrated America's military might.[cdxxxvi] It was a huge win for George H. W. Bush, and *a very strong example of George Bush taking bold action after careful and innovative thought, under PRES Rule #4, to rid Kuwait of Saddam Hussein.*

While Bush was highly successful in foreign affairs, he struggled and was ineffective at home, most particularly with the economy. One of the few major pieces of legislation that Bush signed while in office was the Americans With Disabilities Act,[cdxxxvii] *which was clearly an example of George Bush working for the common good of all of our citizens, consistent with PRES Rule #1.*

Throughout his tenure, Bush was aggravated by a struggling economy. Commercial real estate had collapsed after the passage of Reagan's Tax Simplification Act in 1986, and Bush reacted slowly to the problem. His inability to work with Congress after his tremendous success in the Gulf War (when his approval ratings were more than 82%) proved to be his ultimate nemesis. Like his one-term presidential predecessors, Herbert Hoover and Jimmy Carter, Bush's inability to work effectively with Congress was an instrumental factor in his defeat in 1992.

THE PRES RANKINGS

As described in Chapter 2, George H.W. Bush finished a below-average seventh place in our PRES Rankings, consistently finishing in the bottom half of each economic pillar and each economic indicator. He placed a distant eighth under the U.S. Financial Health Pillar, tied for seventh with his son George W. under the Personal Wealth Pillar, and tied again for seventh with Carter under the Business Prosperity Pillar. His performance is graphically illustrated below. His only bright spot was the stock market, which did very well during his tenure, with an average annual compound return of 12.11%, second best in our rankings.

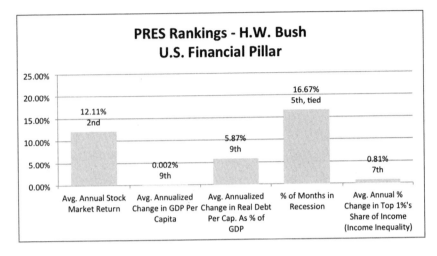

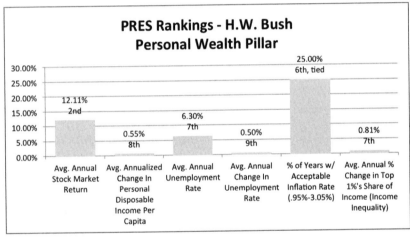

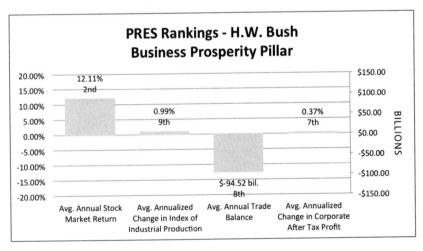

PRES Rankings - H.W. Bush

U.S. Financial Health Pillar	Personal Wealth Pillar	Business Prosperity Pillar	Overall
8th	7th, tied	7th, tied	7th

At a press conference in 1990, Bush expressed his frustration with the economy when he actually told reporters that he found "foreign policy more enjoyable to work on."[cdxxxviii] The economy slowed considerably under Bush's stewardship, with the overall GDP grinding to a virtual standstill during his four-year tenure. *His failure to take bold action when he had the opportunity to do so was a serious problem that only became worse, a clear violation of PRES Rule #4.* Bush inherited significant budget deficits and a growing national debt from his predecessor, Ronald Reagan. Bush tried to curtail this trend early in his presidency, but he struggled to build any consensus among a deeply divided Congress. Ultimately, Bush reneged on his "no new taxes" pledge by signing a bill that raised marginal tax rates from 28% to 31% and phasing out exemptions for high-income taxpayers.[cdxxxix] The bill also raised the earnings cap on Social Security and Medicare from $53.4K to $125K,[cdxl] which angered many of his own GOP base. Bush lost support from conservatives, prompting him to later express regret for having signed the bill into law.[cdxli] Despite approving higher tax rates for the wealthy, Bush presided over an economy in which the income gap widened between the bottom 99% and top 1% of income earners, fifth-worst in our study.

George Herbert Walker Bush accumulated significant debt during his term as well. The national debt as a percentage of GDP increased by an average of 5.87% per year. By and large, this was caused by the savings and loan bailout in 1989 as well as expensive military operations in Panama and the Persian Gulf. Corporate profits, industrial production and personal income stagnated, showing negligible growth during his presidency. His only bright spot was the stock market, which we pointed out earlier. The economy showed some modest signs of recovery in late 1992; however, as with Herbert Hoover, it was too little too late for his hopes of re-election.

CHAPTER 11 ENDNOTES

[cdxvii] Notable Quotes, George H. W. Bush Quotes. Accessed December 12, 2011. http://www.notable-quotes.com/b/bush_george_h_w.html.

[cdxviii] Miller Center of Public Affairs, "Essays on George H.W. Bush and His Administration." Accessed December 3, 2011. http://millercenter.org/academic/americanpresident/bush/essays/biography/2.

[cdxix] Naval Historical Center, "Lieutenant Junior Grade George Bush, USNR." Accessed December 3, 2011. http://www.history.navy.mil/faqs/fag10-1.htm.

[cdxx] Miller Center of Public Affairs, "Essays on George H.W Bush and His Administration." Accessed December 3, 2011. http://millercenter.org/academic/americanpresident/bush/essays/biography/2.

[cdxxi] National First Ladies Library, "Barbara Bush Biography." Accessed December 3, 2011. http://www.firstladies.org/biographies/firstladiesaspx?biography=42.

[cdxxii] The White House, "George H.W. Bush." Accessed December 3, 2011. http://www.whitehouse.gov/about/presidents/georgehwbush.

[cdxxiii] Miller Center of Public Affairs, "Essays on George H.W. Bush and His Administration." Accessed December 3, 2011. http://millercenter.org/academic/americanpresident/bush/essays/biography/2.

[cdxxiv] Spartacus Educational, "George H.W. Bush Biography." Accessed December 3, 2011. http://www.spartacus.schoolnet.co.uk/jfkbushg.htm.

[cdxxv] Learning to Give, "Bush, George Herbert Walker Bush." Accessed December 3, 2011. http://learning to give.org/papers/paper396.html.

[cdxxvi] "George H.W. Bush," www.whitehouse.gov/about/presidents/georgehwbush. Accessed December 3, 2011.

[cdxxvii] Ibid

[cdxxviii] Hatfield, Mark with the Senate Historical Office (1997). "Vice President of the United States: George H.W. Bush." (1981-1989) Page 9, Washington D.C.; U.S. Government Printing Office. Accessed December 4, 2011.

[cdxxix] The American Presidency Project. "Election of 1980." http://www.presidency.ucsb.edu/showelection.php?year=1980.

[cdxxx] Miller Center of Public Affairs, "Essays on George H.W. Bush and His Administration." Accessed December 4, 2011. http://millercenter.org/academic/americanpresident/bush/esays/biography/3.

[cdxxxi] "Poll Gives Large Lead to Dukakis Over Bush." The New York Times, Published June 17, 1988. Accessed December 4, 2011.

[cdxxxii] Miller Center of Public Affairs, "Essays on George H.W. Bush and His Administration." Accessed December 4, 2011. http://millercenter.org/ecademic/americanpresident/bush/essays/biography/3.

[cdxxxiii] "Story on Mrs. Dukakis Is Denied by Campaign." The New York Times, August 26, 1988. Accessed December 4, 2011.

[cdxxxiv] Andrew Rosenthal, "Dukakis Releases Medical Details to Stop Rumors on Mental Health," The New York Times, August 4, 1988. Accessed December 4, 2010. www.nytimes.com/1988/08/04/us/dukakis-releases-medical-details-to-stop-rumors-on-mental-health.html .

CHAPTER 11 ENDNOTES

[cdxxxv] William R. "Willie" Horton is an American convicted felon who, while serving a life sentence for murder, without the possibility of parole, was the beneficiary of a Massachusetts weekend furlough program supported by then Massachusetts Governor Michael Dukakis. He did not return from his furlough, and ultimately he committed assault, armed robbery and rape. Television advertisements depicting this story were used by the Bush campaign, led by Lee Atwater, against Dukakis in the 1988 election campaign. John Brady. "I'm Still Lee Atwater," Washington Post, December 1, 1996. Accessed December 4, 2011.

[cdxxxvi] http://www.whitehouse.gov/?q=taxonomy/term/86. Accessed December 4, 2011.

[cdxxxvii] Miller Center of Public Affairs, "Essays on George H.W. Bush and His Administration." Accessed December 4, 2011. http://millercenter.org/president/bush/essays/biography/4.

[cdxxxviii] "George Herbert Walker Bush." MSN Encarta. Retrieved March 29, 2008. Archived at the Wayback Machine.

[cdxxxix] Bill King, "Facts don't support belief that tax cuts spur growth." Houston Chronicle. August 18, 2011. Accessed December 4, 2011.

[cdxl] Janemarie Mulvey. "Social Security: Raising or Eliminating the Taxable Earnings Base." September 24, 2010. Congressional Research Service. Aging.senate.gov/crs/559.pdf.

[cdxli] DC World Affairs, The. http://diplomatdc.wordpress.com/category/u-s-presidents/george-h-w-bush/.

CHAPTER 12

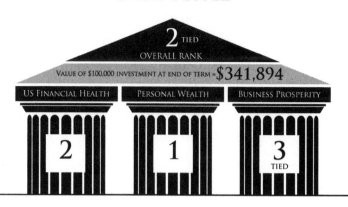

WILLIAM JEFFERSON CLINTON

A CHARISMATIC LEADER BRINGS ECONOMIC PROSPERITY TO THE NATION

★ ★ ★ ★ ★ ★ ★ ★ ★ ★ ★ ★

"America just works better when more people have a chance to live their dreams."

– Bill Clinton,
speech at Democratic National Convention,
July 26, 2004 [cdxlii]

★ ★ ★ ★ ★ ★ ★ ★ ★ ★ ★ ★

W illiam Jefferson Clinton was born on August 19, 1946 in the small Arkansas town of Hope, aptly named for what this man would strive to bring to the country. His father, William Jefferson Blythe, died in a car crash a few months before Clinton's birth, leaving Bill and his mother Virginia to cope alone. She was forced to pursue a nursing degree after her husband's death so Bill was raised by his grandmother, Edith Cassidy, who instilled the importance of a good education and taught Bill to read by age three.[cdxliii]

Clinton's mother returned to Hope in 1950 as a registered nurse and married an automobile salesman named Roger Clinton, who adopted Bill. The family moved to Hot Springs, Arkansas, where young Bill attended church and fell in love with gospel music, inspiring him to learn to play the saxophone. Bill was an excellent student and a member of the jazz band at his high school. His high school principal recommended that Bill attend Arkansas Boys State, and from there he was elected the Arkansas representative to the American Legion's Boys Nation, where he qualified for a trip to Washington D.C. This is where he met and shook hands with President John F. Kennedy. A photograph of their handshake has become an iconic image exhibiting the passing of the baton between generations of leadership. On this same trip, Clinton would also meet another of his political heroes, William Fulbright, chair of the Senate Foreign Relations Committee. Clinton once remarked, "I admired him to no end; he had a real impact on my wanting to be a citizen of the world."[cdxliv]

Clinton demonstrated his first signs of political acuity at Georgetown University, where he was elected president of both his freshman and sophomore classes. He also worked as a clerk for Senator Fulbright during this time. After graduating from Georgetown in 1968, Clinton won a Rhodes scholarship, permitting him to study abroad for two years at Oxford University before ultimately returning home to attend Yale Law School.[cdxlv] There, Bill would meet and fall in love with Hillary Rodham, who shared his political ideology and ambition. They married in 1975 and moved back to Arkansas.

Bill entered politics shortly after and was elected Arkansas' attorney general. In 1978, he would go on to win Arkansas' gubernatorial race, becoming one of the youngest governors in American history at the age of 32. Clinton lost his re-election bid in 1980 to Republican Frank White, but reclaimed his job as governor in the 1982 election, holding the office for three additional terms.[cdxlvi]

Clinton set his sights on a White House bid in 1992. By the summer of that year, Bush's popularity had plummeted from a post-Gulf War high of 87% to a low of 39%.[cdxlvii] Bush had reneged on his promise to not raise taxes – hurting his approval with members of Congress and his own constituents. Clinton secured the Democratic Party's nomination and handily defeated incumbent George H.W. Bush and Independent candidate Ross Perot. Clinton's successful campaign focused on economic issues, a focus epitomized by the simple message posted at his national campaign headquarters that read: *"It's the economy, stupid."* [cdxlviii] That same message would resonate today in the run-up to the 2012 presidential election.

THE PRESIDENTIAL YEARS

Bill Clinton was sworn into office in January of 1993 – the first United States president born during the baby boom.[cdxlix] Over the next eight years, Bill Clinton would preside over the longest period of peacetime economic expansion in United States history.[cdl] His economic stewardship was outstanding, resulting in increased prosperity for individual Americans and as well as the business community. He created large budget surpluses for the U.S. government during his tenure as well. The Congressional Budget Office reported budget surpluses of almost half a trillion dollars during Clinton's last three years in office.[cdli] We will review and evaluate his economic performance in detail at the end of this chapter.

Clinton had many other successes on the domestic front. Despite opposition from a GOP controlled Congress during the last six years of his tenure, Clinton demonstrated, like most of the presidents who performed in the top tier of our PRES Rankings, that he was able to work with Congress and reach across the aisle to forge agreements between both parties.[cdlii] Just two weeks into his first term, Clinton signed into law the Family and Medical Leave Act (FMLA) of 1993, a landmark law that protects families by requiring large employers to grant their employees up to 12 weeks of unpaid leave for the care of a newborn child or for the care of family members suffering serious medical conditions.[cdliii] *Clearly, his support of FMLA demonstrated his recognition that it was in the best interests of the country to advance the common good and build a strong middle class, values espoused by PRES Rules #1 and #2.* He also pushed for the passage of the Brady Bill, which imposed a five-day waiting period on handgun purchases;[cdliv] he compromised on welfare reform that emphasized training and transition from welfare back to the labor force;[cdlv] and he increased the minimum wage twice during his tenure, up to $5.15 an hour by 1997.[cdlvi] Clinton also formed the Children's Health Insurance Program, providing health care coverage for five million uninsured children.[cdlvii] And despite opposition from protectionists within the GOP and his own party for that matter, Clinton supported the North

American Free Trade Agreement (NAFTA), which fostered free trade among the U.S., Mexico and Canada.[cdlviii]

Clinton's most significant legislative failure was his inability to pass sweeping health care reform, which would have brought health care to more Americans.[cdlix] The complexity and size of the proposed reform bill, the inability of the Clinton administration to sell it effectively, and some fierce Republican attack ads doomed the intended reform.[cdlx]

Much like JFK's early disaster with the Bay of Pigs Invasion, Clinton's inexperience in the realm of foreign affairs was evident in his first term. He came under scrutiny for a humanitarian mission that turned into a bloodbath in Somalia; he failed to stop genocide in Rwanda; and was unable to oust a brutal military dictator from Haiti. [cdlxi] However, Clinton, like JFK and Reagan before him, was astute and he learned from his mistakes. He understood that the success of his presidency would require a cohesive, stable foreign policy, so he created his doctrine of "democratic enlargement." This strategy was based on the idea of expanding the community of free market democracies around the world via embracing free trade, multilateral peacekeeping efforts, and international alliances. In Clinton's second term, the doctrine helped guide his administration to bring peace to war-torn Yugoslavia and forced Russian troops to withdraw from the Baltic Republics of Estonia and Latvia.[cdlxii]

Clinton's successes at home and abroad were marred by allegations of impropriety from a Republican Congress. The earliest attacks on Clinton charged him with a financial cover-up involving a real estate deal gone bad called Whitewater. The GOP Congress appointed Special Investigator Ken Starr to head an open-ended investigation into every corner of Clinton's life. Starr became a macabre bedbug to Clinton, but at the end of the day, his investigations were unable to prove any criminal wrongdoing. Starr's report ultimately alleged that Clinton lied under oath to cover up a sexual encounter with Monica Lewinski.[cdlxiii] Clinton's adversaries in the House used Starr's charges to adopt articles of impeachment against him, which they did during the lame duck session in 1998. In the end, the Senate acquitted Clinton on all charges and he was allowed to finish out his second term.[cdlxiv] The stock market and the economy dismissed the entire event as a charade, and neither faltered at all during this time, as they had during the Watergate scandal and the near-impeachment of Richard Nixon in 1974.

THE PRES RANKINGS

Bill Clinton is one of the brightest stars in our PRES Ranking System, finishing in a second-place tie overall with FDR. He had a first-place finish under our Personal Wealth Pillar, a second-place finish under our U.S. Financial Health Pillar, and tied for third place with Reagan under our Business Prosperity Pillar. Indeed, Clinton finishes at or near the top of most categories. He finished first in returns of the stock market, at 16.61%, and the country did not experience any recessionary months during his tenure – the only president in our study who could make that claim. Clinton also had the largest percentage of years (87.5%) of his term with an acceptable inflation rate. The only indicators for which Clinton turned in a meager performance were: (1) the Average Trade Balance, as he presided over an average annual deficit of nearly $210 billion; and (2) the average annual percentage change in the income gap between the bottom 99% and the top 1%, which widened 2.61% per year, second-worst to Reagan's unrivaled 6.43% annual increase in the income gap. His free trade legislation with NAFTA, coupled with a very strong dollar during his tenure, contributed to a large trade deficit during his term. cdlxv The growth of technology companies during the 1990s and the tech bubble experienced by the stock market may have led to the widening income gap.cdlxvi

Clinton's stellar performance as economic steward of this country, as measured by our PRES Ranking System, is depicted in the graphs below.

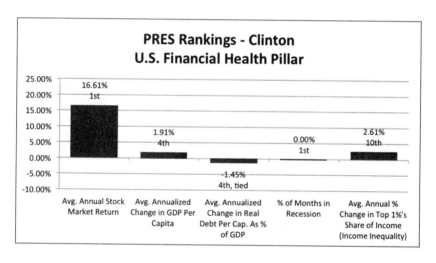

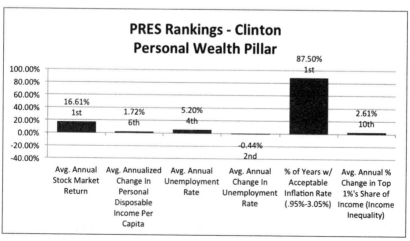

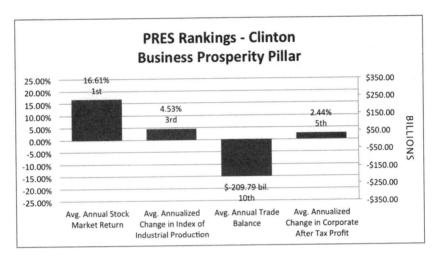

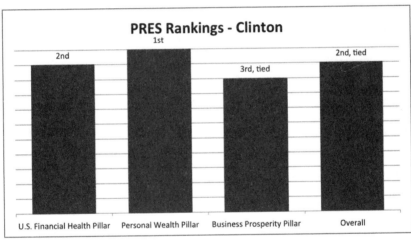

Clinton's most enduring legacy was that he presided over a booming economy during peacetime and his administration created more than 23 million jobs during his eight years in the White House. cdlxvii Many economists credit the commencement of the boom cycle that took root under Clinton with the passage of the Omnibus Budget Reconciliation Act – also called the Deficit Reduction Act (DRA) of 1993. Instead of cutting taxes for all classes as he originally had planned, Clinton changed gears and attacked the budget deficit and the national debt, which had exploded under Reagan and George Bush.[cdlxviii]

In his first State of the Union Address, in 1993, Clinton proclaimed: "Tonight I want to talk with you about what government can do – because I believe government must do more. But let me say first that the real engine of economic growth in this country is the private sector, and second, that each of us must be an engine of growth and change." He went on to say, "Our immediate priority must be to create jobs and create jobs now. Some people say, 'Well, we're in a recovery, and we don't have to do that.' Well, we all hope we're in a recovery, but we're sure not creating new jobs. And there's no recovery worth its salt that doesn't put the American people back to work!"[cdlxix] His peremptory speech demonstrated that Clinton was not happy being complacent early in his tenure when the economy was still tenuous. *By his words and his actions early in his presidency, Clinton demonstrated adherence to all of our PRES Rules, foreshadowing the economic prosperity that he would preside over:*

- *Advance the common good and not solely the interests of the advantaged few.*
- *The middle class is the engine that drives the economy.*
- *The federal government plays a vital role in creating and maintaining a healthy economy.*
- *Take bold action after careful and innovative thought.*
- *Lead as a statesman, not as a partisan.*

The Deficit Reduction Act of 1993 put an end to trickle-down economics as we had known it, an economic philosophy that runs counter to our PRES Rules, and shifted the tax burden away from the middle class and back to more affluent Americans who could, theoretically, afford it;[cdlxx] expanded the earned income tax credit for America's working poor; and cut taxes for 15 million low-income families.[cdlxxi] The DRA also provided favorable tax treatment on gains from the sale of stock of small businesses (with revenues of under $5 million)[cdlxxii] and increased the top corporate tax rate to 35%.[cdlxxiii] Finally, the act raised taxes modestly on the wealthiest 1.2% of taxpayers by increasing the top marginal tax rate.[cdlxxiv]

Reagan's passage of TEFRA in 1982[cdlxxv] and the passage of the DRA in 1993 created uncanny and similar results. Both laws raised taxes modestly, the DRA created more parity for the middle and lower income classes, but both bills mandated the affluent to pay a little bit more. *Clinton's actions again showed adherence to our PRES Rules, often prompted by his recognition that an effective federal government can play a unique and vital role in protecting and stabilizing our national economy.* Both TEFRA and DRA, when they became law, created a positive result for the economy. Because of the Republicans' reluctance to raise taxes on the affluent, the DRA passed in 1993 without a single Republican voting in favor of it. The Deficit Reduction Act is credited with having had a positive net effect on the economy for the ensuing seven years. After its passage, the nation's economy enjoyed a period of unprecedented and extraordinary peacetime expansion:

- Unemployment, which was 6.8% in August of 1993 at the signing of the bill, dropped to 3.9% by the time Bill Clinton departed seven years later.[cdlxxvi]
- Personal income for the middle class increased by 7.5% per year – a historical record.[cdlxxvii]
- Industrial production for business rose by 5.6% per year. [cdlxxviii]
- The stock market appreciated by more than tripling its value in just five years.[cdlxxix] If one had invested $100,000 in

the stock market at Clinton's inauguration, his or her account would have appreciated to $341,894 by the time he departed office in 2001. This is based on the stellar average annual compound return of the stock market of 16.61% during the Clinton presidency under our PRES Rankings.

One of the criticisms leveled against Bill Clinton's economic stewardship was the passage of the Gramm-Leach-Bliley Act late in his second term, which he signed begrudgingly.[cdlxxx] It repealed some portions of the Glass-Steagall Act of 1934 and deregulated parts of the financial services and banking industries.[cdlxxxi] Clinton stressed that he would veto any legislation attached to the Gramm-Leach-Bliley Act that would scale back minority lending. Critics believe that this action and subsequent mistakes made by the Bush administration contributed significantly to the mortgage crisis that started the Great Recession in 2008.[cdlxxxii]

The economic boom under Bill Clinton, including the significant budget surplus and national debt reduction that took place due to his efforts, would be squandered by his successor, George W. Bush. We will discuss how that happened in our next chapter, where we describe the second-worst economic performance in our study, by our country's 43rd president, George W. Bush.

CHAPTER 12 ENDNOTES

cdxlii Bill Clinton's Remarks to the Democratic National Convention, July 26, 2004. Accessed January 10, 2012. http://www.nytimes.com/2004/07/27/politics/campaign/27TEXT-BCLINTON. html?pagewanted=all. .

cdxliii Miller Center of Public Affairs, "Essays on Bill Clinton and His Administration." Accessed December 12, 2011. http://millercenter.org/president/clinton/essays/biography/2.

cdxliv Ibid

cdxlv Ibid

cdxlvi Whitehouse.gov Biography of William Jefferson Clinton. Accessed January 10, 2012. http://www.whitehouse.gov/about/presidents/williamjclinton.

cdxlvii Job Performance Ratings for President Bush (G.H.W.) Accessed January 4, 2012. http://webapps.ropercenter.uconn.edu/CFIDE/roper/presidential/webroot/presidential_rating_detail.cfm?allRate=True&presidentName=Bush%20(G.H.W.)#.TwyNqZjaHNk.

cdxlviii Biography.com. William Jefferson Clinton. Accessed December 12, 2011.

http://www.biography.com/people/bill-clinton-9251236?page=3.

cdxlix Ibid

cdl William J. Clinton Presidential Center. "Clinton-Gore Economics: Understanding the Lessons of the 1990s." Accessed December 12, 2011. http://clintonpresidentialcenter.org/georgetown/resource_clintoneratimeline.php.

cdli Congressional Budget Office, Office of Management and Budget, "Budget and Economic Outlook Historical Budget Data." Table F-1, January 2010. Accessed December 14, 2011. http://www.cbo.gov/ftpdocs/108.

cdlii No. HS-53. Political Party Affiliations in Congress and the Presidency: 1899 to 2003. Accessed January 10, 2012. http://www.census.gov/statab/hist/HS-53.pdf.

cdliii Statement on Signing the Family and Medical Leave Act of 1993 (February 5, 1993) pp. 50-51. Public Papers of the Presidents: William J. Clinton. Last Accessed January 10, 2012.

cdliv Brady Campaign to Prevent Gun Violence. Accessed December 12, 2011. http://www.bradycampaign.org/legislation/backgroundchecks/bradylaw.

cdlv Miller Center of Public Affairs, "Essays on Bill Clinton and His Administration." Accessed December 12, 2011. http://millercenter.org/president/clinton/essays/biography/4.

cdlvi "The Low-Wage Labor Market: Challenges and Opportunities for Economic Self-Sufficiency. Does the Minimum Wage Help or Hurt Low-Wage Workers?" Accessed December 12, 2011. http://aspe.hhs.gov/hsp/lwlm99/turner.htm. Last modified 1/14/00.

cdlvii "The State Children's Health Insurance Program." Congressional Budget Office. May 2007. Accessed December 12, 2011. http://www.cbo.gov/ftpdocs/80xx/doc8092/05-10-SCHIP.pdf.

cdlviii Miller Center of Public Affairs, "Essays on Bill Clinton and His Administration." Accessed December 12, 2011. http://millercenter.org/president/clinton/essays/biography/4.

CHAPTER 12 ENDNOTES

[cdlix] Miller Center of Public Affairs, "American President: A Reference Resource."Accessed December 12, 2011. http://millercenter.org/academic/americanpresident/clinton/essays/biography/1.

[cdlx] "The Evolution of Hillary Clinton," *New York Times*, July 13, 2005. Accessed December 12, 2011. http://www.nytimes.com/2005/07/13/nyregion/13hillary.ready.html?pagewanted=print.

[cdlxi] Biography.com. William Jefferson Clinton. Accessed December 12, 2011.http://www.biography.com/people/bill-clinton-9251236?page=4.

[cdlxii] Douglas Brinkley, "Democratic Enlargement: The Clinton Doctrine," JSTOR: Foreign Policy, No. 106 (Spring, 1997), pp. 110-127. Accessed December 12, 2011. http://www.jstor.org/pss/1149177.

[cdlxiii] Communication from Kenneth W. Starr, H. Doc. 105-310, (September 11, 1998).

[cdlxiv] Biography.com. William Jefferson Clinton. Accessed December 12, 2011. http://www.biography.com/people/bill-clinton-9251236?page=3 and http://www.biography.com/people/bill-clinton-9251236?page=4.

[cdlxv] Miller Center of Public Affairs, "Essays on Bill Clinton and His Administration," Accessed December 12, 2011. http://millercenter.org/president/clinton/essays/biography/4.

[cdlxvi] James K. Galbraith, Income Distribution and the Information Technology Bubble, Accessed January 11, 2012. http://utip.gov.utexas.edu/papers/utip_27.pdf.

[cdlxvii] Wall Street Journal Staff, "Bush on Jobs: The Worst Track Record on Record," Wall Street Journal (2009). Accessed December 13, 2011. http://blogs.wsj.com/economics/2009/01/09/bush-on-jobs-the-worst-track-record-on-record/.

[cdlxviii] Welcome to the White House. "The Clinton Presidency: Historic Economic Growth," Accessed December 13, 2011. http://clinton5.nara.gov/WH/Accomplishments/eightyears-03.html.

[cdlxix] Bill Clinton (February 17, 1993). "William J. Clinton: Address Before a Joint Session of Congress on Administration Goals," Accessed December 13, 2011.http://www.presidency.ucsb.edu/ws/index.php?pid=47232#axzz1gRAnUU5t.

[cdlxx] Bill Clinton (January 25, 1994). "William J. Clinton: Address Before a Joint Session of the Congress on the State of the Union," Accessed December 13, 2011. http://www.presidency.ucsb.edu/ws/index.php?pid=50409#axzz1VKZJJKA6.

[cdlxxi] "The Clinton Record: Clinton's State-by-State Economic Progress," Accessed December 13, 2011. http://www.perkel.com/politics/clinton/accomp.htm.

[cdlxxii] The Library of Congress, Bill Summary & Status, 103rd Congress (1993-1994) H.R.2264 CRS Summary. Accessed December 16, 2011. http://thomas.loc.gov/cgi-bin/bdquery/z?d103:HR02264:@@@D&summ2=m&.

[cdlxxiii] "Tax Policy Center: Tax Legislation," Accessed December 13, 2011. http://www.taxpolicycenter.org/legislation/allyears.cfm.

[cdlxxiv] "The Clinton Record: Clinton's State-by-State Economic Progress," Accessed December 13, 2011. http://www.perkel.com/politics/clinton/accomp.htm.

[cdlxxv] "The Library of Congress THOMAS: Bill Summary and Status 97th Congress (1981-1982) H.R. 4961," Accessed December 13, 2011. http://thomas.loc.gov/cgi-bin/bdquery/z?d097:H.R.4961:.

CHAPTER 12 ENDNOTES

cdlxxvi "Meet the Facts." Accessed December 16, 2011. http://meetthefacts.com/tag/omnibus-budget-reconciliation-act-of-1993.

cdlxxvii Ibid

cdlxxviii Ibid

cdlxxix Welcome to the White House. "The Clinton Presidency: Historic Economic Growth." Accessed December 13, 2011. http://clinton5.nara.gov/WH/Accomplishments/eightyears-03.html.

cdlxxx "U.S. Government Printing Office, Public Law 106-102 Gramm-Leach-Bliley Act." Accessed December 13, 2011. http://www.gpo.gov/fdsys/pkg/PLAW-106publ102/content-detail.html.

cdlxxxi Daily Kos, "Banking Deregulation and Clinton." Accessed December 13, 2011. http://www.dailykos.com/story/2008/03/17/475756/-Banking-Deregulation-and-Clinton.

cdlxxxii Stephen Labaton, "Agreement Reached on Overhaul of U.S. Financial System." The New York Times On The Web. October 23, 1999. Accessed December 14, 2011. http://partners.nytimes.com/library/financial/102399banks-congress.html

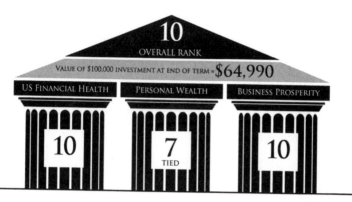

GEORGE WALKER BUSH

THE WEAKEST ECONOMIC PERFORMANCE OF ALL CONTEMPORARY PRESIDENTS

"I will not yield; I will not rest; I will not relent in waging this struggle for freedom and security for the American people."

– George W. Bush,
speaking before a joint session of Congress
on September 20, 2001 ^{cdlxxxiii}

L abeling himself a "compassionate conservative" while campaigning in 2000,[cdlxxxiv] George W. Bush would enter the White House with a budget surplus, a prosperous economy, and a vibrant middle class.[cdlxxxv] Eight years later, Bush departed the Oval Office, leaving the economy, stock market, and the nation's budget in utter tatters.[cdlxxxvi] Bush consistently ranks near the bottom of all pillars of the PRES Ranking System – finishing ahead of only Herbert Hoover in the overall rankings. We will further analyze his poor economic stewardship under our PRES Ranking System at the end of this chapter.

George W. Bush was born in New Haven, Connecticut, on July 6th, 1946, a descendant of political nobility.[cdlxxxvii] His grandfather was a Republican senator from Connecticut for 11 years, and his father, George Herbert Walker Bush, was the 41st president of the United States.[cdlxxxviii] George's mother, Barbara Pierce Bush, was a descendant of Franklin Pierce, the 14th president.[cdlxxxix] In addition to the family ties, Franklin Pierce and George W. Bush share one other characteristic: Both men consistently rank near the bottom of all historical rankings of United States presidents.

George W. Bush, or "W," as family and friends affectionately called him, was an average student. After graduating from Yale, where he admittedly had more success in athletics and fraternity life than in academia,[cdxc] Bush went on to Harvard University, where he acquired an MBA, making him the only U.S. president to hold that degree.[cdxci] George joined the Texas Air National Guard prior to graduating from Yale in 1968.[cdxcii] George was selected as a pilot despite his pilot test score of 25, the lowest possible grade. Critics alleged that George received favorable treatment because of his family's political connections. He served in the Guard at a time when many men were desperately trying to avoid being sent to Vietnam.

Despite the suspicious circumstances surrounding his service, the allegations of favorable treatment were never proven and George was honorably discharged from the Air National Guard in 1974.[cdxciii]

George met Laura Welch in the summer of 1977 at a friend's barbeque. The two had a short courtship and he acted decisively by proposing in September; they married in November. Bush's foray into politics began a year later when he ran for a House seat representing Texas' 19th district. He was narrowly defeated.[cdxciv] George was subsequently summoned to Washington by his father to campaign for him in his successful 1988 presidential run. This is where George would meet political consultants Lee Atwater and Karl Rove.[cdxcv] Upon his father's victory, George returned to Dallas, where he created an investment syndicate to purchase the Texas Rangers baseball team. While George's equity interest in the team was only $800K, he was named managing general partner.[cdxcvi] Bush would sell his interest five years later for a cool $15 million.[cdxcvii]

George made a bid for the governorship of Texas in 1994 against incumbent Ann Richards.[cdxcviii] George won the race; however, the nefarious style of his political campaign would foreshadow more aggressive tactics in future Bush campaigns. Karl Rove's political advisory firm developed a technique called push polling for Bush – asking prospective Texas voters by telephone whether they would be "more or less likely to vote for Governor Richards if they knew her staff was dominated by lesbians or if they knew she had appointed avowed homosexuals to state jobs." Rove's firm also started a whispering campaign accusing Governor Richards of being a lesbian herself; she was not.[cdxcix] The smear campaign was successful, and despite Rove denying any involvement with the attack, similar attacks permeated Rove's presidential campaigns for George W. Bush in 2000 and 2004.

The despicable standards of conduct implemented by his advisors deviated drastically from the PRES Rule of acting like a statesman.

George Bush was one of 12 Republican candidates to put his hat in the ring for a White House bid in 2000. By January of 2000 it was neck-and-neck between two men: Senator John McCain and Bush. Bush's advisors mounted an assault against McCain in South Carolina, alleging he had fathered a black child out of wedlock, that his wife, Cindy, was a drug addict, he was a homosexual, and that he might be the "Manchurian Candidate" as well having been a prisoner in the "Hanoi Hilton" during the Vietnam War. The child in question was actually the daughter he and his wife had adopted from Bangladesh in 1989, and all of the other allegations were utterly untrue as well.[d] Despite these lies, and Rove's denial of any involvement, the smear campaign worked for George W. Bush. He won the South Carolina primary by 11 points, clearing the way for his nomination as the Republican presidential candidate in 2000.[di]

THE PRESIDENTIAL YEARS

In one of the closest and most contentious presidential elections in American history, former Vice President and Democratic candidate Al Gore won the national popular vote by 543,895, but narrowly lost the Electoral College to George W. Bush. The U.S. Supreme Court would decide the election, giving Bush Florida's 25 electoral votes and victory in the presidential election by only five electoral votes. [dii diii] This was one of only four times in the history of the United States in which the winner of the popular tally lost the electoral vote. [div] Bush would go on to be inaugurated on January 20, 2001, with tens of thousands of demonstrators protesting the inaugural parade and throwing objects at the presidential limousine.[dv]

Economically speaking, George W. Bush followed in the footsteps of Herbert Hoover and Calvin Coolidge by predicting an over-optimistic vision of the future. Bush predicted in his first State of the Union speech that there would be a $5.6 trillion surplus over the next 10 years and he then insisted this money belonged to the people and needed to be returned to them.[dvi] This projected surplus was wishful thinking on the part of Bush and it turned out to be pathetic speculation. *Moreover, mere speculation without careful and innovative thought followed by bold action deviates from our PRES Rule #3 that prescribes such behavior.* Despite Federal Reserve Chairman Alan Greenspan's argument that a recession was imminent, Bush disavowed his concern, insisting that lower tax rates and a laissez-faire regulatory environment for business would stimulate the economy and create jobs.[dvii] Instead of staying on the economic trajectory that Bill Clinton had established – reducing the national debt and building a surplus during prosperous times, Bush veered in the opposite direction, selling the American people on the notion that the surplus was "the people's money." The passage of the first round of the Bush tax cuts in 2001 to return this supposed surplus to the people would be the beginning of a wild roller coaster ride for the U.S. economy that would last for eight years.

Ironically, Bush's first treasury secretary, Paul O'Neill, opposed many of these tax cuts, stating they would contribute to much greater budget deficits and would threaten the solvency of Social Security. In 2002, O'Neill suggested that the United States might face future federal budget deficits of more than $500 billion. He also predicted that sharp tax increases, massive spending cuts, or both would be necessary if the United States were to meet benefit promises to future generations.[dviii] It turned out that O'Neill's clairvoyance would be accurate. Ron Suskind's book *The Price of Loyalty* illustrates that O'Neill was curious and thoughtful and wanted to discuss his concerns with Bush, but Vice President Dick Cheney and others summarily dismissed the views of their treasury secretary. O'Neill remarks in the book that Bush was somewhat unquestioning and uncurious, and that the war in Iraq was planned from the very first National Security Council meeting, even though Bush had promised not to engage in the concept of nation building.[dix] For his dissent and attempts to create a meaningful dialogue, Paul O'Neill would be fired on December 31, 2002.[dx] Contrary to O'Neill's advice, Bush heralded and implemented a second round of tax cuts in 2003. *Based on his actions, Bush deviated dramatically from the fundamentals of PRES Rule #3 – careful and innovative thought.*

The attacks by Al-Qaeda on September 11, 2001, would mark a genuine turning point for the Bush administration. On September 14, George W. Bush visited Ground Zero, meeting with New York City Mayor Rudy Giuliani, firefighters, and police. In one of the most compelling moments of any President in our nation's history, Bush addressed the gathering by bullhorn, standing on a heap of rubble at the World Trade Center and reassuring a frightened nation: "I can hear you. The rest of the world hears you. And the people who knocked these buildings down will hear all of us soon." George W. Bush's speech before Congress on September 20 would be one of the very best of his tenure.[dxi] Wall Street, being so close to the attacks, was closed for one week. When the markets reopened the following week, the Dow fell precipitously, losing 685 points (or 7%) on the first day, its largest one-day point decline ever, and more than 14% for the week.[dxii]

Despite 9/11, the markets showed much improvement by March 2002, with the Dow Jones Industrial Average increasing by 34%, to 10,600.[dxiii] The next descent in "Bush's Wild Ride" would then begin. The country faced a firestorm of corporate and accounting scandals over the balance of 2002. There were 23 major corporate scandals that year including Enron, Adelphia, AOL, Bristol Myers, Duke Energy, Freddie Mac, Global Crossing, Halliburton, Kmart, Merck, Merrill Lynch, Tyco, and Arthur Andersen, among many others.[dxiv] Of the 50 most notable corporate and accounting scandals over the past 40 years, 68% of these took place during George W. Bush's tenure. Sadly, President Bush did not exercise the bully pulpit to reassure or calm the markets or the public, instead believing that laissez-faire policies should prevail, nor did he do anything to assure the nation that an Enron episode would never happen again. *His failure to act boldly was not in line with PRES Rules #4 and #5, which advocate taking bold action after careful and innovative thought and leading as a statesman.* President Bush did not act at all, but the stock market did react – crashing in 2002, worse than the crash after 9/11, with the DOW Industrial Average losing 29% of its value in fewer than six months.[dxv] In fact, the S&P 500 and NASDAQ, from peak to trough, plummeted 31% and 55.3%, respectively, in the same six months.[dxvi]

The economy began to show signs of improvement in the third year of Bush's first term, although job growth remained stagnant.[dxvii] Overriding Secretary O'Neill and Chairman Greenspan's counsel, Bush proposed a second large tax cut that was passed in 2003.[dxviii] Nothing Bush did would stop the economic roller coaster ride that the American public experienced during his tenure in office. Over the course of eight years, the volatility in the stock market would be unprecedented. Starting at 10,587 when Bush entered office, the Dow dropped below 8,000 after 9/11; then rose sharply, hitting 10,600 in March of 2002; until falling again to 7,528 in October of 2002; peaking again precisely five years later, at 14,164 in 2007. When Bush left office 17 months later, the Dow stood at 7,949, one of the lowest levels during his tenure.[dxix]

Laissez-faire, hands-off government was the infatuation of George W. Bush and his administration in a manner unseen since the 1920s era of Harding, Coolidge, and Hoover. Sadly, for those who presume that we had learned from the mistakes of our past, we had not. The Bush administration flirted with many of the impetuous and reckless polices that brought chaos three generations before. George W. Bush and his policies fostered excessive leverage on Wall Street;[dxx] subprime lending in tandem with easy credit, which led to a massive housing bubble;[dxxi] predatory lending through mortgage brokers who had no rules, transparency, or oversight to govern them;[dxxii] deregulation of the financial markets at a level not seen since the Great Depression;[dxxiii] financial innovation that increased volatility;[dxxiv] a boom and collapse of the banking system due to a credit crunch that was unprecedented,[dxxv] and finally excessive speculation in oil and gas, real estate, and hedge funds.[dxxvi]

To cover all of the above topics in their entirety would exceed the scope of this book, so instead we will focus on a couple of economic developments under Bush that had a significant adverse impact on the average consumer, shareholder and business owner – those Americans for whom we have written this book. During the stewardship of the George W. Bush administration:

- The national economy witnessed an unprecedented commodity boom and bust in the price of oil and gasoline. The price of oil over a 30-year window had fluctuated in a trading range of approximately $2 (between $1.50 and $3.60 per barrel) between WW II and 1973. Before the invasion of Iraq in January of 2002, crude oil was only 16.65 per barrel, but the lead up to the invasion of Iraq started a long and steady rise to a high of $145.16 by July of 2008.[dxxvii] The irony of this is that one of the Bush administration's selling points for the invasion of Iraq was to maintain lower oil prices in the vicinity of $20 per barrel.[dxxviii] Again, this prediction proved to be dead wrong. Like before, *Bush struggled to act consistently with our PRES Rule #4, which requires careful and innovative thought.* When Bush began his second year in office in January 2002 the average price for a gallon of gas was $1.08. By 2008 average prices had risen to over $4.00 @ gallon.[dxxix] After the election in 2008, President Bush released oil into the market from the nation's strategic oil reserve, sending the price plummeting back down to $35 per barrel by December of 2008.[dxxx]

• Hedge funds, which are speculative by definition, are held by accredited (e.g. affluent) investors and, therefore, are exempt from many of the public disclosure requirements of federal securities law.[dxxxi] Such investments had been a virtual non-entity prior to 2001.[dxxxii] During the tenure of the Bush administration, hedge funds exploded from being a $250 billion enterprise to a $2.5 trillion behemoth as affluent investors saw there was a lot of money to be made.[dxxxiii] Lax enforcement of securities laws by the SEC helped hedge funds explode as managers utilized techniques like "naked short selling" to make profits on the backs of middle class retail investors, who suffered substantial losses. In essence, "naked short selling" occurs when investors hope to profit by borrowing and selling a company's shares at a higher price than the price at which it will repurchase the shares at a later date, but do so with no risk in the transaction. Specifically, hedge fund managers could bring large profits to their investors by taking advantage of a lax SEC run by Christopher Cox, a man who had no business being the SEC Chairman to begin with. Rules like naked short selling, the uptick rule and the "Specialist" being removed from the floor of the NYSE among others enabled hedge funds to drive a good company's stock price down precipitously and have no risk in the transaction whatsoever.[dxxxiv] The value of private hedge funds skyrocketed through the Bush years leaving their targeted stocks in decimated ruin, bringing much happiness to affluent hedge fund owners and tremendous grief to millions of average retail investors.[dxxxv] *Clearly, George W. Bush deviated dramatically from all of our PRES Rules through most of his presidency. Most importantly, he did not: (1) engage in careful and innovative thought prior to taking action; (2) recognize the importance of the middle class as the engine of the nation's economy; or (3) strive for the common good of all citizens instead of the advantaged few.* The abuse caused by hedge funds could have been avoided if Bush had recognized that the government has a viable role in protecting average investors through reasonable regulation, transparency and oversight. He clearly deviated from the *PRES Rule, which recognizes how effective federal government policy can play a vital role in creating and maintaining a healthy economy.*

By prescribing adherence to our PRES rules, we are not suggesting that the government should babysit anyone. To the contrary. If an individual wants to make a high-risk investment, he or she should be able to do so as long the government ensures a fair and level playing field for all of the parties involved. However, rules that permit affluent investors to pool their money, without transparency or oversight, in order to move the market in their favor, while avoiding public scrutiny and being able to do so anonymously, is not a fair or level playing field whatsoever. The hard-working American who is striving to save money for his or her retirement or child's education – in their 401(k), IRA, 403(b) or their 529 plan – should be able to do so with a degree of relative security. Allowing hedge fund managers to decimate a specific stock, with no risk in the transaction, to the detriment of the shareholders and investors holding that stock, is unethical and it is wrong. *George W. Bush and Chris Cox looked the other way, to the detriment of middle class investors, deviating from PRES Rule #2 that recognizes the importance of the middle class to our nation's economy.*

The ride on George W. Bush's roller coaster would come to a tumultuous close. Historically, presidential election years are upbeat and positive years for the market; however, 2008 was anything but calm or upbeat. The Bush administration's reckless policies, acts and omissions contributed to the creation of the perfect storm in 2008 and the chaos that would ensue. The fallout from that storm was a roller coaster that included the following:

- February of 2008 – Fannie Mae, the largest financial institution for U.S. home loans, reports a $3.55 billion loss for fourth quarter 2007, three times what was expected.[dxxxvi]

- On the verge of collapse and under pressure by the Fed in March, Bear Stearns accepts a buyout by JP Morgan Chase. The purchase is a federal bailout backed by a $30 billion loan from the Federal Reserve.[dxxxvii]

- The Carlyle Group defaults on $16.6 billion debt.[dxxxviii]

- The U.S. government frees up $200 billion to support troubled Fannie Mae and Freddie Mac.[dxxxix]
- In April, the International Monetary Fund projects a $945 billion loss from the financial crisis. G7 finance ministers agree to institute a new wave of financial regulations to better deal with the growing crisis.[dxl]
- In June, home repossessions in the United States more than double as the housing and mortgage crisis persists.[dxli] Hundreds of individuals, including two Bear Stearns managers, are charged with fraud related to the collapse of the subprime mortgage market.[dxlii]
- July – The price of oil hits an all-time high at $145 per barrel while the average price of gas tops $4 per gallon.[dxliii]
- Mortgage lender IndyMac collapses. Fannie Mae and Freddie Mac continue to worsen. The U.S. Treasury and the Federal Reserve move to guarantee the debts of Fannie Mae and Freddie Mac. President Bush defends the move, telling Americans to take a deep breath and to have confidence in the mortgage markets.[dxliv]
- Secretary of the Treasury Hank Paulson perfidiously reassures Wall Street and the American public of the economy's strength, saying in March 2007 that, "the global economy is more than sound: it's as strong as I've seen it in my business career".[dxlv]
- Early September – The U. S. government seizes control of Fannie Mae and Freddie Mac.[dxlvi]
- Sunday night September 17 – The nation's second-oldest investment bank, Lehman Brothers, declares bankruptcy. Merrill Lynch, on the brink also, is forced to be acquired by Bank of America.[dxlvii]

- September 17 – The U.S. government bails out insurance behemoth AIG for $85 billion.[dxlviii]
- The White House, through Treasury Secretary Hank Paulson, requests a $700 billion (no-strings-attached) bailout plan from Congress for all financial firms with bad mortgage securities to free up credit.[dxlix]
- The last two standing investment banks, Morgan Stanley and Goldman Sachs, are forced by the Fed to convert to bank holding companies, allowing the two to borrow directly from the Fed discount window to address their short-term liquidity needs.[dl]
- September 26 – The Federal government seizes Washington Mutual in America's largest-ever U.S. bank failure.[dli]
- September 29 – The Republican-led House rejects President Bush's mammoth $700 billion bailout.[dlii]
- Wachovia Bank nears collapse and starts negotiations with Citigroup for a takeover.[dliii]
- The largest government bailout in history clears the U.S. House of Representatives, becoming law with President Bush's signature.[dliv]
- Week of October 6 to 10 – The Dow drops a record 2,031 points for a record weekly loss of 19.67%.[dlv]
- November 4, 2008 – Barack Obama is elected 44th president of the United States. The economy shrinks in the third and fourth quarter of 2008 by 9%, signaling what would become the worst recession since the Great Depression of Herbert Hoover and 1929.[dlvi]

THE PRES RANKINGS

Over his two terms, George W. Bush would preside over one of *the* worst and most volatile periods in our nation's economic history for the consumer, business owner, and the general economy. Bush's failure to adhere to any of our PRES Rules led to his dismal performance as steward of the U.S. economy and your wallet – finishing second-to-last overall in our PRES Rankings as described at the beginning of this chapter and as graphically depicted below.

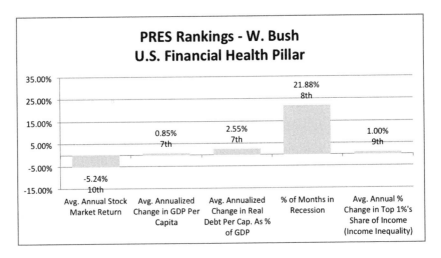

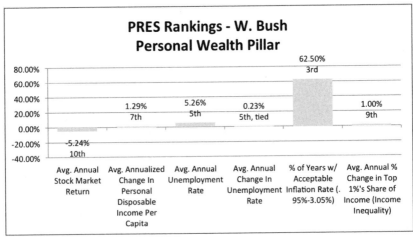

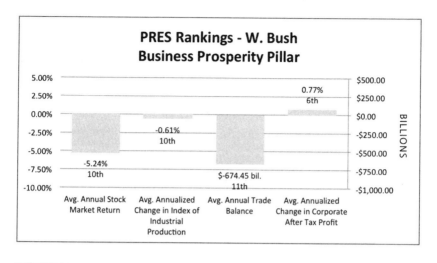

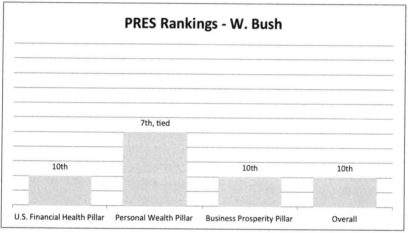

George Bush finished near the bottom of most of the economic indicators in our rankings, including a last place ranking in average annual trade balance, accumulating an average annual trade deficit of more than $674 billion. Notably, he finished second-to-last in: (1) our measurement of stock market returns, the only president since Hoover to preside over a negative return for the financial markets for his eight-year term; and (2) our measurement of industrial production, again the only president since Hoover to preside over a drop in industrial production for his term. It's also notable that the income gap widened approximately 1% per year under Bush, the third-worst result of any president in our study.[dlvii] Bush's lone bright spot was under our inflation measure.

Bush failed as an effective leader and steward of the nation's economy and your wallet. Bush's successor, Barack Obama, would inherit an economic mess created by Bush that was unlike any United States President had seen since Franklin Delano Roosevelt inherited a similar set of circumstances from Herbert Hoover. Because we had only two years of economic data available to us, we have not included President Obama in our PRES Rankings and have not written a separate chapter on him. We will address Obama's economic performance in our next book. Americans will make a judgment as to that performance when they vote on November 6, 2012. Hopefully, our readers will consider some of the insights from this book when they cast their ballots in the future.

CHAPTER 13 ENDNOTES

[cdlxxxiii] Kenneth T Walsh. Posted 9/23/01. "'I will not yield. I will not rest'" U.S. News and World Report. Accessed December 16, 2011. http://www.usnews.com/usnews/news/articles/0110001/archive_006738.htm.

[cdlxxxiv] Miller Center of Public Affairs, "George W. Bush: Campaigns and Elections." Accessed December 15, 2011. http://millercenter.org/president/gwbush/essays/biography/3.

[cdlxxxv] Robert Creamer, "Obama Isn't Trying to Start 'Class Warfare' – He wants to End the Republican War on the Middle Class," Huffington Post: Politics, September 2, 2011 (11:01 AM). Accessed December 15, 2011. http://www.huffingtonpost.com/robert-creamer/obama-isnt-trying-to-star_b_971617.html.

[cdlxxxvi] Peggy Noonan, "It's His Rubble Now," The Wall Street Journal, October 22, 2009. Accessed December 15, 2011. Retrieved from http://www.peggynoonan.com/article.php?article=494.

[cdlxxxvii] The White House, "George W. Bush." Accessed December 15, 2011. http://www.whitehouse.gov/about/presidents/georgewbush.

[cdlxxxviii] Archives: Family History Made Simple & Affordable, "George W Bush Genealogy." Accessed December 15, 2011. http://www.archives.com/genealogy/president-george-w-bush.html.

[cdlxxxix] Ronald Kessler, Laura Bush: An Intimate Portrait of the First Lady, p 23 (Broadway Books 2006).

[cdxc] George W. Bush, Decision Points pp. 11-15 (Broadway Books 2010).

[cdxci] James P. Pfiffner, "The First MBA President: George W. Bush as Public Administrator," Public Administration Review, January/February 2007. Accessed December 15, 2011. Retrieved from http://www.library.eiu.edu/ersvdocs/4734.pdf.

[cdxcii] George Lardner Jr. and Lois Romano, "At Height of Vietnam, Bush Picks Guard," Washington Post, July 28, 1999. Accessed December 15, 2011. http://www.washingtonpost.com/wp-srv/politics/campaigns/wh2000/stories/bush072899.htm.

[cdxciii] Robert A. Rogers, "The Smoking Jet: Bush's Military Record Reveals Grounding and Absence for Two Full Years," Democrats.com, October 4, 2000. Accessed December 15, 2011. http://archive.democrats.com/display.cfm?id=154.

[cdxciv] Famous Texans, "George Walker Bush." Accessed December 15, 2011. http://www.famoustexans.com/georgewbush.htm.

[cdxcv] Frontline on PBS, "Karl Rove's Life and Political Career." Accessed December 15, 2011. http://www.pbs.org/wgbh/pages/frontline/shows/architect/rove/cron.html.

[cdxcvi] Misc. Baseball: Gathering Assorted Items of Baseball History and Trivia, "George W. Bush, Part-Owner of the Texas Rangers, 1989 to 1998." Accessed December 15, 2011. http://miscbaseball.wordpress.com/2010/11/10/george-w-bush-part-owner-of-the-texas-rangers-1989-to-1998/.

[cdxcvii] Brooks Jackson, "Bush as Businessman: How the Texas Governor Made his Millions," CNN, May 13, 1999 (6:00 PM). Accessed December 15, 2011. http://www.cnn.com/ALLPOLITICS/stories/1999/05/13/president.2000/jackson.bush/.

[cdxcviii] Wayne Slater, "Bush as Governor," Frontline on PBS, October 12, 2004. Accessed December 15, 2011. http://www.pbs.org/wgbh/pages/frontline/shows/choice2004/bush/governor.html.

CHAPTER 13 ENDNOTES

cdxcix Richard Gooding, "The Trashing of John McCain." Vanity Fair, November 2004. Accessed January 11, 2012. http://www.vanityfair.com/politics/features/2004/11/mccain200411.print

d Martin Frost, "Frost Meditations: John McCain." Accessed December 15, 2011. http://www.martin-frost.ws/htmlfiles/jan2008/john_mccain.html.

di 2000 Presidential Primary Election Results. Last Accessed January 11, 2012. http://www.fec.gov/pubrec/fe2000/2000presprim.htm

dii 2000 Official Presidential General Election Results. Last Accessed January 11, 2012. http://www.fec.gov/pubrec/2000presgeresults.htm

diii Bush v. Gore, 531 U.S. 98 (2000).

div Kevin Bonsor, "How the Electoral College Works," How Stuff Works, November 6, 2000. Accessed December 15, 2011. http://history.howstuffworks.com/american-history/electoral-college5.htm.

dv Dee Finney, comp., "Bush Protests: Inauguration Day – 2005," Great Dreams. Accessed December 15, 2011. http://www.greatdreams.com/political/bush-protests-inauguration.htm.

dvi USA-presidents, "George W. Bush: State of the Union Address (February 27, 2001)." Accessed December 15, 2011. http://www.usa-presidents.info/union/gwbush-1.html.

dvii Steven Horwitz, "Rhetoric, Reality, and the Recession: Misdiagnosis Leads to Bad Prescriptions," The Freeman: Ideas on Liberty, October 20, 2011. Accessed December 15, 2011. http://www.thefreemanonline.org/headline/rhetoric-reality-recession/.

dviii Chris J. Dolan, John P. Frendreis, and Raymond Tatalovich, The Presidency and Economic Policy (Maryland: Rowman and Littlefield Publishers, Inc., 2008). Accessed on December 15, 2011. Retrieved from http://books.google.com/books. Page 84.

dix Ron Suskind, The Price of Loyalty: George W. Bush, the White House, and the Education of Paul O'Neill (New York: Simon & Schuster, 2004).

dx Rebecca Leung, "Bush Sought 'Way' to Invade Iraq?," CBS, February 11, 2009. Accessed December 15, 2011. http://www.cbsnews.com/stories/2004/01/09/60minutes/main592330.shtml.

dxi Lee Banville, "Candidates: George W. Bush: Sept. 11, 2001," PBS: Online Newshour, 2004. Accessed December 15, 2011. http://www.pbs.org/newshour/vote2004/candidates/can_bush-sept11.html.

dxii The Wall Street Journal, "Crash Comparison Outlook." Accessed January 12, 2012. http://online.wsj.com/public/resources/documents/info-StockCrash_0710-14.html

dxiii March 2002 Dow Jones Industrial Average Historical Prices/Charts, Accessed December 16,2011. http://futures.tradingcharts.com/historical/DJ/2002/3/linewchart.html

dxiv Penelope Patsuris, "The Corporate Scandal Sheet," Forbes, August 26, 2002 (5:30 PM). Accessed December 15, 2011. http://www.forbes.com/2002/07/25/accountingtracker.html.

dxv Danielxx, "The 10 Worst Stock Market Crashes in U.S. History," Bull and Bears: Tales of the Zoo, October 3, 2006 (7:17 AM). Accessed December 15, 2011.

CHAPTER 13 ENDNOTES

[dxvi] "Stock Market Volatility Since 1994: The Swings to the Upside Were Speculative, Debt Ridden, Bear Market Traps," *Comstock Partner, Inc.*, September 6, 2011. Accessed December 15, 2011. http://www.comstockfunds.com/default.aspx?act=newsletter.aspx&category=specialreport&AspxAutoDetectCookieSupport=1.

[dxvii] Employment, Hours, and Earnings from the Current Employment Statistics survey (National). 1-Month Net Change. Series CES0000000001. United States Department of Labor, Bureau of Labor Statisitics. http://data.bls.gov/pdq/SurveyOutputServlet.

[dxviii] Mark Thoma, "The 2003 'Jobs and Growth' Plan (Tax Cuts) Didn't Work," *Economist's View,* January, 25, 2009 (2:25 PM). Accessed December 15, 2011. http://economistsview.typepad.com/economistsview/2009/01/the-2003-jobs-and-growth-plan-tax-cuts-didnt-work.html.

[dxix] MD Leasing Corp., "History of Dow Jones Industrial Average." Accessed December 15, 2011. http://www.mdleasing.com/djia.htm.

[dxx] "Financial Meltdown Was 'Avoidable' Says Inquiry," *New York Times*, January 26, 2011. Accessed December 15, 2011. http://blog.wallstreetgrand.com/2011/01/financial-meltdown-was-%E2%80%98avoidable%E2%80%99-says-inquiry/.

[dxxi] Katalina M. Bianco for the CCH, "The Subprime Lending Crisis: Causes and Effects of the Mortgage Meltdown." Accessed December 16, 2011. http://business.cch.com/bankingfinance/focus/news/Subprime_WP_rev.pdf.

[dxxii] John Atlas, "The Conservative Origins of the Sub-Prime Mortgage Crisis," The American Prospect, December 17, 2007. Accessed December 16, 2011. http://prospect.org/article/conservative-origins-sub-prime-mortgage-crisis-0.

[dxxiii] The New York Times, "Glass-Steagall Act (1933)." Accessed December 16, 2011. http://topics.nytimes.com/topics/reference/timestopics/subjects/g/glass_steagall_act_1933/index.html.

[dxxiv] The New York Times, "Economic Crisis and Market Upheavals," October 3, 2011. Accessed December 16, 2011. http://topics.nytimes.com/top/reference/timestopics/subjects/c/credit_crisis/index.html.

[dxxv] Michael Medved, "Opinion: Which is the Real Prosperity Party?," *AOL News*, August 12, 2010 (5:18 AM). Accessed December 16, 2011. http://www.aolnews.com/2010/08/12/opinion-which-is-the-real-prosperity-party/.

[dxxvi] Chad Garrison, "Report: Wall Street Speculators Drive Up Oil Prices," *Riverfront Times*, May 16, 2011 (7:40 AM). Accessed December 16, 2011. http://blogs.riverfronttimes.com/dailyrft/2011/05/wall_street_speculators_oil_prices.php.

[dxxvii] Spot Prices for Crude Oil and Petroleum Products Last Accessed January 11, 2012. http://www.eia.gov/dnav/pet/xls/PET_PRI_SPT_S1_D.xls

[dxxviii] Joseph Lazzaro, "Another George W. Bush Legacy: $150 Oil," Daily Finance, August 24,2009. Accessed December 16, 2011. http://www.dailyfinance.com/2009/08/24/another-legacy-of-president-george-w-bush-150-oil/.

[dxxix] U.S. All Grades, Areas and Formulations. Last Accessed January 11, 2012. http://www.eia.gov/petroleum/gasdiesel/xls/pswrgvwall.xls.

CHAPTER 13 ENDNOTES

dxxx Fed Prime Rate, "Crude Oil Price History." Accessed December 16, 2011. http://www.nyse.tv/crude-oil-price-history.htm.

dxxxi Magnum Funds: Top Performing Hedge Funds and Funds of Hedge Funds, "What is a Hedge Fund?" Accessed December 16, 2011. http://www.magnum.com/hedgefunds/abouthedgefunds.asp.

dxxxii Ross Barry, "Hedge Funds: A Walk Through the Graveyard," *Applied Finance Centre of Macquarie University*, September 20, 2002. Accessed December 16, 2011. http://www.hedgefundprofiler.com/Documents/168.pdf.

dxxxiii Janet Bush, "Sell-out: Why Hedge Funds Will Destroy the World," *New Statesman*, July 31, 2006. Accessed December 16, 2011. http://www.newstatesman.com/200607310033.

dxxxiv James R. Hedges, IV, *Hedges on Hedge Funds: How to Successfully Analyze and Select an Investment* (New Jersey: John Wiley & Sons, Inc, 2005). Accessed December 16, 2011. http://www.wiley.com/WileyCDA/WileyTitle/productCd-0471625108,descCd-google_preview.html.

dxxxv Robert Kuttner, "The Bubble Economy," The American Prospect, September 21, 2007. Accessed December 16, 2011. http://prospect.org/article/bubble-economy.

dxxxvi Protiviti, "Global Financial Crisis Bulletin," October 16, 2008, Page 5. Accessed December 16, 2011. http://www.aswa-sf.org/Global_Financial_Crisis.pdf.

dxxxvii Bryan Burrough, "Bringing Down Bear Stearns." Vanity Fair, August, 2008. Accessed January 11, 2011. http://www.vanityfair.com/politics/features/2008/08/bear_stearns200808-2.print

dxxxviii Protiviti, "The Current Financial Crisis: Frequently Asked Questions," January 14, 2009, Page 7. Accessed December 16, 2011. http://www.knowledgeleader.com/KnowledgeLeader/content.nsf/dce-93ca8c1f384d6862571420036f06c/bd9d6611635ff94f882575e0006200fa/$FILE/The%20Current%20Financial%20Crisis%20FAQ%27s%20-%203rd%20Edition.pdf.

dxxxix Ibid

dxl Protiviti, "Global Financial Crisis Bullentin," October 16, 2008, Page 6. Accessed December 16, 2011. http://www.aswa-sf.org/Global_Financial_Crisis.pdf.

dxli Les Christie, "Six months, 343,000 lost homes", CNN, July 10, 2008. Last Accessed January 11, 2012. http://money.cnn.com/2008/07/10/real_estate/foreclosures_no_break/index.htm.

dxlii "Hundreds indicted in mortgage fraud probe." Accessed December 16, 2011. http://www.msnbc.msn.com/id/25259083/ns/business-real_estate/t/hundreds-indicted-mortgage-fraud-probe/#.Tw39CJjaHNk

dxliii Spot Prices for Crude Oil and Petroleum Products. Last Accessed January 11, 2012. http://www.eia.gov/dnav/pet/xls/PET_PRI_SPT_S1_D.xls

dxliv "Chronology: US Financial Crisis," *Monsters and Critics*, October 4, 2008. Accessed December 16, 2011. http://www.monstersandcritics.com/news/business/news/article_1434735.php/CHRONOLOGY_US_financial_crisis.

dxlv Matt Kibbe, "The Federal Reserve Deserves Blame for the Financial Crisis," *Forbes*, June 7, 2011. Accessed December 16, 2011. http://www.forbes.com/sites/mattkibbe/2011/06/07/the-federal-reserve-deserves-blame-for-the-financial-crisis/.

CHAPTER 13 ENDNOTES

[dxlvi] David Ellis, "U.S. Seizes Fannie and Freddie: Treasury Chief Paulson Unveils Historic Government Takeover of Twin Mortgage Buyers," *CNN Money*, September 7, 2008. Accessed December 16, 2011. http://money.cnn.com/2008/09/07/news/companies/fannie_freddie/index.htm.

[dxlvii] Robert Dougherty, "Lehman Brothers File for Bankruptcy as Merrill Lynch is Bought Out and AIG Struggles," *Yahoo! Voices*, September 15, 2008. Accessed December 16, 2011. http://voices.yahoo.com/lehman-brothers-file-bankruptcy-as-merrill-lynch-1944686.html.

[dxlviii] Amy Goodman, "US Seizes Control of AIG with $85 Billion Bailout," *Democracy Now*, September 17, 2008. Accessed December 16, 2011. www.democracynow.org/2008/9/17/us_seizes_control_of_aig_with.

[dxlix] David M. Herszenhorn, "Administration Is Seeking $700 Billion for Wall Street." New York Times, September 20, 2008. Accessed January 11, 2012. http://www.nytimes.com/2008/09/21/business/21cong.html?pagewanted=all

[dl] Tami Luhby, "New World on Wall Street: Goldman Sachs and Morgan Stanley to Face More Oversight from the Federal Reserve," *CNN Money*, September 22, 2008 (7:19 AM). Accessed December 16, 2011. http://money.cnn.com/2008/09/21/news/companies/goldman_morgan/index.htm.

[dli] Robin Sidel, David Enrich and Dan Fitzpatrick, "WaMu is Seized, Sold off to J.P. Morgan, in Largest Failure in U.S. Banking History," *The Wall Street Journal: Deals and Deal Makers*, September 26, 2008. Accessed December 16, 2011. http://online.wsj.com/article/SB122238415586576687.html.

[dlii] Chris Isidore, "Bailout Plan Rejected – Supporters Scramble: House Leaders Trade Partisan Words after Historic Financial Rescue goes Down in Defeat," *CNN Money*, September 29, 2008. Accessed December 16, 2011. http://money.cnn.com/2008/09/29/news/economy/bailout/index.htm.

[dliii] "Chronology: Financial Crisis Spreads from US to World Markets," *Deutsche Welle*, began on April 10, 2008. Accessed December 16, 2011. http://www.dw-world.de/dw/article/0,,3689713,00.html.

[dliv] Mu Xuequan, ed., "Financial Bailout Plan Wins House Approval, Bush's Signature into Law Same Day," *Xinhua News Agency*, October 4, 2008. Accessed December 16, 2011. http://news.xinhuanet.com/english/2008-10/04/content_10146313.htm.

[dlv] Money-Zine, "Stock Market Crash of 2008." Accessed December 16, 2011. http://www.money-zine.com/Investing/Stocks/Stock-Market-Crash-of-2008/.

[dlvi] Cctvupload, "US Economy Shrinks in Q3," *CNBC: Money Control*, October 31, 2008. Accessed December 16, 2011. http://www.moneycontrol.com/news-topic/domestic-economic-slowdown/video-us-economy-shrinks-in-q3_vj597288Smo.html.

[dlvii] Arloc Serman and Chad Stone, "Income Gaps Between Very Rich and Everyone Else More than Tripled in Last Three Decades, New Data Show," *Center on Budget and Policy Priorities*, June 25, 2010. Accessed December 16, 2011. http://www.cbpp.org/cms/?fa=view&id=3220.

CHAPTER 14

DONKEYS
VS.
ELEPHANTS

★ ★ ★ ★ ★ ★ ★ ★ ★ ★ ★ ★

*"Should any political party attempt to abolish
Social Security, unemployment insurance, and eliminate
labor laws and farm programs, you would not hear of that
party again in our political history. There is a tiny splinter
group, of course, that believes you can do these things . . .
Their number is negligible and they are stupid."*

– Dwight D. Eisenhower [dlviii]

★ ★ ★ ★ ★ ★ ★ ★ ★ ★ ★ ★

I n Chapter 2, we ranked the economic stewardship of each presidential administration during our 80-year study utilizing our Presidential Rankings of Economic Stewardship (PRES Rankings). During that time period, in which Democrats and Republicans occupied the Oval Office for 40 years each, we ranked each respective administration's performance using objective economic indicators, calculating both an overall ranking and rankings under each of the PRES Rankings' three economic pillars – the U.S.

Financial Health Pillar, the Personal Wealth Pillar, and the Business Prosperity Pillar. Surprisingly, despite the conventional wisdom that the Republican Party is the fiscally responsible party, the PRES Rankings told a much different story, with Democratic Presidents JFK/LBJ, Clinton and FDR holding the top three spots and Republican Presidents Hoover, George W. Bush, and Nixon/Ford trailing the pack in the last three spots. In this chapter we take a closer look at the donkey vs. elephant statistics and summarize the findings.

In Chapters 3 through 13, we provided insights into the lives of the men who served as CEO's of this great country, noting events and individuals who shaped and influenced them, along with their respective successes and failures while in office. With inspiration from our unsung American hero, Marriner Eccles, we explained some of those economic successes and failures by demonstrating how that president followed or deviated from one or more of our Presidential Rules for Economic Success (PRES Rules).

In Appendix A, a spreadsheet of our PRES Rankings shows that the Democratic Party fared better than the Republican Party on each of the three economic pillars and on all but one of our economic indicators – an unbelievable and surprising result. Even more surprising is the huge gap in performance with respect to almost all of the indicators. Most statisticians would concur that such large and consistent differences are more than random. That conclusion was, in fact, reached by statisticians Pedro Santa Clara and Rossen Valkanov with respect to the superior performance of the stock market under Democratic presidents. Their study found that most Democratic presidencies are associated with higher than average returns and that most Republican presidencies are associated with significantly lower than average returns and greater volatility or standard deviations. Through regression analysis, Santa Clara and Valkanov "attribute the difference in returns to the stock market being systematically and positively surprised by Democratic policies." Based on 80 years of quantifiable data, we find it curious that the market continues to be "surprised" that Democratic policies are generally better for the economy.[dlix] One of the likely reasons: the Democratic Party has done a poor job of standing on its historical economic record. We hope this book will help correct that problem.

In order to fairly compare the economic stewardship of the political parties, we calculated each economic indicator as an "annual average" during their respective 40 years in the Oval Office. Specifically, we multiplied the economic indicator for each presidential administration by the number of years that administration held office, added those products together for the administrations from the same political party, and divided by 40; i.e., the number of years that each political party held the highest office. As we said in Chapter 2, the results were indeed a landslide for the Democrats. Graphical illustrations of this one-sided comparison are presented below.

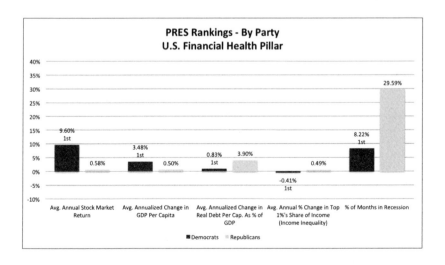

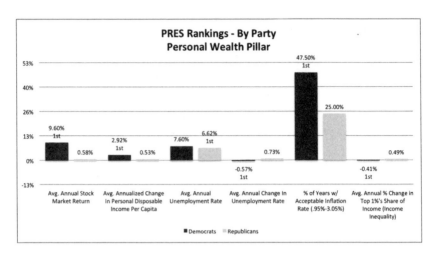

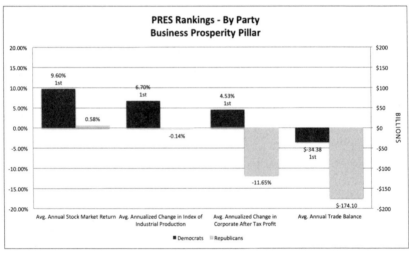

STEWARDSHIP SCORE
OVERALL: PRES ECONOMIC

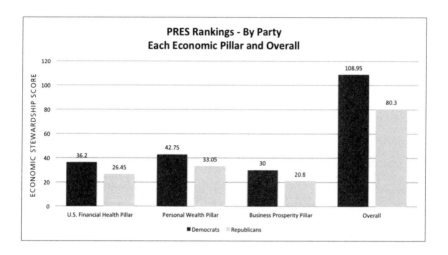

What difference does this significant disparity make to the average American? Let's use stock market returns under each party as an example – the Democrats presided over a very respectable average annual compound return of 9.60% during their 40 years, compared with a surprisingly negligible 0.58% return for the Republicans. If an employee's 401(k) plan was fully invested in stocks and had a value of $100,000 at the beginning of the employee's 40-year working career, the amount of the employee's nest egg at retirement would have differed tremendously depending upon which political party held office during those 40 years, as follows:

Retirement Nest Egg under Republican presidents: $126,027

Retirement Nest Egg under Democratic presidents: $3,912,210

On the other hand, if an employee invested $5,000 per year in stocks as part of his or her 401(k) plan over a 40-year working career, the amount of the employee's nest egg at retirement again would have differed tremendously depending upon which political party held office during those 40 years, as follows:

Retirement Nest Egg under Republican presidents: $224, 375
Retirement Nest Egg under Democratic presidents: $1,985,526
The differences are astounding![dlx]

In completing our research, we were especially surprised by how the parties fared in regard to the Business Prosperity Pillar of our PRES Rankings. Although conventional wisdom for decades has been that the Republican Party is best for the business owner, our PRES Rankings indicate the opposite to be true. Under Democratic presidents, corporate profits have been higher, industrial production has been greater, and the trade balance has been more favorable. The various Chambers of Commerce throughout the country may need to rethink their customary political strategy of promoting Republican candidates and their economic philosophies. Those candidates and philosophies have not fared well – at least when it comes to economic stewardship of our national economy for traditional business.

Please note that the income gap between the bottom 99% and the top 1% has widened considerably under Republican presidents (an average of .49% per year) and narrowed considerably under Democratic presidents (an average of .41% per year). In other words, during the 40-year period that each party held the Oval Office, the income gap widened 19.6% under Republican presidents and narrowed 16.4% under Democratic presidents, a difference of 36%!

During our 80-year study, we compiled some other surprising statistical data that were not used in our PRES Rankings but indicate the superiority of the economic stewardship provided by Democratic presidents and some of the economic failings of the Republican Party. Did you know that the Republican Party has accumulated more than 2.5 times more national debt than the Democratic Party when serving in the Oval Office – $7.1 trillion under Republican presidents and $ 2.8 trillion under Democratic presidents?[dlxi] These amounts are adjusted for inflation and stated in 2010 dollars. Our findings are contrary to the GOP's self-proclamation of economic dominance; in fact it is a misnomer to call the GOP the party of fiscal responsibility and smaller government when in fact the opposite is true.

Sadly, our 80-year study ends where it began, with the country in dire and tumultuous economic times, with high unemployment, slow GDP growth, a skyrocketing debt burden, and the income-gap between the socioeconomic classes widening. Hopefully, current President Barack Obama, future presidents, and our country's political leaders will come together as statesmen, learn from these great leaders of the past like Eccles and FDR, Reagan and O'Neill, and do what is right for our great country. We firmly believe the economic policies that are consistent with our PRES Rules are the recipe for success. In our final chapter, we will discuss that belief in more detail and take a closer look at the role each party has played in creating a political climate that stifles progress. The current adversarial climate must change if the United States is going to regain its stature as the world's premier economic powerhouse, and a place where average families can live comfortably and strive to achieve their dreams.

CHAPTER 14 ENDNOTES

dlviii "The Presidential Papers of Dwight D. Eisenhower," Document #1147; November 8, 1954. Accessed December 13, 2011. http://www.eisenhowermemorial.org/presidential-papers/first-term/documents/1147.cfm.

dlix "The Presidential Puzzle: Political Cycles and the Stock Market." Accessed December 14, 2011. http://personal.anderson.ucla.edu/rossen.valkanov/Politics.pdf and The Journal of Finance, Vol.LVIII, No. 5, October 2003.

568 Detail of calculations is set forth in "Presidential Stock Returns Data" in Appendix A. Calculations apply the annual compound rate of return of our PRES rankings for each president rather than the overall AACR of 9.60% for the Democratic Party and .58% for the Republican Party.

569 United States Department of the Treasury. "Historical National Debt Outstanding." June 17, 2011. Accessed December 14, 2011. http://www.treasurydirect.gov/govt/reports/pd/histdebt/histdebt.htm.

CHAPTER 15

MAKE YOUR VOTE COUNT: YOUR FINANCIAL FUTURE DEPENDS ON IT

★ ★ ★ ★ ★ ★ ★ ★ ★ ★ ★ ★

*"By wiping out the middle classes
and separating society into the two classes of the property –
less on the one hand and the rich speculators on the other,
[inflation] paved the way for fascism and communism
on the continent of Europe. It is a destroyer almost as evil
as war itself. In the eyes of those who want to destroy
democracy and capitalistic institutions,
it is a cheap way of achieving their collapse."*

– Senator Paul Douglas
of Illinois on the Senate floor,
February 22, 1951 [dlxii]

★ ★ ★ ★ ★ ★ ★ ★ ★ ★ ★ ★

Writing this book has been a great learning experience for both of us. We have discovered information about our country's CEOs that has confirmed our pre-existing beliefs, surprised us, generated feelings of pride, and at times caused great anger and frustration. We unearthed many of the facts behind the hyperbole and mantra that we hear every day from the 24/7 media and discovered the characteristics that make a strong steward of our nation's economy. We also came to realize how human our presidents have been – all of them possessing strengths and weaknesses like each and every one of us. It has been our pleasure to share with you all that we have learned over four years. We hope you have enjoyed reading our book as much as we enjoyed writing it and we also hope that you feel better prepared today to make the most informed decision possible when casting your ballot for president in 2012 and beyond.

In this final chapter, we summarize lessons we hope you have learned from *Bulls, Bears, and the Ballot Box* and "take off the gloves" if you will. We are striving to provide fodder for discussion and lively debate in America – detailing what we believe is wrong with our political process and the current political climate of our country and making recommendations as to why we need to revisit our past in order to regain our stature as a country where dreams can come true for all Americans.

THE MYTH OF REPUBLICAN ECONOMIC DOMINANCE

In our review of the past 80 years of American political and economic history, one of the themes that emerges is clear: *Things are not always as they seem.* Conventional wisdom over time has been that the Republican Party, being the party of business, supposedly produces the best results for the general economy and the stock market, and presides over fewer months of recession when it occupies the White House. The GOP has created an illusion that it is the party that performs best for the overall economy because they bring a greater sense of business acumen, financial acuity and economic prowess to the table. We found through our research that the Republican legend of economic superiority and dominance is no more than a myth. As discussed earlier, it is clear that Democratic presidents, over the past 80 years, have been far better stewards of the U.S. economy and your wallet. In fact, the top three spots in our PRES Rankings are all filled by Democratic presidents and the bottom three spots are all filled by Republicans. This is not a coincidence. Historically, the policies of Democratic presidents have aligned more closely with the *PRES Rules, which are:*

1. *Advancing the common good of all citizens and not solely the interests of the advantaged few.*
2. *The middle class is the engine that drives the economy.*
3. *The federal government plays a vital role in creating and maintaining a healthy economy.*
4. *Take bold action after careful and innovative thought.*
5. *Lead as a statesman, not as a partisan.*

If we compare Barack Obama's first term to conservative icon Ronald Reagan's first term, the Obama administration outperforms Reagan on many key economic measures. The stimulus packages and the bailout and federal loan to GM and Chrysler demonstrated Obama's *recognition of the vital role the federal government can play in creating and maintaining a healthy economy.* Consistent with the philosophies and actions taken by Marriner Eccles and FDR during the Great Depression, Obama realized the importance of deficit spending to stimulate economic recovery in the midst of chaos. The 'Stimulus', as it is called, established a floor for the financial markets so they wouldn't decline further. Many forget that in the last 17 months of George W's tenure, the stock market saw an historical loss of 58% from peak to trough. This was worse than any rolling 17-month period during the crash of the market in the Great Depression. Under President Obama's tenure, to date, we have seen an impressive recovery in the equity markets, making up most of the losses accrued under Bush. Today we stand about 1300 points from the highpoint of the DOW of 14,156.53 set on October 9th, 2007. Obama's actions placed a tourniquet on the bleeding and the steep downward spiral occurring when he took office. Most notably:

- Obama ultimately did stop the hemorrhaging of jobs that was taking place when he took office. During the final twelve months of George W. Bush's administration, the country lost 4.43 million jobs, the worst job loss for any U.S. president since Herbert Hoover during the Great Depression.[dlxiii]

- Obama stopped the precipitous and lethal decline in the stock market, which had lost 14 years of gains during George W. Bush's final 17 months in office.[dlxiv] Let us repeat that fact. The stock market retraced the lows back to 1996 and lost 14 years of gains in less than 17 months. In any rolling 17-month period in our nation's history, including the Great Depression, the market had never lost so much in value.[dlxv] Moreover, Obama's actions helped restore consistency and stability to a market that desperately needed both. The equity markets posted a record total gain of 105% through April of 2011 during Barrack Obama's first 27 months in office.[dlxvi]

- Obama stopped what would have been the devastating ripple effect in the economy of losing two of the world's largest automakers, General Motors and Chrysler. If he had not taken this bold action in the midst of the chaos he inherited, unemployment and the stock market would have taken another huge hit that would have been more difficult, if not impossible from which to recover.[dlxvii]

- Obama stopped the decline in corporate profits that started under George W. Bush, achieving an increase of 22% per year during his first two years in office.

- Barack Obama surpasses most of his predecessors, including Bill Clinton and Ronald Reagan, relative to the stewardship of our financial markets during his first term. The average annual compound returns for the Dow, S&P 500, and NASDAQ have been 17.2%, 25.3% and 31.7% respectively in Obama's first 3.3 years. This compares to Reagan's first term results (for the same indices and time period) of 6.86%, 6.16%, and 7.02% respectively.

Although the economy is trending in a positive direction under President Obama, more recovery needs to take hold before the average American family will feel financially secure once again. We do not believe the stimulus package administered by the Obama administration – the American Recovery and Reinvestment Act of 2009 – provided enough direct relief and support for middle class America. Moreover, Obama has continued with the Bush tax cuts, which clearly benefit the wealthiest in America, while not securely protecting programs that primarily benefit middle and lower class Americans. Most importantly, President Obama has not found a way to work effectively with the Republican-dominated House of Representatives, and he has compromised on some of his core principles, evidence of his struggles *to lead effectively.* Admittedly, Barack Obama has had to work with the most dysfunctional and vitriolic Congress and political climate in modern history, one in which partisanship and salesmanship are rewarded over statesmanship and doing what is right for the American people. A recalcitrant Congress has made Obama's job extremely difficult; nonetheless, consistent with our approach to presidential evaluation, Obama takes the credit or blame for what happens during his tenure in office. Suffice it to say, the entire story of President Obama's first term and his economic legacy is yet to be concluded.

INCOME INEQUALITY – THE NEMESIS OF A STRONG ECONOMY

One of the economic indicators used in our PRES Rankings is a measure of income inequality – the percentage by which the income gap has widened or narrowed between the bottom 99% and top 1% of income earners. Why is that measure so important? We answered that question in Chapter 1, when Marriner Eccles astutely recognized that a strong economy is dependent upon money being in the hands of people who will spend it in order to create demand for products and services (the bottom 99% of us) rather than in the hands of those who will save and hoard it. There are two sides to the economic equation of supply and demand. We must focus on both and not one at the exclusion of the other. Eccles recognized that a greater degree of income equality will lead all of us, both the 99% and the top 1%, to more prosperous times.[dlxviii] As we pointed out in earlier chapters, the largest income gaps ever seen by this country occurred in the late 1920s and again today, in the late 2000s – just prior to the two worst economic debacles ever seen in this country: the Great Depression and the Great Recession.[dlxix] This is NOT mere coincidence.

History has demonstrated that the federal government can and should play a role in determining the size of that income gap.[dlxx] Its tax policies, legislative enactments like the GI Bill, regulations, and, perhaps most importantly, its diligence or laissez-faire approach to enforcing regulations intended to protect American investors, all determine whether that gap widens or narrows and, accordingly, whether our national economy is unstable and at risk, or stable and sound.

As we discussed earlier, the Bush administration's laissez-faire approach to enforcing regulations in the financial markets led to hedge fund investors making huge profits and average retail investors suffering as a consequence. This is a good example of how government can play a significant role in influencing the size of the income gap. Like the Bush administration, many politicians and Americans, especially those on the far-right, believe that less government and less regulation is always best for the American people. We beg to differ. During our 80-year study, we learned that reasonable and sensible government regulation is necessary to protect the public in order to create a level playing field for all of the American people.

Imagine for just a moment that you were told that the state and federal governments were going to take down from our roadways and highways all of the guard rails, speed limit signs, stop and yield signs, all traffic signals, pedestrian signs, school and railroad crossing signs and signals, and suspend all state troopers and county sheriffs for one month. Can you imagine the chaos that would ensue on our roadways in one day, let alone one month? It would be *Mad Max Beyond Thunderdome* and it would not be starring Mel Gibson either. In essence, that is precisely what was done on Wall Street in the six years leading up to the Great Recession of 2008. Having a sensible amount of government regulation and oversight, in tandem with adequate enforcement of the rules and regulations that are already on the books can go a long way to ensure that all Americans are protected and have a fair and level opportunity to achieve financial success.

Sadly, as stated earlier, our 80-year study ended where it began, with the average American family struggling to make ends meet and to create a brighter financial future for their children. If only our politicians and leaders would learn from history and our past mistakes, we all would experience less pain and suffering.

THE REPUBLICAN ADVANTAGE

With the superior economic performance of Democratic presidents, why is it that Republicans have occupied the White House for 28 of the last 40 years of our study – 70% of the time – and continue to have the upper hand on the economic argument? One explanation is that most voters are not as informed as perhaps they should be. It is our hope that our book will lead to a better informed electorate. Another explanation is that many voters do not vote based on economic issues alone; instead voters factor in additional issues, including many social issues. We recognize that issues surrounding gay rights, religious rights and beliefs, the right to bear arms, and abortion (among many others) are of importance to many, and we have the utmost respect for the individuals who value these concerns. However, it is our view that economic issues directly impact everyone and we believe a candidate's views on economic policy and other financial and tax issues should be explored and considered first and foremost, including issues relating to:

- Sound tax and investment policies that create a level playing field for all.
- Climate change and an effective energy policy.
- Creating and funding a top-notch education system for all students that permits them to compete more effectively on the world stage.
- Creating a positive dynamic between government and the private sector where a small amount of government spending spurs larger private sector investment.
- Putting policies in place that ensure an enduring and viable middle class.
- Having an effective and rational national security and immigration policy.
- Improving the country's infrastructure – roads, bridges, dams – so that we can compete effectively in the world.

It is in the best interest that voters make decisions after full consideration of the candidate's views, qualifications, and historical performance. By doing so, we can minimize the chance of electing an unworthy candidate whose actions during his or her presidential term will adversely impact you.

We discuss in the following paragraphs what we believe are the primary reasons Republican presidential candidates have experienced success despite their economic record; namely the campaign failures of their Democratic opponents and their own well-planned, clever, brash, and sometimes deceitful campaign strategies. Republican candidates have mastered the use of the red herring, which the Merriam-Webster Dictionary defines as "something that distracts attention from the real issue at hand." Despite their inferior economic record, Republicans are very effective at using salesmanship, concise messaging, hyperbole, fear and red herrings to get elected and re-elected time and again.

From creating doubts about whether Barack Obama is an American citizen to the so-called death panels supposedly created by Obama's health care plan, Republicans have proven to be the masters of use of the red herring to their advantage. One of the most effective uses of this strategy occurred in the hotly contested 2004 presidential election between incumbent George W. Bush and Democratic nominee Senator John Kerry. In order to distract voters from some important issues of the day – the failing war in Iraq, America's loss of respect internationally, and the rampant corruption occurring in corporate America – the Republican Party, led by Karl Rove and Ken Mehlman, inserted a red herring into the election: the issue of same-sex or gay marriage.[dlxxi] Republican strategists made sure that many battleground states put same-sex marriage amendments on 21 state ballots. This campaign strategy galvanized the conservative base and even caused some Kerry supporters to alter their vote and vote contrary to their own economic interest based upon that one single issue. This red herring worked especially well in Ohio, our home state, that decided the election in favor of George W. Bush. Whether you believe such campaign tactics are clever and masterful or dirty politics, it is important that you recognize them for what they are – tactics designed to distract you from the important issues that can significantly impact your and your family's economic future.

THE MEEK SHALL NOT INHERIT THE EARTH

Where the Republican Party has evolved into a party that conducts slick, sometimes deceitful presidential campaigns, the Democratic Party has evolved over the past decade into a party that struggles to craft a simple, consistent and effective message that people can relate to. Instead of boldly and confidently conveying their record of achievement, including a superior economic record, Democratic candidates often come across as meek. In our view, the meek are *not* likely to inherit the earth, or the White House! The reality is that the moderate to progressive wing of the Democratic Party has produced substantive economic results for the American electorate and the middle class over the past 80 years. Business owners, consumers, and shareholders, owners of IRAs and 401(k)s have all benefited from the equity returns and economic results generated when Democratic presidents have been CEOs. What is shocking is that so few Democrats are able to score on this impressive set of facts. When it comes to economic issues, Democratic presidential candidates need not devise clever campaign slogans and strategies – they can merely stand on their record and state the facts. Unfortunately, for the American electorate and their own party, this has not happened.

THE REMEDY FOR TODAY'S VENOMOUS POLITICAL CLIMATE IS STATESMANSHIP

In the lifetimes of the two authors, we can say together that we have never seen a more venomous and vitriolic political climate than the one which exists today. Rather than intelligently discussing important issues and showing mutual respect for one another, even when there is disagreement, politicians today often let their discourse slide into personal attacks and name-calling, which means no progress for the American people. In today's political discourse and the media coverage of it, there is too much heckling and cynicism and not enough productive debate and discussion. This phenomenon was analyzed in the 2007 movie documentary entitled *Heckler* by Jamie Kennedy, which provided insights into the relationship between hecklers, comedians and their audience. The movie delivers the message that heckling truly is an unproductive use of time, often ruining a comedic performance, for both the comedian and his or her audience. We think today's politicians can learn from this message, not because their performance is comedic (which it sometimes is!), but because their behavior is often unproductive and stifles the progress for our country and its people. As we have seen during the Obama presidency, Republicans in particular have learned how to play the role of cynic, heckler and Monday-morning quarterback all too well, but in reality, what good does heckling do for the future of our country and its people?" Furthermore, we ask, when did it become an acceptable American value to heckle and chide the President of the United States every single day and root for him to fail, no less. This is a new phenomenon in the past twenty years that needs to be repudiated and done away with. *We believe that regardless of whom our president is, whether that individual is Ronald Reagan or*

Bill Clinton, George W. Bush or Barack Obama, we should support our president and hope that he or she succeeds, period."

Our country needs a lot less heckling and salesmanship and a lot more statesmanship to the extent we intend to remain the dominant world player we have been over the past century. To this end, one thing that both parties need to purge is the vitriol and hatred being spewed into the public domain. This is a relatively new phenomenon that began some 25 years ago with the advent of the Rupert Murdoch era. If we want to re-establish integrity and statesmanship back into our political process, then it is time for the American people to stand up and say NO to the charades, deceit and red herrings that dominate politics today, and demand that both parties work together for the common good of all of our citizens.

Consistent with our PRES Rule #5, our country is in desperate need of statesmanship. Those presidents who consistently produced the best PRES rankings in our study had several common threads among them. First and foremost, they believed in creating and sustaining a stable and viable middle class that could thrive and prosper. The most successful presidents in our study reached across the aisle and found a way to work cooperatively with their own and other members of Congress in order to attain positive results for the American people. *These men – Roosevelt, Kennedy, Reagan, Eisenhower, Johnson and Clinton – define the word statesmanship.*

A CALL TO ACTION

So where do we go from here? We know the 2012 presidential campaign is going to be ugly. Lies, Super Pac money, negative ads, misdirection, and red herrings will be relentlessly thrown at us in an effort to drown out rational thought, meaningful dialogue, and sound decision making.

Most of us wear our labels very proudly: labels like Methodist, Jewish, African American, parent, Republican, Democrat, veteran, union worker, business owner and American. Sadly, political mantra and red herrings have replaced the hard work and values that have made our country great. We need a return to our core values of pragmatism, hammering out compromise, and working together cooperatively as a team (not as vitriolic adversaries). Of late, it has seemingly become more patriotic to drive the country off a cliff while waving the flag than it is to solve our nation's problems with thoughtful compromise. Our Founding Fathers would be spinning in their graves to see us corrupting the great gift that they bestowed upon us – a Federal Republic – which offers great hope and opportunity to all of its citizens.

In our book we have presented numerous charts, graphs, and statistics; and we hope all of the numbers are not overwhelming. Our core message is simple and sincere:

If members of both major political parties work together cooperatively and put statesmanship above partisanship and salesmanship – as Eccles and Roosevelt once did – the way forward for us is clear.

What is your role in this great process? Cast aside the mantra and red herrings and become an independent thinker. Get your news from a variety of sources, not just radio and TV. Read books and articles from both ends, as well as the middle, of the political spectrum. Give respect where it has been earned and poke fun only where it is deserved. Open your mind and exercise your ability to chart your own course. We recommend that you consider the historical performance and results of our presidents when you vote, in the same way you would pick a money manager who is managing your IRA or 401(k) – with thoughtful due diligence. We've provided plenty of thought-provoking facts in our book. We recommend that you digest the facts, consider your specific economic situation, and cast a vote that will keep the middle class strong, the economy robust, and your future bright.

CHAPTER 15 ENDNOTES

[dlxii] Senator Douglas, "Proceedings and Debates of the 82nd Congress, First Session: Congressional Report." 97 Congressional Record 1471 (February 22, 1951). Accessed December 19, 2011.

[dlxiii] The U.S. Department of Labor. Accessed December 14, 2011. *www.dol.gov/.*

[dlxiv] Yahoo Finance! Accessed December 14, 2011. *finance.yahoo.com/.*

[dlxv] Yahoo Finance! Accessed December 14, 2011. *finance.yahoo.com/.*

[dlxvi] Yahoo Finance, S&P 500, March 9, 2009 to April 25, 2011, Accessed December 19, 2011. finance.yahoo.com/.

[dlxvii] David Welch, "Doing the Math on Obama's Detroit Bailout," *Bloomberg Businessweek*, August 2, 2010. Accessed December 14, 2011. http://www.businessweek.com/autos/autobeat/archives/2010/08/doing_the_math_on_obamas_detroit_bailout.html.

[dlxviii] Yves Smith, "Marriner Eccles on the Need to Save the Rich From Themselves," *Naked Capitalism*, September 25, 2011 (3:39 am). Accessed December 14, 2011. http://www.nakedcapitalism.com/2011/09/marriner-eccles-on-the-need-to-save-the-rich-from-themselves.html.

[dlxix] Barry Eichengreen and Kevin H. O'Rourke, "What do the new data tell us?" *Vox: Research-based policy analysis and commentary from leading economists*, March 8, 2010. Accessed December 14, 2011. http://www.voxeu.org/index.php?q=node/3421.

[dlxx] Vito Tanzi, comp., "International Monetary Fund: Fundamental Determinants of Inequality and the Role of Government," December 1998. Accessed December 14, 2011. http://www.imf.org/external/pubs/ft/wp/wp98178.pdf.

[dlxxi] John Hawkins, "The Top Eleven Reasons Why John Kerry Lost the Election," *Rightwing News*, November 15, 2004 (12:01 AM). Accessed December 14, 2011. http://www.rightwingnews.com/archives/week_2004_11_14.PHP#003142.

APPENDIX A
TABLE OF CONTENTS

ECONOMIC PILLARS/INDICATORS

U.S. FINANCIAL HEALTH PILLAR

PRESIDENT	HOOVER	FDR	TRUMAN	EISENHOWER	JFK/LBJ	NIXON/FORD	
AVG. ANNUAL STOCK MARKET RETURN	-34.96%	8.69%	7.96%	9.59%	5.94%	0.10%	
PRES INDICATOR SCORE (11=BEST, 1=WORST)	1	6	5	8	4	3	
AVG. ANNUALIZED CHANGE IN GDP PER CAPITA	-7.80%	8.39%	-0.78%	1.89%	3.56%	1.53%	
PRES INDICATOR SCORE (11=BEST, 1=WORST)	1	11	2	7	10	6	
AVG. ANNUALIZED CHANGE IN REAL DEBT PER CAP. AS % OF GDP	26.65%	8.81%	-2.74%	-3.65%	-4.32%	-1.45%	
PRES INDICATOR SCORE (11=BEST, 1=WORST)	1	2	9	10	11	7.5	
% OF MONTHS IN RECESSION	89.58%	8.95%	20.37%	28.13%	1.04%	28.13%	
PRES INDICATOR SCORE (11=BEST, 1=WORST)	1	9	5	2.5	10	2.5	
AVG. ANNUAL % CHANGE IN TOP 1%'S SHARE OF INCOME (INCOME INEQUALITY)	-5.63%	-2.87%	-0.80%	-1.88%	0.00%	-0.68%	
PRES INDICATOR SCORE (11=BEST, 1=WORST)	11	10	8	9	6	7	
PRES PILLAR SCORE	15	38	29	36.5	41	26	
PRES PILLAR RANKING (1=BEST, 11 =WORST)	11	3	6.5	4	1	9	

CARTER	REAGAN	HW BUSH	CLINTON	W BUSH	DEMOCRAT WEIGHTED BY LENGTH OF TERM	REPUBLICAN WEIGHTED BY LENGTH OF TERM
8.92%	9.86%	12.11%	16.61%	-5.24%	9.60%	0.58%
7	9	10	11	2	6.50	5.50
0.26%	2.13%	0.002%	1.91%	0.85%	3.48%	0.50%
4	9	3	8	5	7.70	5.80
-1.08%	5.78%	5.87%	-1.45%	2.55%	0.83%	3.90%
6	4	3	7.5	5	6.70	5.70
12.50%	16.67%	16.67%	0.00%	21.88%	8.22%	29.59%
8	6.5	6.5	11	4	8.70	3.85
0.90%	6.43%	0.81%	2.61%	1.00%	-0.41%	0.49%
4	1	5	2	3	6.60	5.60
29	29.5	27.5	39.5	19	36.20	26.45
6.5	5	8	2	10	1	2

ECONOMIC PILLARS/INDICATORS

PERSONAL WEALTH PILLAR

PRESIDENT	HOOVER	FDR	TRUMAN	EISENHOWER	JFK/LBJ	NIXON/FORD
AVG. ANNUAL STOCK MARKET RETURN	-34.96%	8.69%	7.96%	9.59%	5.94%	0.10%
PRES INDICATOR SCORE (11=BEST, 1=WORST)	1	6	5	8	4	3
AVG. ANNUALIZED CHANGE IN AVG. PERSONAL DISPOSABLE INCOME PER CAPITA	-10.45%	6.48%	-0.51%	1.95%	3.44%	2.02%
PRES INDICATOR SCORE (11=BEST, 1=WORST)	1	11	2	7	10	8
AVG. ANNUAL UNEMPLOYMENT RATE	12.85%	13.87%	3.88%	4.88%	4.85%	5.83%
PRES INDICATOR SCORE (11=BEST, 1=WORST)	2	1	11	9	10	6
AVG. ANNUAL CHANGE IN UNEMPLOYMENT RATE	5.10%	-1.87%	0.23%	0.31%	0.24%	0.51%
PRES INDICATOR SCORE (11=BEST, 1=WORST)	1	11	6.5	4	5	2
% OF YEARS W/ ACCEPTABLE INFLATION RATE (.95%-3.05%)	0.00%	25.00%	37.50%	37.50%	75.00%	0.00%
PRES INDICATOR SCORE (11=BEST, 1=WORST)	2	5.5	7.5	7.5	10	2
AVG. ANNUAL % CHANGE IN TOP 1%'S SHARE OF INCOME (INCOME INEQUALITY)	-5.63%	-2.87%	-0.80%	-1.88%	0.00%	-0.68%
PRES INDICATOR SCORE (11=BEST, 1=WORST)	11	10	8	9	6	7
PRES PILLAR SCORE	18	44.5	40	44.5	45	28
PRES PILLAR RANKING (1=BEST, 11 =WORST)	11	3.5	5	3.5	2	9.5

CARTER	REAGAN	HW BUSH	CLINTON	W BUSH	DEMOCRAT WEIGHTED BY LENGTH OF TERM	REPUBLICAN WEIGHTED BY LENGTH OF TERM
8.92%	9.86%	12.11%	16.61%	-5.24%	9.60%	0.58%
7	9	10	11	2	6.50	5.50
0.42%	2.35%	0.55%	1.72%	1.29%	2.92%	0.53%
3	9	4	6	5	7.20	6.30
6.53%	7.54%	6.30%	5.20%	5.26%	7.60%	6.62%
4	3	5	8	7	6.50	5.70
-0.15%	-0.20%	0.50%	-0.44%	0.23%	-0.57%	0.73%
8	9	3	10	6.5	8.40	4.70
0.00%	12.50%	25.00%	87.50%	62.50%	47.50%	25.00%
2	4	5.5	11	9	7.55	5.25
0.90%	6.43%	0.81%	2.61%	1.00%	-0.41%	0.49%
4	1	5	2	3	6.60	5.60
28	35	32.5	48	32.5	42.75	33.05
9.5	6	7.5	1	7.5	1	2

ECONOMIC PILLARS/INDICATORS

BUSINESS PROSPERITY PILLAR

PRESIDENT	HOOVER	FDR	TRUMAN	EISENHOWER	JFK/LBJ	NIXON/FORD	
AVG. ANNUAL STOCK MARKET RETURN	-34.96%	8.69%	7.96%	9.59%	5.94%	0.10%	
PRES INDICATOR SCORE (11=BEST, 1=WORST)	1	6	5	8	4	3	
AVG. ANNUALIZED CHANGE IN INDEX OF IN-DUSTRIAL PRODUCTION	-14.29%	12.10%	2.37%	1.85%	7.08%	2.28%	
PRES INDICATOR SCORE (11=BEST, 1=WORST)	1	11	6	4	10	5	
AVG. ANNUAL TRADE BALANCE/DEFICIT (BILLIONS)	2.33	1.22	39.14	11.39	30.69	11.45	
PRES INDICATOR SCORE (11=BEST, 1=WORST)	7	6	11	8	10	9	
AVG. ANNUALIZED CHANGE IN CORPORATE AFTER TAX PROFIT	-143.50%	12.15%	0.31%	4.14%	6.27%	-0.77%	
PRES INDICATOR SCORE (11=BEST, 1=WORST)	1	11	4	8	9	3	
PRES PILLAR SCORE	10	34	26	28	33	20	
PRES PILLAR RANKING (1=BEST, 11=WORST)	11	1	6	5	2	9	
PRES ECONOMIC STEWARDSHIP SCORE (CUMULATIVE BY INDICATOR)	43	116.5	95	109	119	74	
OVERALL PRES RANKING	11	2.5	5	4	1	9	

	CARTER	REAGAN	HW BUSH	CLINTON	W BUSH	DEMOCRAT WEIGHTED BY LENGTH OF TERM	REPUBLICAN WEIGHTED BY LENGTH OF TERM
	8.92%	9.86%	12.11%	16.61%	-5.24%	9.60%	0.58%
	7	9	10	11	2	6.50	5.50
	2.76%	2.44%	0.99%	4.53%	-0.61%	6.70%	-0.14%
	8	7	3	9	2	9.10	4.00
	-67.5	-172.78	-94.52	-209.79	-674.45	-34.38	-174.10
	5	3	4	2	1	6.90	5.30
	-9.17%	9.16%	0.37%	2.44%	0.77%	4.53%	-11.65%
	2	10	5	7	6	7.50	6.00
	22	29	22	29	11	30	20.8
	7.5	3.5	7.5	3.5	10	1	2
	79	93.5	82	116.5	62.5	108.95	80.3
	8	6	7	2.5	10	1	2

SOURCES OF THE DATA USED IN COMPILING THE STATISTICS SET FORTH ON THIS SPREADSHEET ARE
IDENTIFIED ON THE NEXT PAGE OF THIS APPENDIX A. DUE TO INSUFFICIENT DATA (ONLY 2 YEARS),
OBAMA IS NOT INCLUDED IN THE PRES RANKINGS.

PRES RANKINGS – SOURCES OF DATA COMPILED

SOURCE OF DATA/HOW INDICATOR WAS CALCULATED

ECONOMIC INDICATOR

Average Annual Stock Market Return

Calculated average annual compound return (AACR) per year using blended dollar values of Dow Jones Industrial Average, S&P 500, and NASDAQ, as those indices came into existence. The Dow existed for the entire 80-year period reviewed, S &P 500 started on March 4, 1957, and NASDAQ started on Feb. 8, 1971. See spreadsheet of Presidential Returns Data in Appendix. Values were sourced from Yahoo Finance: http://finance.yahoo.com

Average Annual Compound Return = ((blended value of indices at end of term/blended value of indices at beginning of the term) to an exponential power equal to 1/n, where n is the length of the president's term in years) minus 1.

Average Annualized Change in GDP Per Capita

Calculated real GDP per capita in 2010 dollars using: (1) GDP data from United States Bureau of Economic Analysis. "Current-Dollar and Real Gross Domestic Dollar, 1929-2010." n.d. June 7, 2011 www.bea.gov/national.xls/gdplev.xls.); (2) inflation data from United States Department of Labor—Bureau of Labor Statistics. "Table Containing History of CPI-U U.S. All Items Indexes and Annual Percent Changes From 1913 to Present" available at ftp://ftp.bls.gov/pub/special.requests/cpi/cpiai.txt; and (3) population data from United States Department of Labor—Bureau of Labor Statistics. "Historical National Population Estimates: July 1, 1900 to July 1, 1999" and United States Bureau of Economic Analysis "Table 7.1. Selected Per Capita Product and Income Series in Current and Chained Dollars." April 28, 2011.

Annualized Change=((Real GDP per capita in 2010 dollars at end of term/Real GDP per capita in 2010 dollars at beginning of term) to an exponential power equal to 1/n, where n is the length of the president's term in years) minus 1.

Average Annualized Change in Real Debt Per Capita As % of GDP

Calculated real debt per capita using: (1) national debt data from United States Department of the Treasury. "Historical National Debt Outstanding." June 17, 2011. http://www.treasurydirect.gov/govt/reports/pd/histdebt/histdebt.htm; (2) inflation data from source described above; and (3) population data from sources described above.

Annualized change = ((Real debt per capita in 2010 dollars as a percentage of GDP at the end of the term/Real debt per capita at the beginning of the term as a percentage of GDP) to an exponential power equal to 1/n, where n is the length of the president's term in years) minus 1.

ECONOMIC INDICATOR

SOURCE OF DATA/HOW INDICATOR WAS CALCULATED

% of Months in Recession

Calculated using monthly recession data from: http://www.nber.org/cycles.html
Recession "definition": http://www.nber.org/cycles/recessions.html

Average Annual % Change in Top 1% Share of Income

Calculated based on data from academic paper: Emmanuel Saez, Income Inequality in the United States from 1913-1998, Quarter Journal of Economics, V. 118, No. 1 (2003). Data set was updated with data up to 2008 in July 2010 http://elsa.berkeley.edu/~saez/TabFig2008.xls

Annual % Change = % by which the 1%'s share of income increased or decreased during president's term/number of years in term

Average Annualized Change in Average Real Disposable Inc. Per Capita

Calculated real disposable income per capita using: (1) data on disposable personal income per capita from United States Bureau of Economic Analysis. "Table 2.1. Personal Income and Its Disposition." April 28, 2011; and (2) inflation data from source described above.

Annualized change =((Real disposable income per capita in 2010 dollars at end of term/Real disposable income per capita in 2010 dollars at beginning of term) to an exponential power equal to 1/n, where n is the length of the president's term in years) minus 1.

Average Unemployment Rate

Calculated using unemployment data from United State Department of Labor—Bureau of Labor Statistics. "Employment status of the civilian noninstitutional population, 1940 to date" available at: http://www.bls.gov/cps/cpsaat01.htm
Historical Statistics of the United States, series D-9, p. 126, for data before 1940

Average = sum of annual unemployment rates for each year of president's term/number of years in term

Average Annual Change in Unemployment Rate

Calculated using unemployment data listed above.

Avg. Annual Change = the difference between the annual unemployment rate of the year president left office and the year before he took office/number of years in term

PRES RANKINGS – SOURCES OF DATA COMPILED

SOURCE OF DATA/HOW INDICATOR WAS CALCULATED

ECONOMIC INDICATOR

% of Years of Acceptable Inflation

Calculated using inflation data cited above.

Acceptable Year = Inflation rate of .95%-3.05% This is known in economics as the Taylor Rule.

Average Annualized Change in Industrial Production Index

Calculated using data on industrial production from Board of Governors of the Federal System, Series ID: INDPRO, Release: G.17 Industrial Production and Capacity Utilization (Updated 6/15/2011)

Annualized change = (((Industrial Production Index at end of term/Industrial Production Index at beginning of term) to an exponential power equal to 1/n, where n is the length of the president's term in years) minus 1

Average Trade Balance/Deficit

Calculated using import/export data from Historical Statistics of the United States Millennial Edition Online. Table Ee376-384. Exports and imports of goods and services: 1929-2002 and http://www.bea.gov/international/index.htm for 1992-2008

Avg. Trade Balance/Deficit = Sum of trade balances/deficits for each year of president's term/number of years in term

Average Annualized Change in Corporate Profits

Calculated using data from: (1) U.S, Dept. of Commerce, Bureau of Economic Affairs, National Income and Product Accounts Tables Table 1.14. Gross Value Added of Domestic Corporate Business in Current Dollars and Gross Value Added of Nonfinancial Domestic Corporate Business Current and Chained Dollars; and inflation data from source described above.

Annualized Change = ((Corporate after tax profits at end of term/ Corporate after tax profits at beginning of term) to an exponential power equal to 1/n, where n is the length of the president's term in years) minus 1

PRES RANKINGS

★ ★ ★ ★ ★ ★ ★ ★ ★ ★ ★ ★

RANK	OVERALL	U.S. FIN'L HEALTH PILLAR	PERSONAL WEALTH PILLAR	BUSINESS PROSPERITY PILLAR
1	JFK/LBJ	JFK/LBJ	Clinton	FDR
2	Clinton (Tie)	Clinton	JFK/LBJ	JFK/LBJ
3	FDR (Tie)	FDR	Eisenhower (Tie)	Clinton (Tie)
4	Eisenhower	Eisenhower	FDR (Tie)	Reagan (Tie)
5	Truman	Reagan	Truman	Eisenhower
6	Reagan	Truman (Tie)	Reagan	Truman
7	H.W. Bush	Carter (Tie)	W. Bush (Tie)	H.W. Bush (Tie)
8	Carter	H.W. Bush	H.W. Bush (Tie)	Carter (Tie)
9	Nixon/Ford	Nixon/Ford	Carter (Tie)	Nixon/Ford
10	W. Bush	W. Bush	Nixon/Ford (Tie)	W. Bush
11	Hoover	Hoover	Hoover	Hoover

|||||||||||||||||||||||||||||||| ★ ||||||||||||||||||||||||||||||||||||||

PRESIDENTIAL STOCK MARKET RETURNS DATA

PRESIDENT	START DATE	END DATE	DOW JONES INDUSTRIAL AVERAGE				
			START	END	YRS	EXPONENT	AACR
HOOVER	3/4/29	3/4/33	319.12	57.11	4	0.2500	-34.96%
FDR	3/4/33	4/12/45	57.11	158.48	12.25	0.0816	8.69%
TRUMAN	4/12/45	1/20/53	158.48	286.97	7.75	0.1290	7.96%
EISENHOWER	1/20/53	1/20/61	286.97	632.39	8	0.1250	10.38%
JFK/LBJ	1/20/61	1/20/69	632.39	935.54	8	0.1250	5.02%
NIXON/FORD	1/20/69	1/20/77	935.54	968.67	8	0.1250	0.44%
CARTER	1/20/77	1/20/81	968.67	970.99	4	0.2500	0.06%
REAGAN	1/20/81	1/20/89	970.99	2,239.11	8	0.1250	11.01%
BUSH	1/20/89	1/20/93	2,239.11	3,255.99	4	0.2500	9.81%
CLINTON	1/20/93	1/20/01	3,255.99	10,581.90	8	0.1250	15.87%
BUSH	1/20/01	1/20/09	10,581.90	8,279.63	8	0.1250	-3.02%
OBAMA	1/20/09	5/10/12	8,279.63	12,855.04	3.4	0.2941	13.81%

AACR = AVERAGE ANNUAL COMPOUND RETURN

PRESIDENT	START DATE	END DATE	S&P 500				
			START	END	YRS	EXPONENT	AACR
HOOVER	3/4/29	3/4/33	-	-	-	-	-
FDR	3/4/33	4/12/45	-	-	-	-	-
TRUMAN	4/12/45	1/20/53	-	-	-	-	-
EISENHOWER	1/20/53	1/20/61	44.06	59.96	4	0.2500	8.01%
JFK/LBJ	1/20/61	1/20/69	59.96	102.03	8	0.1250	6.87%
NIXON/FORD	1/20/69	1/20/77	102.03	103.85	8	0.1250	0.22%
CARTER	1/20/77	1/20/81	103.85	134.37	4	0.2500	6.65%
REAGAN	1/20/81	1/20/89	134.37	286.90	8	0.1250	9.95%
BUSH	1/20/89	1/20/93	286.90	435.13	4	0.2500	10.97%
CLINTON	1/20/93	1/20/01	435.13	1,342.54	8	0.1250	15.12%
BUSH	1/20/01	1/20/09	1,342.54	850.12	8	0.1250	-5.55%
OBAMA	1/20/09	5/10/12	850.12	1,144.03	2.75	0.3636	11.40%

S&P 500 STARTED ON MARCH 4, 1957 (44.06)

||||||||||||||||||||||||||||||||||||★|||||||||||||||||||||||||||||||||||||

PRESIDENTIAL STOCK MARKET RETURNS DATA

PRESIDENT	START DATE	END DATE	NASDAQ START	END	YRS	EXPONENT	AACR
HOOVER	3/4/29	3/4/33	-	-	-	-	-
FDR	3/4/33	4/12/45	-	-	-	-	-
TRUMAN	4/12/45	1/20/53	-	-	-	-	-
EISENHOWER	1/20/53	1/20/61	-	-	-	-	-
JFK/LBJ	1/20/61	1/20/69	-	-	-	-	-
NIXON/FORD	1/20/69	1/20/77	100	97.08	6	0.1667	-0.49%
CARTER	1/20/77	1/20/81	97.08	201.58	4	0.2500	20.04%
REAGAN	1/20/81	1/20/89	201.58	391.10	8	0.1250	8.64%
BUSH	1/20/89	1/20/93	391.10	696.81	4	0.2500	15.53%
CLINTON	1/20/93	1/20/01	696.81	2,770.38	8	0.1250	18.83%
BUSH	1/20/01	1/20/09	2,770.38	1,529.33	8	0.1250	-7.16%
OBAMA	1/20/09	5/10/12	1,529.33	2,460.51	2.75	0.3636	18.88%

NASDAQ STARTED ON FEBRUARY 8, 1971

PRESIDENT	START DATE	END DATE	BLENDED BY CHAPTER AACR	YRS	BEGIN	END
HOOVER	3/4/29	3/4/33	-34.96%	4	100,000.00	17,896.09
FDR	3/4/33	4/12/45	8.69%	12.25	100,000.00	277,499.56
TRUMAN	4/12/45	1/20/53	7.96%	7.75	100,000.00	181,076.48
EISENHOWER	1/20/53	1/20/61	9.59%	8	100,000.00	208,047.03
JFK/LBJ	1/20/61	1/20/69	5.94%	8	100,000.00	158,710.17
NIXON/FORD	1/20/69	1/20/77	0.10%	8	100,000.00	100,839.96
CARTER	1/20/77	1/20/81	8.92%	4	100,000.00	140,729.24
REAGAN	1/20/81	1/20/89	9.86%	8	100,000.00	212,233.55
BUSH	1/20/89	1/20/93	-12.11%	4	100,000.00	157,945.24
CLINTON	1/20/93	1/20/01	16.61%	8	100,000.00	341,832.92
BUSH	1/20/01	1/20/09	-5.24%	8	100,000.00	64,997.93
OBAMA	1/20/09	5/10/12	14.70%	2.75	100,000.00	145,801.23

BLENDED RATE EQUALLY WEIGHTS ALL OF THE MAJOR AVERAGES (DOW, S&P 500, NASDAQ) THAT WERE IN EXISTENCE DURING EACH RESPECTIVE PRESIDENCY

AACR BY PARTY (USING DOW)

REPUBLICANS	START	END	AACR	YRS
HOOVER	$100,000.00	$17,894.61	-0.3496	4
IKE	$17,894.61	$39,431.68	0.1038	8
NIXON/FORD	$39,431.68	$40,841.24	0.0044	8
REAGAN	$40,841.24	$94,188.03	0.1101	8
BUSH	$94,188.03	$136,950.39	0.0981	4
BUSH	$136,950.39	$107,157.04	-0.0302	8
AACR	$100,000.00	$107,157.04	0.17%	0.025

DEMOCRATS	START	END	AACR	YRS
FDR	$100,000.00	$277,538.01	0.0869	12.25
TRUMAN	$277,538.01	$502,469.55	0.0796	7.75
JFK/LBJ	$502,469.55	$743,508.37	0.0502	8
CARTER	$743,508.37	$745,294.40	0.0006	4
CLINTON	$745,294.40	$2,423,236.20	0.1588	8
AACR	$100,000.00	$2,423,236.20	8.30%	0.025

AACR BY PARTY (USING DOW)
(WITHOUT WORST TERM)

REPUBLICANS	START	END	AACR	YRS
IKE	$100,000.00	$220,355.11	0.1038	8
NIXON/FORD	$220,355.11	$228,232.11	0.0044	8
REAGAN	$228,232.11	$526,348.72	0.1101	8
BUSH	$526,348.72	$765,316.61	0.0981	4
BUSH	$765,316.61	$598,823.14	-0.0302	8
AACR	**$100,000.00**	**$598,823.14**	**5.10%**	**0.027778**

DEMOCRATS	START	END	AACR	YRS
FDR	$100,000.00	$277,538.01	0.0869	12.25
TRUMAN	$277,538.01	$502,469.55	0.0796	7.75
JFK/LBJ	$502,469.55	$743,508.37	0.0502	8
CLINTON	$743,508.37	$2,417,429.15	0.1588	8
AACR	**$100,000.00**	**$2,417,429.15**	**9.25%**	**0.027778**

AACR USING BLENDED RATE

$100K INVESTMENT BY PARTY

PARTY	RETURN	YEARS	START	END
REPUBLICANS	0.0058	40	100,000.00	126,027.48
DEMOCRATS	0.096	40	100,000.00	3,912,210.06

AACR USING BLENDED RATE

$5K INVESTMENT PER YEAR BY PARTY

PARTY	RETURN	YEARS	START	END
REPUBLICANS	0.0058	40	100,000.00	224,374.83
DEMOCRATS	0.096	40	100,000.00	1,985,526.07